CANONS AND DECREES

OF THE

COUNCIL OF TRENT

CANONS AND DECREES

OF THE

COUNCIL OF TRENT

ENGLISH TRANSLATION

By

REV. H. J. SCHROEDER, O.P.

(NOTE: The original 1941 edition contained the Latin text and the English translation. This edition contains only the English translation because few can read Latin any more. Plus, this issue is aimed at a wider readership.)

TAN Books
Charlotte, North Carolina

Nihil Obstat: Fr. Humbertus Kane, O.P.
                     Fr. Alexius Driscoll, O.P.

Imprimi Potest: Fr. Petrus O'Brien, O.P.
                     Prior Provincialis

Nihil Obstat: Sti. Ludovici, die 5. Septembris, 1941
                     A. A. Esswein,
                     Censor Deputatus

Imprimatur: Sti. Ludovici, die 5. Septembris, 1941
                 ✠ Joannes J. Glennon,
                 Archiepiscopus

Cover Design by Milo Persic

Cover Art: *Seduta del Concilio di Trento nella chiesa di S. Maria Maggiore,* with the consent of the Castello del Buonconsiglio Monumenti e collezioni provinciali. This image may not be reproduced or reprinted in any manner without prior written consent of the museum.

Printed and bound in the United States of America.

TAN Books
Charlotte, North Carolina
www.TANBooks.com
2011

Translator's Foreword

Some fifteen years ago the writer formed the intention of making accessible to English readers the disciplinary decrees of the ecumenical or general councils of the Church, a work which, with the exception of the Council of Trent, had up to that time received no attention. The fact that the last of these, that of the Vatican, did not issue any such decrees narrowed my field of labor to nineteen councils, leaving, nevertheless, a field still large enough to make anyone who has taken sufficient time to look carefully over the ground hesitant about undertaking the work. The results of these labors, covering the first eighteen councils, appeared in 1937 under the title, *Disciplinary Decrees of the General Councils*. The present volume covers the Council of Trent, giving the translation and text of its canons and decrees.

The original intention of limiting myself to the disciplinary decisions of the councils could not very well be carried out in the case of Trent without producing a one-sided work amounting almost to a monstrosity. In the list of general councils Trent holds the first place, not only because of its restatement of Catholic doctrine and its initiation of a genuine reform, but also because of its extraordinary influence both within and without the Church. Its purpose was twofold, to define the doctrines of the Church in reply to the heresies of the Protestants, and to bring about a thorough reform of the inner life of Christians. We have become so accustomed to look upon the two parts as one that either without the other seems incomplete. Moreover, it is scarcely necessary to state that the translation of these dogmatic decisions will be of immense advantage not only to the clergy but also and especially to the seminarian and the educated layman. In them the council proclaimed to the world the doctrines that were committed to the keeping of the Church on the day of Pentecost. They are a sign erected on everlasting foundations indicating to the passer-by the straight road along which the Church has traveled ever since that day and along which she will continue to travel till the Day of Judgment. She recognizes no detours, for these lead only

to destruction. Again, many of the Council's dogmatic decrees
are gems, masterpieces of theology reduced to the briefest
possible form, yet sufficiently complete to leave nothing wanting. I make mention particularly of the famous decree on
justification, in the working out and formulation of which
"the spirit of God is easily discernible." The Council spent
seven months of arduous labor in formulating that decree
as we have it today. There had been no decisions on that
point of Catholic doctrine by earlier councils by which to be
guided or on which to lean. In the works of the Fathers we
look in vain for a definite and satisfactory exposition. The
older theologians incorporated what they had to say on that
subject in their treatises on grace, while the controversial
works of later Catholic writers were more or less tainted
by the false doctrine of a twofold formal cause of justification, namely, the *justitia inhaerens* and the *justitia impu-
tata,* a compromise contrivance designed to conciliate the
heretics. In the reform decrees the reader will find the means
employed by the Church to correct and remove prevailing
moral evils and abuses.

The first English translation of the canons and decrees
of the Council of Trent, so far as I am aware, was made by
the Rev. J. Waterworth and published in London in 1848.
As is well known, this work has been out of print and off
the market for many years. As long as it was available it
filled a real need. In 1687 there appeared an anonymous
translation. But the work was so poorly done and so unfaith-
ful to the original that it must be regarded as a travesty
and burlesque rather than as a translation. Another rendi-
tion was made by T. A. Buckley and published in England
in 1851. This I have not seen, and had it not been for an
item in the catalogue of a London antiquarian some years
ago, I would not know of its existence. Whether an English
rendering of Trent has ever been made in this country, I do
not know. A translation of the dogmatic decrees only was
made by an Oxford convert in *Catholic Doctrine as Defined
by the Council of Trent* (Philadelphia, 1869), which is a translation of a series of conferences delivered in Geneva by the
Rev. A. Nampon, S.J., under the title, *Étude de la doctrine
catholique dans le concile de Trente.*

The Latin text of the canons and decrees given in the
second part of this book and upon which the accompanying

translation is based, is that of the Neapolitan edition of 1859, which was made from the Roman edition of 1834 issued by the *Collegium Urbanum de Propaganda Fide*. In transcribing this text typographical errors were corrected by reference to the new edition of the Acts of the council sponsored by the *Görres-Gesellschaft* in so far as it was available and also to the edition of Le Plat (Antwerp, 1779). In the spelling of certain words changes were made to conform to current usage. In the translation I have endeavored to adhere to the text as closely as possible, that is, to make it as literal as the text would permit, without, however, making that adherence a slavish one. Only direct scriptural quotations, not paraphrases, are printed in italics. For the benefit of those who are interested in a wider acquaintance with pre-Tridentine legislation, references to provincial councils and to the *Corpus Juris Canonici* will be found more copious and more complete under the Latin text. The references to a few papal bulls are given to indicate the action of popes to enforce the decrees of Trent.

—Rev. H. J. Schroeder, O.P.

Contents

SEVENTH SESSION

EIGHTH SESSION

NINTH SESSION

TENTH SESSION

ELEVENTH SESSION

TWELFTH SESSION

THIRTEENTH SESSION

FOURTEENTH SESSION

Contents

FIFTEENTH SESSION

SIXTEENTH SESSION

SEVENTEENTH SESSION

EIGHTEENTH SESSION

NINETEENTH SESSION

TWENTIETH SESSION

TWENTY-FIRST SESSION

TWENTY-SECOND SESSION

TWENTY-THIRD SESSION

TWENTY-FOURTH SESSION

TWENTY-FIFTH SESSION

Contents   xxi

BULL OF THE CONVOCATION

OF THE HOLY ECUMENICAL

COUNCIL OF TRENT

under Pope Paul III

Paul, Bishop, servant of the servants of God, for a
perpetual remembrance hereof

Recognizing at the very beginning of our pontificate, which
the divine providence of Almighty God, not for any merit of
our own, but by reason of its own great goodness, has committed to us, to what troubled times and to how many distresses in almost all affairs our pastoral solicitude and
vigilance were called, we desired indeed to remedy the evils
that have long afflicted and well-nigh overwhelmed the Christian commonwealth; but we also, as men *compassed with
infirmity,*[1] felt our strength unequal to take upon ourselves
such a burden. For while we realized that peace was necessary to free and preserve the commonwealth from the
many dangers that threatened it, we found all filled with
hatreds and dissensions, and particularly those princes, to
whom God has entrusted almost the entire direction of affairs,
at enmity with one another. Whilst we deemed it necessary
for the integrity of the Christian religion and for the confirmation within us of the hope of heavenly things, that
there be *one fold and one shepherd*[2] for the Lord's flock, the
unity of the Christian name was well-nigh rent and torn
asunder by schisms, dissensions and heresies. Whilst we
desired the commonwealth to be safe and protected against
the arms and insidious designs of the infidels, yet, because
of our transgressions and the guilt of us all, indeed, because
of the wrath of God hanging over us by reason of our sins,
Rhodes had been lost, Hungary ravaged, war by land and
sea intended and planned against Italy, and against Aus-
tria and Illyria, since the Turk, our godless and ruthless
enemy, was never at rest and looked upon our mutual enmi-

1. *Heb.* 5:2
2. *John* 10:16

1

ties and dissensions as his fitting opportunity to carry out his designs with success. Wherefore, having been called, as we have said, in so great a tempest of heresies, discords and wars and in such restlessness of the waves to rule and pilot the bark of Peter, and not trusting sufficiently our own strength, we first of all *cast our cares upon the Lord,*[3] that He might sustain us and provide our soul with firmness and strength, our understanding with prudence and wisdom. Then, considering that our predecessors, endowed with admirable wisdom and sanctity, had often in the greatest dangers of the Christian commonwealth had recourse to ecumenical councils and general assemblies of bishops as the best and most suitable remedy, we also decided to hold a general council. When, on consulting the opinions of the princes whose consent in this matter we deemed particularly useful and expedient, we found them at that time not averse to so holy a work, we, as our letters and records attest, summoned an ecumenical council and a general assembly of those bishops and fathers, whose duty it is to attend, to be opened in the city of Mantua on the twenty-third of May in the year 1537 of our Lord's incarnation and the third of our pontificate; entertaining almost the assured hope that when we should be assembled there in the name of the Lord, He would, as He promised, *be in our midst*[4] and in His goodness and mercy dispel with ease by the breath of His mouth all the storms and dangers of the times. But, as the enemy of mankind always plots against pious enterprises, at the very outset, contrary to all our hopes and expectations, the city of Mantua was refused us, unless we subscribed to certain conditions which were totally irreconcilable with the ordinances of our predecessors, with the condition of the times, with our own dignity and liberty, and with that of the Apostolic See and the ecclesiastical name, as we have made known in other letters. Wherefore we were obliged to find another place and to choose another city, and since a convenient and suitable one did not immediately present itself, we were constrained to prorogue the celebration of the council to the following first day of November. In the meantime, the Turk, our cruel and everlasting enemy, having attacked Italy with a powerful fleet, captured, sacked

---

3. *Psalms* 54:23
4. *Matt.* 18

and ravaged several cities on the shores of Apulia and carried off as booty the inhabitants, while we, in the greatest fear and general danger, were occupied in fortifying our shores and in furnishing assistance to the nearest neighboring localities. At the same time, however, we did not neglect to consult and exhort the Christian princes to inform us what in their opinion would be a suitable place to hold the council, and since their opinions were various and uncertain, and there seemed to be needless delay, we, with the best intention and, we think, with prudence, chose Vicenza, a populous city, which by reason of the valor, esteem and power of the Venetians, who conceded it to us, offered not only free access but also and especially a free and safe place of residence for all. But since time had already far advanced and the choice of the new city had to be made known to all, the proximity of the first of November precluding any announcement of this change, and winter moreover was near, we were again obliged to prorogue the council to the following spring, that is, to the first of the next May. This having been firmly settled and decreed, we considered, while preparing ourselves and everything else to hold and celebrate that council successfully with the help of God, that it was a matter of prime importance both for the celebration of the council and for Christendom, that the Christian princes be united in peace and concord, and so we did not fail to implore and beseech our most beloved sons in Christ, Charles, ever august Emperor of the Romans, and Francis, the most Christian King, the two chief props and supports of the Christian name, to come together in a conference with us. Both of them we very often urged by letters, nuncios and legates *a latere* selected from the number of our venerable brethren, to lay aside their jealousies and animosities, to agree to an alliance and holy friendship, and to succor the tottering state of Christendom, for the preservation of which especially did God give them power; and in case of neglect to do this and of failure to direct all their counsels to the common welfare of Christendom, they would have to render to Him a strict and severe account. Yielding at last to our petitions they repaired to Nice, whither we also, for the cause of God and of bringing about peace, undertook a long and, to our advanced age, very fatiguing journey. Neither did we neglect in the meantime, as the time set for the council, namely, the first of May, approached, to send to Vicenza three legates *a latere,* men of the greatest worth and esteem, chosen from the number of our brethren, the cardinals of the holy Roman Church, to open the council, to receive the prelates coming from various parts, and to transact and attend to such matters as they should deem necessary, till we ourselves on our return from our journey and mission of peace should be able to direct everything with greater exactness. In the meantime we applied ourselves with all the zeal, love and energy of our soul to that holy and most necessary work, the establishment of peace among the princes. God is our witness, in whose goodness we trusted when we exposed ourselves to the dangers of the journey and of life. Our conscience is witness, and in this matter certainly cannot reproach us with having either neglected or not sought an opportunity to effect a reconciliation. Witnesses are the princes themselves, whom we so often and so urgently implored through our nuncios, letters, legates, admonitions, exhortations and entreaties of every kind to lay aside their jealousies and form an alliance, that with united zeal and action they might aid the Christian commonwealth, already reduced to the greatest immediate danger. Witnesses, moreover, are those vigils and anxieties, those labors and strenuous exertions of our soul by day and night, which we have endured to such large measure in this matter and cause. For all that, our counsels and labors have not yet produced the desired results; for so it pleased the Lord Our God, who, however, we trust will yet look more favorably on our wishes. We ourselves have not in this matter, so far as we could, omitted anything pertaining to the duty of our pastoral office. If there be any who interpret our efforts for peace in any other sense, we are grieved indeed, but in our grief we nevertheless give thanks to Almighty God who, as an example and a lesson of patience to us, willed that His own Apostles should be *accounted worthy to suffer reproach for the name of Jesus who is our peace.*[5] However, though by reason of our sins a true and lasting peace between the two princes could not be effected in our meeting and conference at Nice, nevertheless, a truce of ten years was agreed upon; and hoping that as a result of this

5. *Acts* 5:41; *Eph.* 2:14

the holy council might be celebrated more beneficially and thus by its authority peace be permanently established, we urged the princes to come to the council themselves and to bring with them the prelates who had accompanied them and to summon those absent. On both these points, however, they excused themselves on the grounds that it was necessary for them to return to their kingdoms and that the prelates who had accompanied them, being wearied and exhausted by the journey and its expenses, must recover and recruit themselves, and they besought us to decree yet another prorogation of the time for the opening of the council. While we were rather unwilling to yield in this, we received in the meantime letters from our legates at Vicenza, announcing that though the day for the opening of the council had arrived, indeed had long since passed, hardly more than one or two prelates had repaired to Vicenza from foreign nations. Since we saw on receipt of this information that the council could under no circumstances be held at this time, we yielded to the princes and put off the time for the opening of the council till the following Easter, the feast of the resurrection of the Lord. The decretal letters concerning this our ordinance and prorogation were given and published at Genoa on the twenty-eighth of June in the year of the incarnation of our Lord 1538. This delay we granted the more readily because each of the princes promised to send ambassadors to us at Rome, that those things which remained for the perfect establishment of peace and which on account of the brevity of time could not be accomplished at Nice, might be considered and negotiated more conveniently in our presence at Rome. And for this reason also both requested that the peace negotiations might precede the celebration of the council, for with peace established the council would be much more beneficial and salutary to the Christian commonwealth. It was this hope for peace that moved us always to yield to the wishes of the princes, a hope that was greatly strengthened by the kind and friendly conference between those two princes after our departure from Nice, the news of which, giving us the greatest joy, confirmed us in the good hope, so that we believed God had at last listened to our prayers and received our earnest wishes for peace. This conclusion of peace, therefore, we earnestly desired and urged, and since it was the opinion

not only of the two aforesaid princes but also of our most
dear son in Christ, Ferdinand, King of the Romans, that the
work of the council ought not to be undertaken till peace
had been established, and all urged us by letters and through
their spokesmen to decide on a further prorogation of the
time, particularly insistent being the most illustrious
Emperor, who declared that he had promised those who dis-
sent from Catholic unity that he would consider the matter with us on their behalf to the end that some plan of
agreement might be arranged, which could not be done sat-
isfactorily before his return to Germany, and guided throughout by the same hope of peace and the wishes of such powerful
princes, and above all, seeing that even on the said feast of
the resurrection no other prelates had assembled at Vicenza,
we, now avoiding the word prorogation, which has been so
often repeated in vain, preferred to suspend the celebration
of the general council during our own good pleasure and
that of the Apostolic See. This we therefore did and dispatched letters concerning this suspension to each of the
aforesaid princes on the tenth day of June, 1539, as may be
clearly seen therein. This suspension having been made by
force of circumstances, we looked forward to that more favor-
able time and to some conclusion of peace that would later
bring dignity and numbers to the council as well as a more
immediate safety to the Christian commonwealth. But the
affairs of Christendom meanwhile became worse day by day.
The Hungarians on the death of their king called in the
Turks; King Ferdinand declared war against them; a portion of Belgium was incited to revolt against the Emperor,
who, to crush that rebellion, traversed France into Belgium
on the most friendly and peaceful terms with the most Christian King and with a great manifestation of mutual good
will toward each other. Thence he returned to Germany
where he began to hold diets of the princes and cities of
Germany with a view to discuss that agreement of which
he had spoken to us. But as the hope for peace was already
on the wane and that method of providing and establishing
unity by means of diets seemed rather adapted to produce
greater discord, we were led to return to our former remedy of a general council, and through our legates, cardinals
of the holy Roman Church, proposed this to the Emperor
himself, which we also did later and especially in the Diet

of Ratisbon, at which our beloved son, Gasparo Contarini, Cardinal of St. Praxedes, acted as our legate with great learning and integrity. For since, as we had previously feared, we might be petitioned by a decision of the diet to declare that certain articles maintained by the dissenters from the Church be tolerated till they be examined and decided upon by an ecumenical council, and since neither Christian and Catholic truth, nor our own dignity nor that of the Apostolic See would permit us to yield in this, we chose rather to command that it be proposed openly that a council be held as soon as possible. Neither did we ever have any other intention and wish than that an ecumenical and general council should be convened at the earliest opportunity. For we hoped that thereby peace might be restored to the Christian people and integrity to the Christian religion; yet we desired to hold that council with the good will and favor of the Christian princes. However, while looking forward to this will, while watching for the hidden time, *the time of thy good pleasure, O Lord,*[6] we were at last forced to conclude that all time is pleasing to God when there is question of deliberation on holy things and on such as pertain to Christian piety. Wherefore, beholding with the bitterest grief of our soul that the affairs of Christendom were daily becoming worse, Hungary oppressed by the Turks, Germany endangered, and all other states overwhelmed with apprehension and grief, we resolved to wait no longer for the consent of any prince, but to look solely to the will of the Almighty God and to the good of the Christian commonwealth. Wherefore, since the city of Vicenza was no longer at our disposal, and we desired in our choice of a new place for holding the council to have in mind both the common welfare of Christians and the conveniences of the German nation, and seeing that among the various places proposed these desired the city of Trent, we, though of opinion that everything could be transacted more conveniently in cisalpine Italy, nevertheless yielded with paternal charity to their desires. Accordingly, we have chosen the city of Trent as that in which the ecumenical council is to be held on the following first day of November, selecting that place as a convenient one in which the bishops and prelates from Germany

---

6. *Psalms* 68:14

and from the nations bordering on Germany can assemble very easily and those from France, Spain and other more remote provinces without difficulty. In fixing the day for the council, we considered that there should be time both for the publication of this our decree throughout the Christian nations and to make it possible for all the prelates to arrive. Our reason for not announcing the change of place of the council one year in advance, as has been prescribed by certain constitutions,[7] was this, that we were not willing that the hope of applying some remedy to the Christian commonwealth, afflicted as it is with so many disasters and calamities, should be delayed any longer, though we know the times and recognize the difficulties, and we understand that what may be looked for from our counsels is a matter of uncertainty. But since it is written: *Commit thy way to the Lord, and trust in him, and he will do it,*[8] we have resolved to trust in the clemency and mercy of God rather than distrust our own weakness, for in undertaking good works it often happens that where human counsels fail the divine power succeeds. Wherefore, relying on the authority of Almighty God, Father, Son, and Holy Ghost, and on that of His blessed Apostles Peter and Paul, which we also exercise on earth, and supported also by the advice and assent of our venerable brethren, the cardinals of the holy Roman Church, having removed and annulled the aforesaid suspension, which by the present we remove and annul, we announce, proclaim, convoke, ordain and decree a holy ecumenical and general council to be opened on the first day of November of the present year 1542 from the incarnation of the Lord in the city of Trent, for all nations a commodious, free and convenient place, to be there begun and prosecuted and with the help of God concluded and completed to His glory and praise and the welfare of the whole Christian people; and we summon, exhort and admonish, in whatever country they may be, all our venerable brethren, the patriarchs, archbishops, bishops, and our beloved sons, the abbots, as well as all others who by law or privilege have the right to sit in general councils and express their sentiments therein, enjoining and strictly commanding them by

---

7. Council of Constance, Sess. XXXIX, const. Frequens. Cf. my work, *Disciplinary Decrees of the General Councils* (St. Louis, 1937), pp. 447f
8. *Psalms* 36:5

virtue of their oath to us and to this Holy See, and in virtue
of holy obedience and under other penalties that by law or
custom are usually imposed and proposed in the celebration of councils against absentees, that they attend and be
present personally at this holy council, unless they should
perchance be hindered by a just impediment, of which, however, they shall be obliged to give proof, in which case they
must be represented by their lawful procurators and delegates. Also the aforesaid Emperor and the most Christian
King, as well as the other kings, dukes and princes, whose
presence, if ever, would certainly at this time be very salutary to the most holy faith of Christ and of all Christians,
we beg and beseech by the bowels of the mercy of God and
of Our Lord Jesus Christ, the truth of whose faith and whose
religion are now so violently assailed both from within and
without, that if they wish the Christian commonwealth to
be safe, if they feel themselves bound and under obligation
to the Lord for His great favors toward them, they will not
abandon His cause and interests but will come personally
to the celebration of the holy council, where their piety and
virtue would be greatly conducive to the common good, to
their own and the welfare of others, temporal as well as
spiritual. But if, which we do not wish, they themselves cannot appear, let them at least send distinguished men
entrusted with authority, each of whom may represent in
the council with prudence and dignity the person of his
prince. But above all, and this is for them an easy matter,
let them see to it that the bishops and prelates of their
respective kingdoms and provinces proceed to the council
without tergiversation and delay, a favor that God Himself
and we can in justice claim particularly from the prelates
and princes of Germany; for since it is chiefly on their account
and at their wishes that the council has been summoned,
and in the very city that they desired, let them not regard
it burdensome to celebrate and adorn it with their presence,
so that, God going before us in our deliberations and holding before our minds the light of His wisdom and truth, we
may in the holy ecumenical council, in a better and easier
manner consider, and with the charity of all concurring to
one end, ponder, discuss, execute and bring speedily and
happily to the desired result whatever things pertain to the
purity and truth of the Christian religion, to the restora-

tion of what is good and the correction of bad morals, to the
peace, unity and harmony of Christians among themselves,
of the princes as well as of the people, and whatever is necessary to repulse those attacks of barbarians and infidels
whereby they seek the overthrow of all Christendom. And
that this our letter and its contents may come to the knowledge of all whom it concerns, and that no one may plead
ignorance as an excuse, particularly since there may not
perchance be free access to all to whom it ought to be especially communicated, we wish and command that it be read
publicly and in a loud voice by the messengers of our court
or by some public notaries in the Vatican Basilica of the
Prince of the Apostles and in the Lateran Church, at a time
when the people are accustomed to assemble there to hear
divine services; and after having been read, let it be affixed
to the doors of the said churches, also to the gates of the
Apostolic Chancery and to the usual place in the Campo di
Fiore, where it shall hang openly for some time for the
perusal and cognizance of all; and when removed thence,
copies of it shall still remain affixed in the same places. For
by being thus read, published and affixed, we wish that each
and all whom our aforesaid letter concerns be, after the
interval of two months from the day of being published and
affixed, so bound and obligated as if it had been read and
published in their presence. We command and decree also
that an unshaken and firm faith be given to transcripts
thereof, written or subscribed by the hand of a notary public and authenticated by the seal of some person constituted
in ecclesiastical dignity. Therefore, let no one infringe this
our letter of summons, announcement, convocation, statute,
decree, command, precept and supplication, or with foolhardy boldness oppose it. But if anyone shall presume to
attempt this, let him know that he will incur the indignation of Almighty God and of His blessed Apostles Peter and
Paul. Given at Rome at Saint Peter's in the year 1542 of
the Lord's incarnation on the twenty-second of May, in the
eighth year of our pontificate.

Blosius.

Hier. Dand.

FIRST SESSION

COUNCIL OF TRENT

Celebrated under the sovereign pontiff, Paul III, on the thirteenth day of December in the year of the Lord 1545

DECREE CONCERNING THE OPENING OF THE COUNCIL

Does it please you, for the praise and glory of the holy and undivided Trinity, Father, Son, and Holy Ghost, for the advance and exaltation of the Christian faith and religion, for the extirpation of heresies, for the peace and unity of the Church, for the reform of the clergy and Christian people, for the suppression and destruction of the enemies of the Christian name, to decree and declare that the holy and general Council of Trent begins and has begun?

They answered: It pleases us.

ANNOUNCEMENT OF THE NEXT SESSION

And since the solemnity of the Nativity of Our Lord Jesus Christ is near, and other festivals of the closing and opening year follow thereon, does it please you that the next ensuing session be held on the Thursday after the Epiphany, which will be the seventh of the month of January in the year of the Lord 1546?

They answered: It pleases us.

SECOND SESSION

DECREE CONCERNING THE MANNER OF LIVING AND OTHER MATTERS TO BE OBSERVED DURING THE COUNCIL

The holy Council of Trent, lawfully assembled in the Holy Ghost and presided over by the same three legates of the Apostolic See, recognizing with the blessed Apostle James that *every best gift and every perfect gift is from above, coming down from the Father of lights,*[1] who, to those who ask of Him *wisdom, giveth to all abundantly and upbraided them not;*[2] and knowing also that *the fear of the Lord is the beginning of wisdom,*[3] has ordained and decreed that each and all of the faithful of Christ assembled in the city of Trent be exhorted, as they are hereby exhorted, to amend themselves in the evils and sins hitherto committed and to walk henceforth in the fear of the Lord; *not to fulfill the lusts of the flesh,*[4] to be *instant in prayer,*[5] to confess more often, to receive the sacrament of the Eucharist, to frequent the churches, to observe, so far as each one is able, the commandments of the Lord, and to pray daily in private for peace among the Christian princes and for unity of the Church. The bishops, however, and all others constituted in the sacerdotal order, who are participating in the celebration of the ecumenical council in this city, are to apply themselves diligently to glorifying God, to offer up sacrifices, praises and prayers, to celebrate in accordance with their duty the sacrifice of the mass at least every Sunday, the day on which God made the light, rose from the dead, and poured forth the Holy Ghost upon the disciples;[6] making, as the same Holy Ghost commanded by the Apostle, *supplications, prayers, intercessions and thanksgivings* for our most holy Lord the Pope, for the Emperor, *for kings and others who are placed in high stations, and for all men, that we*

---

1. *James* 1:17
2. *Idem,* 1:5
3. *Psalms* 110:10; *Prov.* 1:7; 9:10; *Eccles.* 1:16
4. *Gal.* 5:16
5. *Romans* 12:12
6. *Acts* 2:1ff.

may lead a quiet and peaceable life,[7] may enjoy peace and witness an increase of the faith. Furthermore, it exhorts that they fast at least every Friday in memory of the passion of the Lord and give alms to the poor. Every Thursday the mass of the Holy Ghost shall be celebrated in the cathedral with the litanies and other prayers assigned for this purpose; in the other churches there shall be said on the same day at least the litanies and the prayers. During the time that the sacred services are being performed, let there be no talking and idle conversation, but let mouth and mind be united with the celebrant. And since *it behooves bishops to be blameless, sober, chaste, ruling well their own household,*[8] it exhorts also that above all things each observe sobriety at table and moderation in diet; and further, since there idle conversations are often wont to arise, that the reading of the Scriptures be introduced at the tables, even at those of the bishops.[9] Let each one instruct and charge his servants not to be contentious, given to wine, disrespectful, covetous, arrogant, blasphemous and lovers of pleasure; finally, let them shun vice and embrace virtue, and in attire, in behavior and in all their actions let them manifest decorum as becomes the servants of the servants of God. Moreover, since it is the chief care, solicitude and intention of this holy council that the darkness of heresies, which for so many years has covered the earth, being dispelled, the light of Catholic truth may, with the aid of Jesus Christ, who is the true light,[10] shine forth in splendor and purity, and that those things that need reform may be reformed, the council exhorts all Catholics here assembled and who will be here assembled, especially those having a knowledge of the Sacred Scriptures, that by sedulous meditation they ponder diligently within themselves, by what ways and means the intention of the council can best be carried out and the desired result obtained; how the things to be condemned may be condemned more promptly and prudently and those to be approved may be approved, so that throughout the whole world all may with one voice and with the same pro-

---

7. Cf. *1 Tim.* 2:1f.
8. *Idem,* 3:2ff.
9. Cf. III Synod of Toledo (589), c.7 (c.11, D.XLIV); II Synod of Reims (813), c.17 (Hardouin IV, 1019) and *infra,* Sess. XXV, chap. 1 de ref.
10. *John* 1:9

fession of faith glorify God and the Father of Our Lord Jesus Christ.[11]

In expressing opinions when the priests of the Lord are assembled in the place of benediction, in conformity with the decree of the Synod of Toledo,[12] no one ought to be boisterous by immoderate shouting or create disturbance by stamping, nor contentious in false, vain and obstinate disputations, but let whatever is said be so tempered with mildness that neither the hearers be offended nor the keenness of correct judgment warped by a disturbed mind.

Moreover, this holy council has ordained and decreed that if it should happen that some during the council do not sit in their proper places and also make known their mind by the word *Placet,* are present at the assemblies and perform any other acts whatsoever, no disadvantage shall thereby accrue to anyone, neither shall anyone thereby acquire a new right.[13]

ANNOUNCEMENT OF THE NEXT SESSION

After this the next session was announced for Thursday, the fourth day of the following February.

---

11. *Romans* 15:6
12. Cf. XI Synod of Toledo (675), c.1
13. Cf. Sess. XXV at the end.

THIRD SESSION

Celebrated on the fourth day of February, 1546

DECREE CONCERNING THE SYMBOL OF FAITH

In the name of the holy and undivided Trinity, Father, Son, and Holy Ghost.

This holy, ecumenical and general Council of Trent, lawfully assembled in the Holy Ghost, the same three legates of the Apostolic See presiding, considering the magnitude of the matters to be dealt with, especially those comprised under the two heads, the extirpation of heresies and the reform of morals, for which purposes it was chiefly assembled, and recognizing with the Apostle that its *wrestling is not against flesh and blood, but against the spirits of wickedness in high places,*[1] exhorts with the same Apostle each and all above all things to be *strengthened in the Lord and in the might of his power, in all things taking the shield of faith, wherewith they may be able to extinguish all the fiery darts of the most wicked one, and to take the helmet of the hope of salvation and the sword of the spirit, which is the word of God.*[2] Wherefore, that this pious solicitude [of the council] may begin and continue by the grace of God, it ordains and decrees that before all else a confession of faith be set forth; following herein the examples of the Fathers, who in the more outstanding councils were accustomed at the beginning of their work to use this shield against heresies, with which alone they have at times drawn unbelievers to the faith, overcome heretics and confirmed the faithful. For this reason it has thought it well that the symbol of faith which the holy Roman Church uses as the cardinal principle wherein all who profess the faith of Christ necessarily agree and as the firm and sole foundation *against which the gates of hell shall never prevail,*[3] be expressed in the same words in which it is read in all the churches, which is as follows: *I believe in one God the Father Almighty, creator of heaven and earth, of all things visible and invisible;*

---

1. *Eph.* 6:12
2. *Ibid.,* 6:10, 16f.
3. *Matt.* 16:18

*and in one Lord Jesus Christ, the only begotten Son of God
and born of the Father before all ages; God of God, light of
light, true God of true God; begotten, not made, consub-
stantial with the Father, by whom all things were made; who
for us men and for our salvation descended from heaven,
and was incarnate by the Holy Ghost of the Virgin Mary,
and was made man; crucified also for us under Pontius
Pilate, he suffered and was buried; and he arose on the third
day according to the Scriptures, and ascended into heaven,
sits at the right hand of the Father; and again he will come
with glory to judge the living and the dead; of whose kingdom there shall be no end; and in the Holy Ghost the Lord
and giver of life, who proceeds from the Father and the Son;
who with the Father and the Son together is adored and
glorified; who spoke by the prophets; and in one holy Catholic
and Apostolic Church. I confess one baptism for the remission of sins; and I look for the resurrection of the dead, and
the life of the world to come. Amen.*

ANNOUNCEMENT OF THE NEXT SESSION

The same holy, ecumenical and general Council of Trent,
lawfully assembled in the Holy Ghost, the same three legates
of the Apostolic See presiding, understanding that many
prelates in various localities are girded for their journey,
and that some also are on their way here; and considering
that the greater the attendance of Fathers in sanctioning
and confirming all that will be decreed by the holy council,
in so much greater esteem and respect will those decrees
be held among all men, has ordained and decreed that the
next session after the present one be held on the Thursday
following the next *Laetare* Sunday. In the meantime, however, the discussion and examination of those things which
the council shall deem necessary to discuss and examine,
shall not be deferred.

FOURTH SESSION

Celebrated on the eighth day of April, 1546

DECREE CONCERNING THE CANONICAL SCRIPTURES

The holy, ecumenical and general Council of Trent, lawfully assembled in the Holy Ghost, the same three legates of the Apostolic See presiding, keeps this constantly in view, namely, that the purity of the Gospel may be preserved in the Church after the errors have been removed. This [Gospel], of old promised through the Prophets in the Holy Scriptures,[1] Our Lord Jesus Christ, the Son of God, promulgated first with His own mouth, and then commanded it to be preached by His Apostles to every creature[2] as the source at once of all saving truth and rules of conduct. It also clearly perceives that these truths and rules are contained in the written books and in the unwritten traditions, which, received by the Apostles from the mouth of Christ Himself, or from the Apostles themselves,[3] the Holy Ghost dictating, have come down to us, transmitted as it were from hand to hand. Following, then, the examples of the orthodox Fathers, it receives and venerates with a feeling of piety and reverence all the books both of the Old and New Testaments, since one God is the author of both; also the traditions, whether they relate to faith or to morals, as having been dictated either orally by Christ or by the Holy Ghost, and preserved in the Catholic Church in unbroken succession. It has thought it proper, moreover, to insert in this decree a list of the sacred books, lest a doubt might arise in the mind of someone as to which are the books received by this council.[4] They are the following: of the Old Testament, the

---

1. *Jer.* 31:22
2. *Matt.* 28:19f.; *Mark* 16:15
3. See *2 Thess.* 2:14; c.5, D.XI
4. For earlier lists, cf. Synod of Laodicea (end of IV cent.), c.60, the genuineness of which canon however is contested (Hefele-Leclercq, *Hist. des conciles,* I, 1026); Synod of Rome (382) under Pope Damasus (Denzinger, *Enchiridion,* no. 84); Synod of Hippo (393), c.36, which the III Synod of Carthage (397) made its own in c.47 (*idem,* no. 92); Innocent I in 405 to Exuperius, bishop of Toulouse (*idem,* no. 96); Eugene IV in the Council of Florence (Mansi, XXXI, 1736; Hardouin, IX, 1023f.). The Tridentine list or decree was the first infallible and effectually promulgated declaration on the Canon of the Holy Scriptures.

five books of Moses, namely, Genesis, Exodus, Leviticus, Numbers, Deuteronomy; Josue, Judges, Ruth, the four books of Kings, two of Paralipomenon, the first and second of Esdras, the latter of which is called Nehemias, Tobias, Judith, Esther, Job, the Davidic Psalter of 150 Psalms, Proverbs, Ecclesiastes, the Canticle of Canticles, Wisdom, Ecclesiasticus, Isaias, Jeremias, with Baruch, Ezechiel, Daniel, the twelve minor Prophets, namely, Osee, Joel, Amos, Abdias, Jonas, Micheas, Nahum, Habacuc, Sophonias, Aggeus, Zacharias, Malachias; two books of Machabees, the first and second. Of the New Testament, the four Gospels, according to Matthew, Mark, Luke and John; the Acts of the Apostles written by Luke the Evangelist; fourteen Epistles of Paul the Apostle, to the Romans, two to the Corinthians, to the Galatians, to the Ephesians, to the Philippians, to the Colossians, two to the Thessalonians, two to Timothy, to Titus, to Philemon, to the Hebrews; two of Peter the Apostle, three of John the Apostle, one of James the Apostle, one of Jude the Apostle, and the Apocalypse of John the Apostle. If anyone does not accept as sacred and canonical the aforesaid books in their entirety and with all their parts, as they have been accustomed to be read in the Catholic Church and as they are contained in the old Latin Vulgate Edition, and knowingly and deliberately rejects the aforesaid traditions, let him be anathema. Let all understand, therefore, in what order and manner the council, after having laid the foundation of the confession of faith, will proceed, and who are the chief witnesses and supports to whom it will appeal in confirming dogmas and in restoring morals in the Church.

DECREE CONCERNING THE EDITION AND
USE OF THE SACRED BOOKS

Moreover, the same holy council considering that not a little advantage will accrue to the Church of God if it be made known which of all the Latin editions of the sacred books now in circulation is to be regarded as authentic, ordains and declares that the old Latin Vulgate Edition, which, in use for so many hundred years, has been approved by the Church, be in public lectures, disputations, sermons and expositions held as authentic, and that no one dare or presume under any pretext whatsoever to reject it.

Furthermore, to check unbridled spirits, it decrees that

no one relying on his own judgment shall, in matters of faith and morals pertaining to the edification of Christian doctrine, distorting the Holy Scriptures in accordance with his own conceptions,[5] presume to interpret them contrary to that sense which holy mother Church, to whom it belongs to judge of their true sense and interpretation,[6] has held and holds, or even contrary to the unanimous teaching of the Fathers, even though such interpretations should never at any time be published. Those who act contrary to this shall be made known by the ordinaries and punished in accordance with the penalties prescribed by the law.

And wishing, as is proper, to impose a restraint in this matter on printers also, who, now without restraint, thinking what pleases them is permitted them, print without the permission of ecclesiastical superiors the books of the Holy Scriptures and the notes and commentaries thereon of all persons indiscriminately, often with the name of the press omitted, often also under a fictitious press-name, and what is worse, without the name of the author, and also indiscreetly have for sale such books printed elsewhere, [this council] decrees and ordains that in the future the Holy Scriptures, especially the old Vulgate Edition, be printed in the most correct manner possible, and that it shall not be lawful for anyone to print or to have printed any books whatsoever dealing with sacred doctrinal matters without the name of the author, or in the future to sell them, or even to have them in possession, unless they have first been examined and approved by the ordinary, under penalty of anathema and fine prescribed by the last Council of the Lateran.[7] If they be regulars they must in addition to this examination and approval obtain permission also from their own superiors after these have examined the books in accordance with their own statutes. Those who lend or circulate them in manuscript before they have been examined and approved, shall be subject to the same penalties as the printers, and those who have them in their possession or read them, shall, unless they make known the authors, be themselves regarded

---

5. St. Jerome, *Comment. on Galatians,* chap. 5, vers. 19-21, PL, XXVI, 445 (c.27, C.XXIV, q.3); c.39 (§ 70) ead
6. Quinisext Council (692), c.19 (Mansi, XI, 951; Hardouin, III, 1667)
7. Cf. the bull "Inter sollicitudines," Schroeder, *Disciplinary Decrees of the General Councils,* p. 504

as the authors. The approbation of such books, however, shall be given in writing and shall appear authentically at the beginning of the book, whether it be written or printed, and all this, that is, both the examination and approbation, shall be done gratuitously, so that what ought to be approved may be approved and what ought to be condemned may be condemned.

Furthermore, wishing to repress that boldness whereby the words and sentences of the Holy Scriptures are turned and twisted to all kinds of profane usages, namely, to things scurrilous, fabulous, vain, to flatteries, detractions, superstitions, godless and diabolical incantations, divinations, the casting of lots and defamatory libels, to put an end to such irreverence and contempt, and that no one may in the future dare use in any manner the words of Holy Scripture for these and similar purposes, it is commanded and enjoined that all people of this kind be restrained by the bishops as violators and profaners of the word of God, with the penalties of the law and other penalties that they may deem fit to impose.

ANNOUNCEMENT OF THE NEXT SESSION

Likewise, this holy council ordains and decrees that the next session will be held and celebrated on the Thursday after the next most sacred feast of Pentecost.

FIFTH SESSION

Celebrated on the seventeenth day of June, 1546

DECREE CONCERNING ORIGINAL SIN

That our Catholic faith, *without which it is impossible to please God,*[1] may, after the destruction of errors, remain integral and spotless in its purity, and that the Christian people may not be *carried about with every wind of doctrine,*[2] since that old serpent,[3] the everlasting enemy of the human race, has, among the many evils with which the Church of God is in our times disturbed, stirred up also not only new but also old dissensions concerning original sin and its remedy, the holy, ecumenical and general Council of Trent, lawfully assembled in the Holy Ghost, the same three legates of the Apostolic See presiding, wishing now to reclaim the erring and to strengthen the wavering, and following the testimonies of the Holy Scriptures, of the holy Fathers, of the most approved councils, as well as the judgment and unanimity of the Church herself, ordains, confesses and declares these things concerning original sin:

1. If anyone does not confess that the first man, Adam, when he transgressed the commandment of God in paradise, immediately lost the holiness and justice in which he had been constituted, and through the offense of that prevarication incurred the wrath and indignation of God, and thus death with which God had previously threatened him,[4] and, together with death, captivity under his power who thenceforth *had the empire of death, that is to say, the devil,*[5] and that the entire Adam through that offense of prevarication was changed in body and soul for the worse,[6] let him be anathema.

2. If anyone asserts that the transgression of Adam injured him alone and not his posterity,[7] and that the holiness and justice which he received from God, which he lost,

---

1. *Heb.* 11:6
2. *Eph.* 4:14
3. *Gen.* 3:1ff.; Apoc. 12:9; 20:2
4. *Gen.* 2:17
5. *Heb.* 2:14
6. Cf. II Synod of Orange (529), c.1. Denzinger, no. 174
7. See *1 Cor.* 15:21f.; II Synod of Orange, c.2. *Ibid.*, no. 175

21

he lost for himself alone and not for us also; or that he, being defiled by the sin of disobedience, has transfused only death and the pains of the body into the whole human race, but not sin also, which is the death of the soul, let him be anathema, since he contradicts the Apostle who says: *By one man sin entered into the world and by sin death; and so death passed upon all men, in whom all have sinned.*[8]

3. If anyone asserts that this sin of Adam, which in its origin is one, and by propagation, not by imitation, transfused into all, which is in each one as something that is his own, is taken away either by the forces of human nature or by a remedy other than the merit of the one mediator, Our Lord Jesus Christ,[9] who has reconciled us to God in his own blood, *made unto us justice, sanctification and redemption;*[10] or if he denies that that merit of Jesus Christ is applied both to adults and to infants by the sacrament of baptism rightly administered in the form of the Church, let him be anathema; *for there is no other name under heaven given to men, whereby we must be saved.*[11] Whence that declaration: *Behold the Lamb of God, behold him who taketh away the sins of the world;*[12] and that other: *As many of you as have been baptized, have put on Christ.*[13]

4. If anyone denies that infants, newly born from their mothers' wombs, are to be baptized, even though they be born of baptized parents, or says that they are indeed *baptized for the remission of sins,*[14] but that they derive nothing of original sin from Adam which must be expiated by the laver of regeneration for the attainment of eternal life, whence it follows that in them the form of baptism for the remission of sins is to be understood not as true but as false, let him be anathema, for what the Apostle has said, *by one man sin entered into the world, and by sin death, and so death passed upon all men, in whom all have sinned,*[15] is not to be understood otherwise than as the Catholic Church has everywhere and always understood it. For in virtue of this rule of faith handed down from the apostles, even infants who could not

8. *Romans* 5:12
9. See *1 Tim.* 2:5
10. See *1 Cor.* 1:30
11. *Acts* 4:12
12. *John* 1:29
13. *Gal.* 3:27
14. *Acts* 2:38
15. *Romans* 5:12

as yet commit any sin of themselves, are for this reason truly baptized for the remission of sins, in order that in them what they contracted by generation may be washed away by regeneration.[16] For, *unless a man be born again of water and the Holy Ghost, he cannot enter into the kingdom of heaven.*[17]

5. If anyone denies that by the grace of Our Lord Jesus Christ which is conferred in baptism, the guilt of original sin is remitted, or says that the whole of that which belongs to the essence of sin is not taken away, but says that it is only canceled or not imputed, let him be anathema. For in those who are born again God hates nothing, because *there is no condemnation to those who are* truly *buried together with Christ by baptism unto death,*[18] *who walk not according to the flesh,*[19] but, putting off the old man and putting on the new one who is created according to God,[20] are made innocent, immaculate, pure, guiltless and beloved of God, heirs indeed of God, joint heirs with Christ;[21] so that there is nothing whatever to hinder their entrance into heaven. But this holy council perceives and confesses that in the one baptized there remains concupiscence or an inclination to sin, which, since it is left for us to wrestle with, cannot injure those who do not acquiesce but resist manfully by the grace of Jesus Christ; indeed, he who shall have *striven lawfully shall be crowned.*[22] This concupiscence, which the Apostle sometimes calls sin,[23] the holy council declares the Catholic Church has never understood to be called sin in the sense that it is truly and properly sin in those born again, but in the sense that it is of sin and inclines to sin. But if anyone is of the contrary opinion, let him be anathema.

This holy council declares, however, that it is not its intention to include in this decree, which deals with original sin, the blessed and immaculate Virgin Mary, the mother of God, but that the constitutions of Pope Sixtus IV, of happy memory, are to be observed under the penalties contained in those constitutions, which it renews.[24]

---

16. C.153, D.IV de cons.
17. *John* 3:5
18. *Romans* 6:4; c.13, D.IV de cons.
19. *Romans* 8:1
20. *Eph.* 4:22, 24; *Col.* 3:9f.
21. *Romans* 8:17
22. See *2 Tim.* 2:5
23. *Romans* 6-8; *Col.* 3
24. Cc. 1, 2, Extrav. comm., De reliq. et venerat. sanct., III, 12

Chapter I

THE ESTABLISHMENT OF LECTURESHIPS IN HOLY SCRIPTURE AND THE LIBERAL ARTS

The same holy council, adhering to the pious decisions of the sovereign pontiffs and of approved councils,[25] and accepting and adding to them, that the heavenly treasure of the sacred books which the Holy Ghost has with the greatest liberality delivered to men may not lie neglected, has ordained and decreed that in those churches in which there exists a prebend or a benefice with an obligation attached, or other income by whatever name it may be known, set aside for instructors in sacred theology, the bishops, archbishops, primates, and other ecclesiastical superiors of those localities compel, even by a reduction of their revenues, those who hold such prebend, benefice or income, to expound and interpret the Holy Scriptures, either personally if they are competent, otherwise by a competent substitute to be chosen by the bishops, archbishops, primates, or other superiors of those places. In the future such prebend, benefice and income shall be conferred only on competent persons and those who can themselves discharge that office; a provision made otherwise shall be null and void. In metropolitan and cathedral churches, however, if the city be an outstanding and populous one, and also in collegiate churches that are situated in a prominent town, even though they do not belong to any diocese, provided the clergy there are numerous, where there is no prebend, benefice or income provided for this purpose, let the prebend that shall first become vacant in any manner whatever, except by resignation, and to which some other incompatible duty is not attached, he understood to be *ipso facto* and forever set aside and devoted to that purpose. And should it happen that in those churches there is not any or no sufficient income,[26] let the metropolitan or the bishop himself, by assigning thereto the revenues of

---

25. C.12 D.XXXVII; cc.1, 4, 5, X, De magistr., V, 5. Cf. also Sess. XXIII, chap. 18 de ref.
26. Sess. XXIV, chap. 15 de ref.

some simple benefice, the duties connected with it being nevertheless discharged, or by contributions of the *beneficiati* of his city and diocese, or otherwise, as may be most convenient, provide in such a way with the advice of the chapter that the instructions in Holy Scripture may be procured; so, however, that all other instructions, whether established by custom or any other agency, be by no means on that account omitted. Churches whose annual revenues are scanty and where the number of clergy and people is so small that instruction in theology cannot be conveniently had therein, may have at least a master, to be chosen by the bishop with the advice of the chapter, to teach grammar gratuitously to clerics and other poor students,[27] so that afterwards they may with the help of God pass on to the study of Holy Scripture. For this purpose let the revenues of some simple benefice be assigned to that master of grammar,[28] which he shall receive so long as he is engaged in teaching (provided, however, that that benefice be not deprived of the services due to it), or let some suitable remuneration be paid him out of the capitular or episcopal income, or finally, let the bishop himself devise some other arrangement suitable to his church and diocese, that this pious, useful and profitable provision may not under any feigned excuse be neglected. In the monasteries of monks also, where this can be conveniently done, let there be instructions in the Holy Scriptures.[29] If abbots prove negligent in this matter, let the bishops of the localities, as the delegates herein of the Apostolic See, compel them thereto by suitable measures. In the convents of other regulars in which studies can conveniently flourish, let there be likewise instructions in the Holy Scriptures, which shall be assigned by the general and provincial chapters to the more worthy masters. In the public gymnasia also where instructions so profitable and of all the most necessary have not thus far been instituted, let them be introduced by the piety and charity of the most religious princes and governments for the defense and increase of the Catholic faith and the preservation and

---

27. C.1, X, De magistr., V, 5; Sess. XXIII, chap. 18 de ref.
28. By the bull *In sacrosancta* of Pius IV (13 Nov., 1564) this master was bound to make a profession of faith.
29. To which Paul V by the constitution *Apostolicae* (1610) added instructions in Hebrew, Greek and Arabic.

propagation of wholesome doctrine, and where once instituted and neglected, let them be restored. And that under the semblance of piety impiety may not be disseminated, the same holy council has decreed that no one be admitted to this office of instructor, whether such instruction be public or private, who has not been previously examined and approved by the bishop of the locality as to his life, morals and knowledge; which, however, is not to be understood of instructions in the monasteries of monks. Moreover, those who teach Holy Scripture, as long as they teach publicly in the schools, and also the students who study in those schools, shall fully enjoy and possess in case of absence all the privileges accorded by the common law with regard to the collection of the incomes of their prebends and benefices.[30]

Chapter II

PREACHERS OF THE WORD OF GOD AND QUESTORS OF ALMS

But since the preaching of the Gospel is no less necessary to the Christian commonwealth than the reading thereof, and since this is the chief duty of the bishops,[31] the same holy council has ordained and decreed that all bishops, archbishops, primates and all other prelates of the churches are bound personally, if not lawfully hindered, to preach the holy Gospel of Jesus Christ. But if it should happen that bishops and the others mentioned above are hindered by a legitimate impediment, they shall be bound, in accordance with the provision of the general council,[32] to appoint competent persons to discharge beneficially this office of preaching. If however anyone through contempt fails to observe this, let him be subject to severe punishment. Archpriests, priests and all who in any manner have charge of parochial and other churches to which is attached the *cura animarum,* shall at least on Sundays and solemn festivals,[33] either personally or, if they are lawfully impeded, through others who are competent, feed the people committed to them with wholesome words in proportion to their own and

---

30. C.5, X, De magistr., V, 5
31. Cf. Sess. XXIV, chap. 4 de ref.; c.6, D.LXXXVIII
32. C. 15, X, De off. jud. ord., I, 31 (IV Lat., c.10)
33. Cf. Sess. XXIV, chap. cit.

their people's mental capacity, by teaching them those things that are necessary for all to know in order to be saved, and by impressing upon them with briefness and plainness of speech the vices that they must avoid and the virtues that they must cultivate, in order that they may escape eternal punishment and obtain the glory of heaven. But if anyone of the above should neglect to discharge this duty, even on the plea that for some reason he is exempt from the jurisdiction of the bishop, even if the churches are said in some way to be exempt, or perhaps annexed or united to some monastery that is outside the diocese, if the churches are really within their dioceses, let not the watchful and pastoral solicitude of the bishops be wanting, lest that be fulfilled: *The little ones have asked for bread, and there was none to break it unto them.*[34] Wherefore, if after having been admonished by the bishop they neglect their duty for a period of three months, let them be compelled by ecclesiastical censures or by other measures at the discretion of the bishop; and should he deem it expedient, let a fair remuneration be paid from the revenues of the benefices to another person to discharge that office, till the incumbent, having come to his senses, shall fulfill his own duty.

But if there should be found parochial churches subject to monasteries that are not in any diocese, and the abbots and regular prelates are negligent in the aforesaid matters, let them be compelled thereto by the metropolitans in whose provinces the dioceses are located, who in this matter shall act as delegates of the Apostolic See, and no custom, exemption, appeal, protest or counteraction shall impede the execution of this decree, till a competent judge, who shall proceed summarily and examine only into the truth of the fact, shall have taken the matter into consideration and given a decision. Regulars of whatever order, unless they have been examined by their superiors regarding life, morals and knowledge and approved by them, may not without their permission preach even in the churches of their order, and they must present themselves personally with this permission before the bishops and ask from these the blessing before they begin to preach. In churches, however, that are not of their orders they must, in addition to the permission of their

---

34. *Lam.* 4:4

superiors, have also that of the bishop, without which they may not under any circumstances preach in churches that do not belong to their orders.[35] This permission the bishops shall grant *gratis*. But if, which heaven avert, a preacher should spread errors or scandals among the people, let the bishop forbid him to preach, even though he preach in his own or in the monastery of another order. Should he preach heresies, let him proceed against him in accordance with the requirement of the law or the custom of the locality, even though that preacher should plead exemption by a general or special privilege; in which case the bishop shall proceed by Apostolic authority and as the delegate of the Apostolic See. But let bishops be careful that a preacher be not annoyed by false accusations or calumnies, or have just cause of complaint concerning such. Moreover, let bishops be on their guard not to permit anyone, whether of those who, being regulars in name, live outside their monasteries and the obedience of their religious institute, or secular priests, unless they are known to them and are of approved morals and doctrine, to preach in their city or diocese, even under pretext of any privilege whatsoever, till they have consulted the holy Apostolic See on the matter; from which See it is not likely that privileges of this kind are extorted by unworthy persons except by suppressing the truth or stating what is false.

Those soliciting alms, who are also commonly known as questors,[36] whatever their state, shall not in any manner presume to preach either *per se* or *per alium,* and shall, notwithstanding any privilege whatsoever, be absolutely restrained by suitable measures by the bishops and ordinaries of the localities.

ANNOUNCEMENT OF THE NEXT SESSION

This holy council also ordains and decrees that the next session be held and celebrated on the Thursday after the feast of the blessed Apostle James.

The session was afterwards prorogued to the thirteenth day of January, 1547.

---

35. C.13 (§ 6), X, De haeret., V, 7; Sess. XXIV, chap. 4 de ref.
36. C.14, X, De poenit. et remis., V, 38; c.11 (§ 2), VI°, De haeret., V, 2; c.2, in Clem., De poenit. et remis., V, 9. By the bull of Pius V, *Etsi Dominici,* (1567) all indulgences which gave occasion for abuse by the questors were withdrawn.

SIXTH SESSION

Celebrated on the thirteenth day of January, 1547

DECREE CONCERNING JUSTIFICATION

Introduction

Since there is being disseminated at this time, not without the loss of many souls and grievous detriment to the unity of the Church, a certain erroneous doctrine concerning justification, the holy, ecumenical and general Council of Trent, lawfully assembled in the Holy Ghost, the most reverend John Maria, Bishop of Praeneste de Monte, and Marcellus, priest of the Holy Cross in Jerusalem, cardinals of the holy Roman Church and legates Apostolic *a latere,* presiding in the name of our most holy Father and Lord in Christ, Paul III, by the providence of God, Pope, intends, for the praise and glory of Almighty God, for the tranquillity of the Church and the salvation of souls, to expound to all the faithful of Christ the true and salutary doctrine of justification, which the *Sun of justice,*[1] Jesus Christ, *the author and finisher of our faith*[2] taught, which the Apostles transmitted and which the Catholic Church under the inspiration of the Holy Ghost has always retained; strictly forbidding that anyone henceforth presume to believe, preach or teach otherwise than is defined and declared in the present decree.

Chapter I

THE IMPOTENCY OF NATURE AND OF THE LAW TO JUSTIFY MAN

The holy council declares first, that for a correct and clear understanding of the doctrine of justification, it is necessary that each one recognize and confess that since all men had lost innocence in the prevarication of Adam,[3] having become unclean,[4] and, as the Apostle says, *by nature chil-*

---

1. *Mal.* 4:2
2. *Heb.* 12:2
3. *Romans* 5:12; *1 Cor.* 15:22
4. *Is.* 64:6

dren of wrath,[5] as has been set forth in the decree on original sin,[6] they were so far *the servants of sin*[7] and under
the power of the devil and of death, that not only the Gentiles by the force of nature, but not even the Jews by the
very letter of the law of Moses, were able to be liberated or
to rise therefrom, though free will, weakened as it was in
its powers and downward bent,[8] was by no means extin-
guished in them.

Chapter II

THE DISPENSATION AND MYSTERY OF THE ADVENT OF CHRIST

Whence it came to pass that the heavenly Father, *the
Father of mercies and the God of all comfort,*[9] *when the blessed
fullness of the time was come,*[10] sent to men Jesus Christ,
His own Son, who had both before the law and during the
time of the law been announced and promised to many of
the holy fathers,[11] *that he might redeem the Jews who were
under the law,*[12] and *that the Gentiles who followed not after
justice*[13] might attain to justice, and that all men might receive
the adoption of sons. Him has God *proposed* as a propitia-
tor *through faith in his blood*[14] *for our sins, and not for our
sins only, but also for those of the whole world.*[15]

Chapter III

WHO ARE JUSTIFIED THROUGH CHRIST

But though *He died for all,*[16] yet all do not receive the
benefit of His death, but those only to whom the merit of
His passion is communicated; because as truly as men would
not be born unjust, if they were not born through propagation of the seed of Adam, since by that propagation they

---

5. *Eph.* 2:3
6. Cf. Sess. V at the beginning.
7. *Romans* 6:17, 20
8. Cf. II Synod of Orange (529), c.25. Hardouin, II, 1101
9. See *2 Cor.* 1:3
10. *Gal.* 4:4
11. *Gen.* 49:10, 18
12. *Gal.* 4:5
13. *Romans* 9:30
14. *Ibid.,* 3:25; Dist. I De poenit., *passim.*
15. See *1 John* 2:2
16. See *2 Cor.* 5:15

contract through him, when they are conceived, injustice as their own, so if they were not born again in Christ, they would never be justified, since in that new birth there is bestowed upon them, through the merit of His passion, the grace by which they are made just. For this benefit the Apostle exhorts us always *to give thanks to the Father, who hath made us worthy to be partakers of the lot of the saints in light, and hath delivered us from the power of darkness, and hath translated us into the kingdom of the Son of his love, in whom we have redemption and remission of sins.*[17]

Chapter IV

A BRIEF DESCRIPTION OF THE JUSTIFICATION OF THE SINNER AND ITS MODE IN THE STATE OF GRACE

In which words is given a brief description of the justification of the sinner, as being a translation from that state in which man is born a child of the first Adam, to the state of grace and of the adoption of the sons of God through the second Adam, Jesus Christ, Our Saviour. This translation however cannot, since the promulgation of the Gospel, be effected except through the laver of regeneration or its desire, as it is written: *Unless a man be born again of water and the Holy Ghost, he cannot enter into the kingdom of God.*[18]

Chapter V

THE NECESSITY OF PREPARATION FOR JUSTIFICATION IN ADULTS, AND WHENCE IT PROCEEDS

It is furthermore declared that in adults the beginning of that justification must proceed from the predisposing grace of God through Jesus Christ, that is, from His vocation, whereby, without any merits on their part, they are called; that they who by sin had been cut off from God, may be disposed through His quickening and helping grace to convert themselves to their own justification by freely assenting to and cooperating with that grace; so that, while God touches the heart of man through the illumination of the

---

17. *Col.* 1:12-14
18. *John* 3:5

Holy Ghost, man himself neither does absolutely nothing while receiving that inspiration, since he can also reject it, nor yet is he able by his own free will and without the grace of God to move himself to justice in His sight. Hence, when it is said in the sacred writings: *Turn ye to me, and I will turn to you,*[19] we are reminded of our liberty; and when we reply: *Convert us, O Lord, to thee, and we shall be converted,*[20] we confess that we need the grace of God.

Chapter VI

THE MANNER OF PREPARATION

Now, they [the adults] are disposed to that justice when, aroused and aided by divine grace, receiving *faith by hearing,*[21] they are moved freely toward God, believing to be true what has been divinely revealed and promised, especially that the sinner is justified by God *by his grace, through the redemption that is in Christ Jesus;*[22] and when, understanding themselves to be sinners, they, by turning themselves from the fear of divine justice, by which they are salutarily aroused, to consider the mercy of God, are raised to hope, trusting that God will be propitious to them for Christ's sake; and they begin to love Him as the fountain of all justice, and on that account are moved against sin by a certain hatred and detestation, that is, by that repentance that must be performed before baptism;[23] finally, when they resolve to receive baptism, to begin a new life and to keep the commandments of God. Of this disposition it is written: *He that cometh to God, must believe that he is, and is a rewarder to them that seek him;*[24] and, *Be of good faith, son, thy sins are forgiven thee;*[25] and, *The fear of the Lord driveth out sin;*[26] and, *Do penance, and be baptized every one of you in the name of Jesus Christ, for the remission of your sins, and you shall receive the gift of the Holy Ghost;*[27] and, *Going, there-*

---

19. *Zach.* 1:3
20. *Lam.* 5:21
21. *Romans* 10:17
22. *Ibid.,* 3:24
23. Cf. Sess. XIV, chap. 4
24. *Heb.* 11:6
25. *Matt.* 9:2; *Mark* 2:5
26. *Ecclus.* 1:27
27. *Acts* 2:38; cc.13, 97, D.IV de cons.

fore, teach ye all nations, baptizing them in the name of the Father, and of the Son, and of the Holy Ghost, teaching them to observe all things whatsoever I have commanded you;[28] finally, *Prepare your hearts unto the Lord.*[29]

Chapter VII

IN WHAT THE JUSTIFICATION OF THE SINNER CONSISTS, AND WHAT ARE ITS CAUSES

This disposition or preparation is followed by justification itself, which is not only a remission of sins but also the sanctification and renewal of the inward man through the voluntary reception of the grace and gifts whereby an unjust man becomes just and from being an enemy becomes a friend, that he may be *an heir according to hope of life everlasting.*[30] The causes of this justification are: the final cause is the glory of God and of Christ and life everlasting; the efficient cause is the merciful God who *washes and sanctifies*[31] gratuitously, signing and anointing *with the holy Spirit of promise, who is the pledge of our inheritance,*[32] the meritorious cause is His most beloved only begotten, Our Lord Jesus Christ, who, *when we were enemies,*[33] *for the exceeding charity wherewith he loved us,*[34] merited for us justification by His most holy passion on the wood of the cross and made satisfaction for us to God the Father, the instrumental cause is the sacrament of baptism, which is the sacrament of faith,[35] without which no man was ever justified finally, the single formal cause is the justice of God, not that by which He Himself is just, but that by which He makes us just, that, namely, with which we being endowed by Him, are *renewed in the spirit of our mind,*[36] and not only are we reputed but we are truly called and are just, receiving justice within us, each one according to his own measure, which the Holy Ghost distributes to everyone as He wills,[37] and

---

28. *Matt.* 28:19f.
29. See *1 Kings* 7:3
30. *Titus* 3:7
31. See *1 Cor.* 6:11
32. *Eph.* 1:13f.
33. *Romans* 5:10
34. *Eph.* 2:4
35. C.76, D.IV de cons.
36. *Eph.* 4:23
37. See *1 Cor.* 12:11

according to each one's disposition and cooperation. For though no one can be just except he to whom the merits of the passion of Our Lord Jesus Christ are communicated, yet this takes place in that justification of the sinner, when by the merit of the most holy passion, *the charity of God is poured forth by the Holy Ghost in the hearts*[38] of those who are justified and inheres in them; whence man through Jesus Christ, in whom he is ingrafted, receives in that justification, together with the remission of sins, all these infused at the same time, namely, faith, hope and charity. For faith, unless hope and charity be added to it, neither unites man perfectly with Christ nor makes him a living member of His body.[39] For which reason it is most truly said that *faith without works is dead*[40] and of no profit, and *in Christ Jesus neither circumcision availeth anything nor uncircumcision, but faith that worketh by charity.*[41] This faith, conformably to Apostolic tradition, catechumens ask of the Church before the sacrament of baptism, when they ask for the faith that gives eternal life, which without hope and charity faith cannot give. Whence also they hear immediately the word of Christ: *If thou wilt enter into life, keep the commandments.*[42] Wherefore, when receiving true and Christian justice, they are commanded, immediately on being born again, to preserve it pure and spotless, as *the first robe*[43] given them through Christ Jesus in place of that which Adam by his disobedience lost for himself and for us, so that they may bear it before the tribunal of Our Lord Jesus Christ and may have life eternal.

Chapter VIII

HOW THE GRATUITOUS JUSTIFICATION OF THE SINNER BY FAITH IS TO BE UNDERSTOOD

But when the Apostle says that man is justified by faith and freely,[44] these words are to be understood in that sense in which the uninterrupted unanimity of the Catholic

---

38. *Romans* 5:5
39. Cf. *infra*, chap. 10
40. *James* 2:17, 20
41. *Gal.* 5:6, 6:15
42. *Matt.* 19:17
43. *Luke* 15:22; c.31, D.II de poenit.
44. *Romans* 3:24; 5:1

Church has held and expressed them, namely, that we are therefore said to be justified by faith, because faith is the beginning of human salvation, the foundation and root of all justification, *without which it is impossible to please God*[45] and to come to the fellowship of His sons; and we are therefore said to be justified gratuitously, because none of those things that precede justification, whether faith or works, merit the grace of justification. For, *if by grace, it is not now by works, otherwise,* as the Apostle says, *grace is no more grace.*[46]

Chapter IX

AGAINST THE VAIN CONFIDENCE OF HERETICS

But though it is necessary to believe that sins neither are remitted nor ever have been remitted except gratuitously by divine mercy for Christ's sake, yet it must not be said that sins are forgiven or have been forgiven to anyone who boasts of his confidence and certainty of the remission of his sins,[47] resting on that alone, though among heretics and schismatics this vain and ungodly confidence may be and in our troubled times indeed is found and preached with untiring fury against the Catholic Church. Moreover, it must not be maintained, that they who are truly justified must needs, without any doubt whatever, convince themselves that they are justified, and that no one is absolved from sins and justified except he that believes with certainty that he is absolved and justified,[48] and that absolution and justification are effected by this faith alone, as if he who does not believe this, doubts the promises of God and the efficacy of the death and resurrection of Christ. For as no pious person ought to doubt the mercy of God, the merit of Christ and the virtue and efficacy of the sacraments, so each one, when he considers himself and his own weakness and indisposition, may have fear and apprehension concerning his own grace, since no one can know with the certainty of faith, which cannot be subject to error, that he has obtained the grace of God.

45. *Heb.* 11:6
46. *Romans* 11:6
47. Cf. *infra,* can. 12 and 13
48. *Infra,* can. 14

Chapter X

THE INCREASE OF THE JUSTIFICATION RECEIVED

Having, therefore, been thus justified and made the friends and *domestics of God,*[49] advancing *from virtue to virtue,*[50] they are *renewed,* as the Apostle says, *day by day,*[51] that is, *mortifying the members*[52] of their flesh, and presenting them as instruments of justice unto sanctification,[53] they, through the observance of the commandments of God and of the Church, faith cooperating with good works, increase in that justice received through the grace of Christ and are further justified, as it is written: *He that is just, let him be justified still;*[54] and, *Be not afraid to be justified even to death;*[55] and again, *Do you see that by works a man is justified, and not by faith only?*[56] This increase of justice holy Church asks for when she prays: "Give unto us, O Lord, an increase of faith, hope and charity."[57]

Chapter XI

THE OBSERVANCE OF THE COMMANDMENTS AND THE NECESSITY AND POSSIBILITY THEREOF

But no one, however much justified, should consider himself exempt from the observance of the commandments; no one should use that rash statement, once forbidden by the Fathers under anathema, that the observance of the commandments of God is impossible for one that is justified. For God does not command impossibilities, but by commanding admonishes thee to do what thou canst and to pray for what thou canst not, and aids thee that thou mayest be able.[58] *His commandments are not heavy,*[59] and *his yoke is sweet and burden light.*[60] For they who are the sons of God love Christ, but they who love Him, keep His command-

---

49. *Eph.* 2:19
50. *Psalms* 83:8
51. See *2 Cor.* 4:16
52. *Col.* 3:5
53. *Romans* 6:13, 19
54. *Apoc.* 22:11
55. *Ecclus.* 18:22
56. *James* 2:24
57. Thirteenth Sunday after Pentecost
58. St. Augustine, *De natura et gratia,* c.43 (50), PL, XLIV, 271
59. See *1 John* 5:3
60. *Matt.* 11:30

ments, as He Himself testifies;[61] which, indeed, with the divine help they can do. For though during this mortal life, men, however holy and just, fall at times into at least light and daily sins, which are also called venial, they do not on that account cease to be just, for that petition of the just, *forgive us our trespasses,*[62] is both humble and true; for which reason the just ought to feel themselves the more obliged to walk in the way of justice, for *being now freed from sin and made servants of God,*[63] they are able, *living soberly, justly and godly,*[64] to proceed onward through Jesus Christ, by whom they have access unto this grace.[65] For God does not forsake those who have been once justified by His grace, unless He be first forsaken by them. Wherefore, no one ought to flatter himself with faith alone, thinking that by faith alone he is made an heir and will obtain the inheritance, even though *he suffer* not *with Christ, that he may be also glorified with him.*[66] For even Christ Himself, as the Apostle says, *whereas he was the Son of God, he learned obedience by the things which he suffered, and being consummated, he became to all who obey him the cause of eternal salvation.*[67] For which reason the same Apostle admonishes those justified, saying: *Know you not that they who run in the race, all run indeed, but one receiveth the prize? So run that you may obtain. I therefore so run, not as at an uncertainty; I so fight, not as one beating the air, but I chastise my body and bring it into subjection; lest perhaps when I have preached to others, I myself should become a castaway.*[68] So also the prince of the Apostles, Peter: *Labor the more, that by good works you may make sure your calling and election. For doing these things, you shall not sin at any time.*[69] From which it is clear that they are opposed to the orthodox teaching of religion who maintain that the just man sins, venially at least, in every good work;[70] or, what is more intolerable, that he merits eternal punish-

61. *John* 14:23
62. *Matt.* 6:12
63. *Romans* 6:18, 22
64. *Titus* 2:12
65. *Romans* 5:1f.
66. *Ibid.*, 8:17
67. *Heb.* 5:8f.
68. See *1 Cor.* 9:24, 26f.
69. See *2 Peter* 1:10
70. Cf. *infra,* can. 25

ment; and they also who assert that the just sin in all works,
if, in order to arouse their sloth and to encourage themselves to run the race, they, in addition to this, that above
all God may be glorified, have in view also the eternal
reward,[71] since it is written: *I have inclined my heart to do
thy justifications on account of the reward;*[72] and of Moses
the Apostle says; that *he looked unto the reward.*[73]

Chapter XII

RASH PRESUMPTION OF PREDESTINATION IS TO BE AVOIDED

No one, moreover, so long as he lives this mortal life,
ought in regard to the sacred mystery of divine predesti-
nation, so far presume as to state with absolute certainty
that he is among the number of the predestined,[74] as if it
were true that the one justified either cannot sin any more,
or, if he does sin, that he ought to promise himself an assured
repentance. For except by special revelation, it cannot be
known whom God has chosen to Himself.

Chapter XIII

THE GIFT OF PERSEVERANCE

Similarly with regard to the gift of perseverance, of which
it is written: *He that shall persevere to the end, he shall be
saved,*[75] which cannot be obtained from anyone except from
Him who is able to make him stand who stands,[76] that he
may stand perseveringly, and to raise him who falls, let no
one promise himself herein something as certain with an
absolute certainty, though all ought to place and repose the
firmest hope in God's help. For God, unless men themselves
fail in His grace, as *he has begun a good work, so will he
perfect it, working to will and to accomplish.*[77] Nevertheless,
let those who think themselves to stand, take heed lest they
fall,[78] and with fear and trembling work out their salva-

71. Cf. *infra,* can. 31
72. *Psalms* 118:112
73. *Heb.* 11:26
74. Cf. c.17, C.XXIV, q.3
75. *Matt.* 10:22; 24:13
76. *Romans* 14:4
77. *Phil.* 1:6; 2:13
78. See *1 Cor.* 10:12

tion,[79] in labors, in watchings, in almsdeeds, in prayer, in fastings and chastity. For knowing that they are born again unto the hope of glory,[80] and not as yet unto glory, they ought to fear for the combat that yet remains with the flesh, with the world and with the devil, in which they cannot be victorious unless they be with the grace of God obedient to the Apostle who says: *We are debtors, not to the flesh, to live according to the flesh; for if you live according to the flesh, you shall die, but if by the spirit you mortify the deeds of the flesh, you shall live.*[81]

Chapter XIV

THE FALLEN AND THEIR RESTORATION

Those who through sin have forfeited the received grace of justification, can again be justified when, moved by God, they exert themselves to obtain through the sacrament of penance the recovery, by the merits of Christ, of the grace lost.[82] For this manner of justification is restoration for those fallen, which the holy Fathers have aptly called a second plank after the shipwreck of grace lost.[83] For on behalf of those who fall into sins after baptism, Christ Jesus instituted the sacrament of penance when He said: *Receive ye the Holy Ghost, whose sins you shall forgive, they are forgiven them, and whose sins you shall retain, they are retained.*[84] Hence, it must be taught that the repentance of a Christian after his fall is very different from that at his baptism, and that it includes not only a determination to avoid sins and a hatred of them, or *a contrite and humble heart,*[85] but also the sacramental confession of those sins, at least in desire, to be made in its season, and sacerdotal absolution, as well as satisfaction by fasts, alms, prayers and other devout exercises of the spiritual life, not indeed for the eternal punishment, which is, together with the guilt, remitted either by the sacrament or by the desire of the sacrament, but for the temporal punishment which, as the

---

79. *Phil.* 2:12
80. See *1 Peter* 1:3
81. *Romans* 8:12f.
82. Cf. *infra*, can. 23 and 29
83. C.72, D.I de poenit.
84. *John* 20:22f.
85. *Psalms* 50:19

sacred writings teach, is not always wholly remitted, as is
done in baptism, to those who, ungrateful to the grace of
God which they have received, have grieved the Holy Ghost[86]
and have not feared to *violate the temple of God.*[87] Of which
repentance it is written: *Be mindful whence thou art fallen;
do penance, and do the first works;*[88] and again, *The sorrow
that is according to God worketh penance, steadfast unto
salvation;*[89] and again, *Do penance, and bring forth fruits
worthy of penance.*[90]

Chapter XV

BY EVERY MORTAL SIN GRACE IS LOST, BUT NOT FAITH

Against the subtle wits of some also, who *by pleasing
speeches and good words seduce the hearts of the innocent,*[91]
it must be maintained that the grace of justification once
received is lost not only by infidelity, whereby also faith
itself is lost, but also by every other mortal sin, though in
this case faith is not lost; thus defending the teaching of
the divine law which excludes from the kingdom of God not
only unbelievers, but also the faithful [who are] *fornicators,
adulterers, effeminate, liers with mankind, thieves, covetous,
drunkards, railers, extortioners,*[92] and all others who commit deadly sins, from which with the help of divine grace
they can refrain, and on account of which they are cut off
from the grace of Christ.

Chapter XVI

THE FRUITS OF JUSTIFICATION, THAT IS, THE MERIT OF GOOD
WORKS, AND THE NATURE OF THAT MERIT

Therefore, to men justified in this manner, whether they
have preserved uninterruptedly the grace received or recov-
ered it when lost, are to be pointed out the words of the
Apostle: *Abound in every good work, knowing that your
labor is not in vain in the Lord.*[93] *For God is not unjust,*

---

86. *Eph.* 4:30
87. See *1 Cor.* 3:17
88. *Apoc.* 2:5
89. See *2 Cor.* 7:10
90. *Matt.* 3:2; 4:17; *Luke* 3:8
91. *Romans* 16:18
92. See *1 Cor.* 6:9f.; *1 Tim.* 1:9f.
93. See *1 Cor.* 15:58

that he should forget your work, and the love which you have shown in his name;[94] and, *Do not lose your confidence, which hath a great reward.*[95] Hence, to those who work well *unto the end*[96] and trust in God, eternal life is to be offered, both as a grace mercifully promised to the sons of God through Christ Jesus, and as a reward promised by God Himself, to be faithfully given to their good works and merits.[97] For this is the crown of justice which after his fight and course the Apostle declared was laid up for him, to be rendered to him by the just judge, and not only to him, but also to all that love his coming.[98] For since Christ Jesus Himself, as the head into the members and the vine into the branches,[99] continually infuses strength into those justified, which strength always precedes, accompanies and follows their good works, and without which they could not in any manner be pleasing and meritorious before God, we must believe that nothing further is wanting to those justified to prevent them from being considered to have, by those very works which have been done in God, fully satisfied the divine law according to the state of this life and to have truly merited eternal life, to be obtained in its [due] time, provided they depart [this life] in grace,[100] since Christ Our Saviour says: *If anyone shall drink of the water that I will give him, he shall not thirst forever; but it shall become in him a fountain of water springing up unto life everlasting.*[101] Thus, neither is our own justice established as our own from ourselves,[102] nor is the justice of God ignored or repudiated, for that justice which is called ours, because we are justified by its inherence in us, that same is [the justice] of God, because it is infused into us by God through the merit of Christ. Nor must this be omitted, that although in the sacred writings so much is attributed to good works, that even *he that shall give a drink of cold water to one of his least ones,* Christ promises, *shall not lose his reward;*[103]

---

94. *Heb.* 6:10
95. *Heb.* 10:35
96. *Matt.* 10:22
97. *Romans* 6:22
98. See *2 Tim.* 4:8
99. *John* 15:1f.
100. *Apoc.* 14:13
101. *John* 4:13f.
102. *Romans* 10:3; *2 Cor.* 3:5
103. *Matt.* 10:42; *Mark* 9:40

and the Apostle testifies that, *That which is at present momentary and light of our tribulation, worketh for us above measure exceedingly an eternal weight of glory;*[104] nevertheless, far be it that a Christian should either trust or glory in himself and not in the Lord,[105] whose bounty toward all men is so great that He wishes the things that are His gifts to be their merits. And since *in many things we all offend,*[106] each one ought to have before his eyes not only the mercy and goodness but also the severity and judgment [of God]; neither ought anyone to judge himself, even though he be not conscious to himself of anything;[107] because the whole life of man is to be examined and judged not by the judgment of man but of God, *who will bring to light the hidden things of darkness, and will make manifest the counsels of the hearts, and then shall every man have praise from God,*[108] who, as it is written, *will render to every man according to his works.*[109]

After this Catholic doctrine on justification, which whosoever does not faithfully and firmly accept cannot be justified, it seemed good to the holy council to add these canons, that all may know not only what they must hold and follow, but also what to avoid and shun.

CANONS CONCERNING JUSTIFICATION

Canon 1. If anyone says that man can be justified before God by his own works, whether done by his own natural powers or through the teaching of the law,[110] without divine grace through Jesus Christ, let him be anathema.

Canon 2. If anyone says that divine grace through Christ Jesus is given for this only, that man may be able more easily to live justly and to merit eternal life, as if by free will without grace he is able to do both, though with hardship and difficulty, let him be anathema.

Canon 3. If anyone says that without the predisposing inspiration of the Holy Ghost[111] and without His help, man

---

104. See *2 Cor.* 4:17
105. See *1 Cor.* 1:31; *2 Cor.* 10:17
106. *James* 3:2
107. See *1 Cor.* 4:3f.
108. *Ibid.,* 4:5
109. *Matt.* 16:27; *Romans* 2:6; *Apoc.* 22:12
110. Cf. *supra,* chaps. 1, 3
111. *Ibid.,* chap. 5

can believe, hope, love or be repentant as he ought,[112] so that the grace of justification may be bestowed upon him, let him be anathema.

Canon 4. If anyone says that man's free will moved and aroused by God, by assenting to God's call and action, in no way cooperates toward disposing and preparing itself to obtain the grace of justification, that it cannot refuse its assent if it wishes, but that, as something inanimate, it does nothing whatever and is merely passive, let him be anathema.

Canon 5. If anyone says that after the sin of Adam man's free will was lost and destroyed, or that it is a thing only in name, indeed a name without a reality, a fiction introduced into the Church by Satan, let him be anathema.

Canon 6. If anyone says that it is not in man's power to make his ways evil, but that the works that are evil as well as those that are good God produces, not permissively only but also *proprie et per se,* so that the treason of Judas is no less His own proper work than the vocation of St. Paul, let him be anathema.

Canon 7. If anyone says that all works done before justification, in whatever manner they may be done, are truly sins, or merit the hatred of God; that the more earnestly one strives to dispose himself for grace, the more grievously he sins, let him be anathema.

Canon 8. If anyone says that the fear of hell,[113] whereby, by grieving for sins, we flee to the mercy of God or abstain from sinning, is a sin or makes sinners worse, let him be anathema.

Canon 9. If anyone says that the sinner is justified by faith alone,[114] meaning that nothing else is required to cooperate in order to obtain the grace of justification, and that it is not in any way necessary that he be prepared and disposed by the action of his own will, let him be anathema.

Canon 10. If anyone says that men are justified without the justice of Christ,[115] whereby He merited for us, or by that justice are formally just, let him be anathema.

Canon 11. If anyone says that men are justified either by the sole imputation of the justice of Christ or by the sole

---

112. *Romans* 5:5
113. *Matt.* 10:28; *Luke* 12:5
114. *Supra,* chaps. 7, 8
115. *Gal.* 2:16; *supra,* chap. 7

remission of sins, to the exclusion of the grace and *the char-ity which is poured forth in their hearts by the Holy Ghost,*[116] and remains in them, or also that the grace by which we are justified is only the good will of God, let him be anathema.

Canon 12. If anyone says that justifying faith is nothing else than confidence in divine mercy,[117] which remits sins for Christ's sake, or that it is this confidence alone that jus-tifies us, let him be anathema.

Canon 13. If anyone says that in order to obtain the remis-sion of sins it is necessary for every man to believe with certainty and without any hesitation arising from his own weakness and indisposition that his sins are forgiven him, let him be anathema.

Canon 14. If anyone says that man is absolved from his sins and justified because he firmly believes that he is absolved and justified,[118] or that no one is truly justified except him who believes himself justified, and that by this faith alone absolution and justification are effected, let him be anathema.

Canon 15. If anyone says that a man who is born again and justified is bound *ex fide* to believe that he is certainly in the number of the predestined,[119] let him be anathema.

Canon 16. If anyone says that he will for certain, with an absolute and infallible certainty, have that great gift of perseverance even to the end, unless he shall have learned this by a special revelation,[120] let him be anathema.

Canon 17. If anyone says that the grace of justification is shared by those only who are predestined to life, but that all others who are called are called indeed but receive not grace, as if they are by divine power predestined to evil, let him be anathema.

Canon 18. If anyone says that the commandments of God are, even for one that is justified and constituted in grace,[121] impossible to observe, let him be anathema.

Canon 19. If anyone says that nothing besides faith is commanded in the Gospel, that other things are indifferent, neither commanded nor forbidden, but free; or that the ten

---

116. *Romans* 5:5
117. *Supra,* chap. 9
118. *Supra,* chap. 9
119. *Ibid.,* chap. 12
120. *Ibid.,* chap. 13
121. *Ibid.,* chap. 11

commandments in no way pertain to Christians, let him be anathema.

Canon 20. If anyone says that a man who is justified and however perfect is not bound to observe the commandments of God and the Church, but only to believe,[122] as if the Gospel were a bare and absolute promise of eternal life without the condition of observing the commandments, let him be anathema.

Canon 21. If anyone says that Christ Jesus was given by God to men as a redeemer in whom to trust, and not also as a legislator whom to obey, let him be anathema.

Canon 22. If anyone says that the one justified either can without the special help of God persevere in the justice received,[123] or that with that help he cannot, let him be anathema.

Canon 23. If anyone says that a man once justified can sin no more, nor lose grace,[124] and that therefore he that falls and sins was never truly justified; or on the contrary, that he can during his whole life avoid all sins, even those that are venial, except by a special privilege from God, as the Church holds in regard to the Blessed Virgin, let him be anathema.

Canon 24. If anyone says that the justice received is not preserved and also not increased before God through good works,[125] but that those works are merely the fruits and signs of justification obtained, but not the cause of its increase, let him be anathema.

Canon 25. If anyone says that in every good work the just man sins at least venially,[126] or, what is more intolerable, mortally, and hence merits eternal punishment, and that he is not damned for this reason only, because God does not impute these works unto damnation, let him be anathema.

Canon 26. If anyone says that the just ought not for the good works done in God[127] to expect and hope for an eternal reward from God through His mercy and the merit of Jesus Christ, if by doing well and by keeping the divine command-

---

122. Cf. chap. cit.
123. *Supra,* chap. 13
124. *Ibid.,* chap. 14
125. *Ibid.,* chap. 10
126. *Ibid.,* chap. 11 at the end.
127. *Ibid.,* chap. 16

ments they persevere to the end,[128] let him be anathema.

Canon 27. If anyone says that there is no mortal sin except that of unbelief,[129] or that grace once received is not lost through any other sin however grievous and enormous except by that of unbelief, let him be anathema.

Canon 28. If anyone says that with the loss of grace through sin faith is also lost with it, or that the faith which remains is not a true faith, though it is not a living one, or that he who has faith without charity is not a Christian, let him be anathema.

Canon 29. If anyone says that he who has fallen after baptism cannot by the grace of God rise again,[130] or that he can indeed recover again the lost justice but by faith alone without the sacrament of penance, contrary to what the holy Roman and Universal Church, instructed by Christ the Lord and His Apostles, has hitherto professed, observed and taught, let him be anathema.

Canon 30. If anyone says that after the reception of the grace of justification the guilt is so remitted and the debt of eternal punishment so blotted out to every repentant sinner, that no debt of temporal punishment remains to be discharged either in this world[131] or in purgatory before the gates of heaven can be opened,[132] let him be anathema.

Canon 31. If anyone says that the one justified sins when he performs good works with a view to an eternal reward,[133] let him be anathema.

Canon 32. If anyone says that the good works of the one justified are in such manner the gifts of God that they are not also the good merits of him justified; or that the one justified by the good works that he performs by the grace of God and the merit of Jesus Christ, whose living member he is, does not truly merit an increase of grace, eternal life, and in case he dies in grace, the attainment of eternal life itself and also an increase of glory, let him be anathema.

Canon 33. If anyone says that the Catholic doctrine of justification as set forth by the holy council in the present

---

128. *Matt.* 24:13
129. *Supra,* chap. 15
130. *Ibid.,* chap. 14
131. Cf. Sess. XIV, chap. 8
132. Cf. Sess. XXV at the beginning.
133. *Supra,* chap. 11 at the end.

decree, derogates in some respect from the glory of God or the merits of Our Lord Jesus Christ, and does not rather illustrate the truth of our faith and no less the glory of God and of Christ Jesus, let him be anathema.

DECREE CONCERNING REFORM

Chapter I

IT IS PROPER THAT PRELATES RESIDE IN THEIR CHURCHES; IF THEY ACT OTHERWISE, THE PENALTIES OF THE EARLIER LAWS ARE RENEWED AGAINST THEM AND NEW ONES ARE PRESCRIBED

The same holy council, the same legates of the Apostolic See presiding, wishing to restore a very much collapsed ecclesiastical discipline and to reform the depraved morals of the clergy and the Christian people, has deemed it proper to begin with those who preside over the major churches, for unblemished character in those who govern is the salvation of those governed.[134] Trusting therefore that by the mercy of Our Lord and God and the prudent vigilance of the vicar of that God on earth, it will surely come about that for the government of the churches, a burden formidable even to the shoulders of angels, those who are most worthy, whose previous life in its every stage, from their youth to their riper years, laudably spent in the services of ecclesiastical discipline, bears testimony in their favor, will be chosen in accordance with the venerable ordinances of the holy Fathers,[135] it admonishes all who under whatever name or title are set over patriarchal, primatial, metropolitan and cathedral churches, and hereby wishes that they be considered admonished, that *taking heed to themselves and to the whole flock, wherein the Holy Ghost hath placed them to rule the Church of God which he hath purchased with his own blood,*[136] that *they be vigilant,* as the Apostle commands, *labor in all things and fulfill their ministry.*[137] Let them know, however, that they cannot fulfill this if like hirelings they desert the flocks committed to them[138] and do not attend to the guardianship of their sheep, whose blood will be required at their hands

---

134. C.5, D.LXI
135. C.4, D.LIX; cc.2, 6, 8, D.LXI
136. *Acts* 20:28
137. See *2 Tim.* 4:5
138. *John* 10:12

by the supreme judge;[139] since it is most certain that the shepherd's excuse will not be accepted if the wolf devours the sheep and he knows it not. And since there are some at this time, which is greatly to be deplored, who, forgetful even of their own salvation and preferring earthly things to the things of heaven and things human to things divine, wander about at divers courts or keep themselves occupied with the care of temporal affairs, their fold forsaken and their watchfulness over the sheep committed to them neglected, it has seemed good to the holy council to renew, as by virtue of the present decree it does renew, the old canons promulgated against non-residents,[140] which on account of the disorders of the times and of men have wellnigh fallen into desuetude; and furthermore, for a more faithful residence of the same and for the reform of morals in the Church, to ordain and decree in the manner following. If anyone, by whatever dignity, rank and pre-eminence distinguished, shall, by remaining outside of his diocese for a continuous period of six months[141] without lawful impediment or just and reasonable causes,[142] be absent from a patriarchal, primatial, metropolitan or cathedral church, under whatever title, cause, name or right committed to him, he shall incur *ipso jure* the forfeiture of a fourth part of one year's revenues, to be applied by the ecclesiastical superior to the church treasury and to the poor of the locality. If he continues to absent himself for another six months, he shall *eo ipso* forfeit another fourth part of the revenues, to be applied in like manner.[143] If the contumacy proceed yet farther, that he may be subject to a severer penalty of the sacred canons, the metropolitan shall be bound to denounce the absent suffragan bishops, and the oldest resident suffragan bishop shall be bound under penalty, to be incurred *ipso facto,* of being forbidden entrance to the church,[144] to denounce the absent metropolitan to the Roman pontiff by letter or messenger within three months, that he, by the authority of his supreme see, may take action against the non-resident prelates, as the degree of contumacy of each may demand, and provide

---

139. *Ezech.* 33:6
140. C.20, C.VII, q. 1 ff.; tit. X, De cler. non resid., III, 4 et in VI°, III, 3
141. C.11, X, De cler. non resid., III, 4
142. Cf. Sess. XXIII, chap. 1 de ref.
143. Cf. Sess. and chap. cit.
144. Cf. Schroeder, *Disciplinary Decrees of the General Councils,* p. 353, no. 60

the churches with more useful pastors, as he shall know in the Lord to be salutary and expedient.

Chapter II

NO ONE HOLDING A BENEFICE THAT REQUIRES PERSONAL RESIDENCE MAY ABSENT HIMSELF EXCEPT FOR A JUST CAUSE TO BE APPROVED BY THE BISHOP, WHO SHALL THEN APPOINT A VICAR FOR THE *CURA ANIMARUM,* WITHDRAWING A PORTION OF THE REVENUES

Those inferior to bishops, who by title or *in commendam* hold any ecclesiastical benefices that by law or custom require personal residence, shall by appropriate measures be compelled by their ordinaries to reside therein, according as it seems expedient to them for the good government of the churches and the increase of divine worship, taking into account the character of places and persons, and to no one shall privileges or perpetual indults in favor of non-residence or the reception of revenues during absence be of avail;[145] temporary permissions and dispensations, however, granted solely on true and reasonable grounds and to be legally proved before the ordinary, shall remain in force; in which cases, nevertheless, it is the duty of the bishops, as delegated in this matter by the Apostolic See, to see to it that the *cura animarum* is in no way neglected by the appointment of competent vicars and the assignment of a suitable portion of the revenues;[146] no privilege or exemption whatever shall be of avail to anyone in this matter.

Chapter III

TRANSGRESSIONS OF SECULAR CLERICS AND OF REGULARS WHO LIVE OUTSIDE THEIR MONASTERIES, SHALL BE CORRECTED BY THE ORDINARY OF THE LOCALITY

The prelates of the churches shall apply themselves prudently and diligently to correct the excesses of their subjects, and no secular cleric under pretext of a personal privilege, or a regular living outside his monastery under pretext of a privilege of his order, shall, if he transgresses,

---

145. C.15, VI°, De rescrip., I, 3
146. C. 34, VI°, De elect., I, 6

be considered exempt from being visited, punished and corrected in accordance with the canonical enactments by the
ordinary of the locality as delegated in this matter by the
Apostolic See.[147]

Chapter IV

BISHOPS AND OTHER MAJOR PRELATES SHALL VISIT ALL
CHURCHES AS OFTEN AS THIS IS NECESSARY; EVERYTHING THAT
MIGHT HINDER THE EXECUTION OF THIS DECREE IS ABROGATED

Chapters of cathedral and of other major churches and
the members thereof shall not by any exemptions, customs,
judicial verdicts, oaths, agreements, which bind only the
originators thereof and not also their successors, shield themselves so that they cannot even with Apostolic authority be
visited, corrected and amended in accordance with the
canonical statutes as often as shall be necessary by their
own bishops and other major prelates, by themselves alone
or with those whom they shall deem fit to accompany them.[148]

Chapter V

BISHOPS SHALL NEITHER EXERCISE ANY PONTIFICAL
FUNCTIONS NOR ORDAIN IN ANOTHER DIOCESE

No bishop is allowed under pretext of any privilege to
exercise pontifical functions in the diocese of another, except
with the expressed permission of the ordinary of the place,
and for those persons only who are subject to the same ordinary.[149] If the contrary is done, the bishop is *ipso jure* suspended from the exercise of pontifical functions and those
so ordained from the exercise of their orders.

ANNOUNCEMENT OF THE NEXT SESSION

Does it please you that the next following session be celebrated on Thursday after the first Sunday of the approaching Lent, which will be the third day of March?
They answered: It pleases us.

---

147. Cf. Sess. XIV, chap. 4 de ref.
148. Cf. Sess. XXIV, chap. 3 de ref. and Sess. XXV, chap. 6 de ref.
149. Cf. Sess. XIV, chaps. 2, 3 de ref. and Sess. XXIII, chap. 8 de ref.

SEVENTH SESSION

Celebrated on the third day of March, 1547

DECREE CONCERNING THE SACRAMENTS

Foreword

For the completion of the salutary doctrine on justification, which was promulgated with the unanimous consent of the Fathers in the last session, it has seemed proper to deal with the most holy sacraments of the Church, through which all true justice either begins, or being begun is increased, or being lost is restored. Wherefore, in order to destroy the errors and extirpate the heresies that in our stormy times are directed against the most holy sacraments, some of which are a revival of heresies long ago condemned by our Fathers, while others are of recent origin, all of which are exceedingly detrimental to the purity of the Catholic Church and the salvation of souls, the holy, ecumenical and general Council of Trent, lawfully assembled in the Holy Ghost, the same legates of the Apostolic See presiding, adhering to the teaching of the Holy Scriptures, to the Apostolic traditions, and to the unanimous teaching of other councils and of the Fathers, has thought it proper to establish and enact these present canons; hoping, with the help of the Holy Spirit, to publish later those that are wanting for the completion of the work begun.

CANONS ON THE SACRAMENTS IN GENERAL

Canon 1. If anyone says that the sacraments of the New Law were not all instituted by Our Lord Jesus Christ, or that there are more or less than seven, namely, baptism, confirmation, Eucharist, penance, extreme unction, order and matrimony,[1] or that any one of these seven is not truly and intrinsically a sacrament, let him be anathema.

Canon 2. If anyone says that these sacraments of the New Law do not differ from the sacraments of the Old Law, except

---

1. Eugene IV in *decr. ad Armenos* (Denzinger, no. 695); Pius IV in the bull *Injunctum nobis* (*idem,* no. 996).

that the ceremonies are different and the external rites are different, let him be anathema.

Canon 3. If anyone says that these seven sacraments are so equal to each other that one is not for any reason more excellent than the other, let him be anathema.

Canon 4. If anyone says that the sacraments of the New Law are not necessary for salvation but are superfluous, and that without them or without the desire of them men obtain from God through faith alone the grace of justification,[2] though all are not necessary for each one, let him be anathema.

Canon 5. If anyone says that these sacraments have been instituted for the nourishment of faith alone, let him be anathema.

Canon 6. If anyone says that the sacraments of the New Law do not contain the grace which they signify, or that they do not confer that grace on those who place no obstacles in its way,[3] as though they are only outward signs of grace or justice received through faith and certain marks of Christian profession, whereby among men believers are distinguished from unbelievers, let him be anathema.

Canon 7. If anyone says that grace, so far as God's part is concerned, is not imparted through the sacraments always and to all men even if they receive them rightly, but only sometimes and to some persons, let him be anathema.

Canon 8. If anyone says that by the sacraments of the New Law grace is not conferred *ex opere operato,* but that faith alone in the divine promise is sufficient to obtain grace, let him be anathema.

Canon 9. If anyone says that in three sacraments, namely, baptism, confirmation and order, there is not imprinted on the soul a character, that is, a certain spiritual and indelible mark, by reason of which they cannot be repeated,[4] let him be anathema.

Canon 10. If anyone says that all Christians have the power to administer the word and all the sacraments,[5] let him be anathema.

Canon 11. If anyone says that in ministers, when they effect and confer the sacraments, there is not required at

2. Cf. Sess. VI, chap. 7 and can. 9
3. Eugene IV in the decr. cited
4. *Ibid.*
5. Cf. Sess. XIV, Penance, chap. 6, and Extr. Unct., chap. 3.

least the intention of doing what the Church does,[6] let him be anathema.

Canon 12. If anyone says that a minister who is in mortal sin, though he observes all the essentials that pertain to the effecting or conferring of a sacrament,[7] neither effects nor confers a sacrament, let him be anathema.

Canon 13. If anyone says that the received and approved rites of the Catholic Church, accustomed to be used in the administration of the sacraments, may be despised or omitted by the ministers without sin and at their pleasure, or may be changed by any pastor of the churches to other new ones, let him be anathema.

CANONS ON BAPTISM

Canon 1. If anyone says that the baptism of John had the same effect as the baptism of Christ,[8] let him be anathema.

Canon 2. If anyone says that true and natural water is not necessary for baptism[9] and thus twists into some metaphor the words of Our Lord Jesus Christ: *Unless a man be born again of water and the Holy Ghost,*[10] let him be anathema.

Canon 3. If anyone says that in the Roman Church, which is the mother and mistress of all churches, there is not the true doctrine concerning the sacrament of baptism,[11] let him be anathema.

Canon 4. If anyone says that the baptism which is given by heretics in the name of the Father, and of the Son, and of the Holy Ghost, with the intention of doing what the Church does, is not true baptism,[12] let him be anathema.

Canon 5. If anyone says that baptism is optional, that is, not necessary for salvation,[13] let him be anathema.

Canon 6. If anyone says that one baptized cannot, even if he wishes, lose grace, however much he may sin, unless he is unwilling to believe, let him be anathema.

Canon 7. If anyone says that those baptized are by baptism made debtors only to faith alone, but not to the obser-

---

6. Eugene IV in the decr. cited
7. Cf. c.98, C.I, q. 1; cc.39, 149, D.IV de cons.
8. Cf. c.135, D.IV de cons.
9. Cf. c.5, X, De bapt., III, 42
10. *John* 3:5
11. C.9, X, De haeret., V, 7
12. Cc.97, 98, C.I, q. 1
13. *John* 3:5

vance of the whole law of Christ, let him be anathema.

Canon 8. If anyone says that those baptized are free from all the precepts of holy Church, whether written or unwritten, so that they are not bound to observe them unless they should wish to submit to them of their own accord, let him be anathema.

Canon 9. If anyone says that the remembrance of the baptism received is to be so impressed on men that they may understand that all the vows made after baptism are void in virtue of the promise already made in that baptism, as if by those vows they detracted from the faith which they professed and from the baptism itself, let him be anathema.

Canon 10. If anyone says that by the sole remembrance and the faith of the baptism received, all sins committed after baptism are either remitted or made venial, let him be anathema.

Canon 11. If anyone says that baptism, truly and rightly administered, must be repeated in the one converted to repentance after having denied the faith of Christ among the infidels, let him be anathema.

Canon 12. If anyone says that no one is to be baptized except at that age at which Christ was baptized, or when on the point of death, let him be anathema.

Canon 13. If anyone says that children, because they have not the act of believing, are not after having received baptism to be numbered among the faithful, and that for this reason are to be rebaptized when they have reached the years of discretion;[14] or that it is better that the baptism of such be omitted than that, while not believing by their own act, they should be baptized in the faith of the Church alone, let him be anathema.

Canon 14. If anyone says that those who have been thus baptized when children, are, when they have grown up, to be questioned whether they will ratify what their sponsors promised in their name when they were baptized, and in case they answer in the negative, are to be left to their own will; neither are they to be compelled in the meantime to a Christian life by any penalty other than exclusion from the reception of the Eucharist and the other sacraments, until they repent, let him be anathema.

---

14. Cf. c.139, D.IV de cons.

CANONS ON CONFIRMATION

Canon 1. If anyone says that the confirmation of those baptized is an empty ceremony and not a true and proper sacrament; or that of old it was nothing more than a sort of instruction, whereby those approaching adolescence gave an account of their faith to the Church, let him be anathema.

Canon 2. If anyone says that those who ascribe any power to the holy chrism of confirmation, offer insults to the Holy Ghost, let him be anathema.

Canon 3. If anyone says that the ordinary minister of holy confirmation is not the bishop alone,[15] but any simple priest, let him be anathema.

DECREE CONCERNING REFORM

The same holy council, the same legates presiding therein, intending to continue, to the praise of God and the increase of the Christian religion, the work begun concerning residence and reform, has thought it well to decree as follows, saving always and in all things the authority of the Apostolic See.

Chapter I

THE COMPETENCY REQUIRED TO CONDUCT CATHEDRAL CHURCHES

No one shall be chosen to govern cathedral churches unless he is born of lawful wedlock, is of mature age, is known for his integrity of morals, and possesses the required knowledge,[16] in accordance with the constitution of Alexander III, which begins, "Cum in cunctis," promulgated in the Lateran Council.[17]

Chapter II

THOSE HOLDING SEVERAL CATHEDRAL CHURCHES ARE COMMANDED TO RESIGN IN A SPECIFIED MANNER AND TIME ALL BUT ONE

No one, by whatever dignity, rank or pre-eminence distinguished, shall presume, in contravention of the sacred

15. Cf. Sess. XXIII, chap. 4
16. Cf. Sess. XXII, chap. 2 de ref.
17. C.7, X, De elect., I, 6

canons,[18] to accept and to hold at the same time several metropolitan or cathedral churches, either by title or *in commendam* or under any other name, since he must be considered exceedingly fortunate who succeeds in ruling one church well, fruitfully and with due interest in the salvation of the souls committed to him. But those who now hold several churches contrary to the tenor of the present decree, shall be bound, retaining the one which they prefer, to resign the rest within six months if they are subject to free disposal by the Apostolic See, in other cases within a year; otherwise those churches, with the sole exception of the one last obtained, shall be *eo ipso* considered vacant.

Chapter III

BENEFICES ARE TO BE CONFERRED ONLY ON COMPETENT PERSONS

Inferior ecclesiastical benefices, especially those to which is attached the *cura animarum,* shall be conferred on worthy and competent persons and on such as can reside in the place and exercise personally the care of souls, in accordance with the constitution of Alexander III in the Lateran Council, which begins, "Quia nonnulli,"[19] and that of Gregory X, published in the General Council of Lyons, which begins, "Licet canon."[20] A collation or provision made otherwise is absolutely null, and let the collating bishop know that he will incur the penalties of the constitution of the general council, which begins, "Grave nimis."[21]

Chapter IV

THE HOLDER OF SEVERAL BENEFICES CONTRARY TO THE CANONS SHALL BE DEPRIVED OF THEM

Whoever shall in the future presume to accept and to hold at the same time several charges or otherwise incompatible ecclesiastical benefices,[22] whether by way of union for life or

---

18. C.2, D.LXX; c.3, C.X, q.3; cc. I, 2, C.XXI, q.1; cc.5, 13, 28, X, De praeb., III, 5; c.32, VI°, De praeb., III, 4
19. C.3, X, De cler. non resid., III, 4
20. C.14, VI°, De elect., I, 16
21. C.29, X, De praeb., III, 5
22. Cf. Sess. XXIV, chap. 17 de ref.

by way of perpetual *commendam* or under any other name or title whatsoever, in contravention of the provision of the sacred canons and especially of the constitution of Innocent III, which begins, "De multa,"[23] shall be *ipso jure* deprived of those benefices in accordance with the provisions of that constitution and also by virtue of the present canon.

Chapter V

HOLDERS OF SEVERAL BENEFICES TO WHICH IS ANNEXED THE *CURA ANIMARUM* MUST EXHIBIT THEIR DISPENSATIONS TO THE ORDINARY, WHO SHALL PROVIDE THE CHURCHES WITH A VICAR, ASSIGNING A SUITABLE PORTION OF THE REVENUES

Local ordinaries shall strictly compel all who hold several charges or otherwise incompatible ecclesiastical benefices to exhibit their dispensations, and adopt other procedures in accordance with the constitution of Gregory X, published in the General Council of Lyons, beginning with "Ordinarii,"[24] which this holy council believes ought to be renewed and does renew; adding, moreover, that the ordinaries are by all means to provide, even by deputing competent vicars and assigning a suitable portion of the revenues, that the *cura animarum* be in no way neglected and that those benefices be by no means defrauded of the services due them; appeals, privileges and exemptions whatsoever, even with the appointment of special judges and their inhibitions, being of no avail to anyone in the aforesaid matter.

Chapter VI

WHAT UNIONS OF BENEFICES SHALL BE CONSIDERED VALID

Perpetual unions,[25] made within forty years, may be investigated by the ordinaries as delegates of the Apostolic See, and such as have been obtained through deceit or deception shall be declared null. Those however must be presumed to have been obtained surreptitiously which, having been granted within the aforesaid period, have not yet been carried into effect in whole or in part; those also which shall henceforth

23. C.28, X, De praeb., III, 5
24. C.3, VI°, De off. ord., I, 16
25. Cf. Sess. XIV, chap. 9 de ref.; Sess. XXIV, chap. 13 de ref; Sess. XXV, chap. 9 de ref.

be made at the instance of any person, unless it is certain that they have been made for lawful and otherwise reasonable causes, which must be verified before the local ordinary, those persons being summoned whose interests are concerned; hence, unless the Apostolic See shall have declared otherwise, they shall be absolutely devoid of force.

Chapter VII

UNITED ECCLESIASTICAL BENEFICES MUST BE VISITED; THE *CURA ANIMARUM* THERETO IS TO BE EXERCISED ALSO BY PERPETUAL VICARS, WITH WHOSE APPOINTMENT A PORTION IS TO BE ASSIGNED EVEN FOR SPECIFIC PURPOSES

Ecclesiastical benefices having the *cura animarum,* which are found to have been always united or annexed to cathedral, collegiate or other churches, or to monasteries, benefices, colleges or to pious places of whatever sort,[26] shall be visited every year by the local ordinaries, who shall zealously see to it that the *cura animarum* is exercised in a praiseworthy manner by competent vicars, also perpetual, unless the ordinaries shall deem it expedient for the good government of the churches to provide otherwise, who shall be appointed to the same by the ordinaries with a portion consisting of a third part of the revenues,[27] or of a greater or less proportion, at the discretion of the ordinaries, also assigned for the specific purpose; appeals, privileges and exemptions, also with the appointment of special judge's and their inhibitions, being of no avail to anyone in the aforesaid matter.

Chapter VIII

CHURCHES SHALL BE REPAIRED; THE *CURA ANIMARUM* DILIGENTLY DISCHARGED

The local ordinaries shall be bound to visit every year with Apostolic authority all churches in whatsoever manner exempt, and to provide by suitable legal remedies that those that need repair be repaired, and that they be not in any way defrauded of the *cura animarum* if such be annexed

---

26. Cf. Sess. XIV, chap. 9 de ref.
27. Cf. *supra,* chap. 5 and Sess. XXV, chap. 16 de ref.

to them or of other services due them;[28] appeals, privileges, customs, even though immemorial, appointment of judges and their inhibitions, being absolutely excluded.

Chapter IX

THE RITE OF CONSECRATION IS NOT TO BE DELAYED

Those promoted to major churches shall receive the rite of consecration within the time prescribed by law,[29] and any delays granted extending beyond a period of six months, shall be of no avail to anyone.

Chapter X

WHEN A SEE IS VACANT, CHAPTERS SHALL NOT GRANT RELEASES TO ANYONE UNLESS HE BE PRESSED FOR TIME BECAUSE OF A BENEFICE OBTAINED OR ABOUT TO BE OBTAINED; VARIOUS PENALTIES AGAINST THOSE WHO ACT OTHERWISE

It shall not be lawful for chapters of churches, when a see is vacant, to grant, either by a provision of the common law or by virtue of a privilege or custom, permission to be ordained or dimissory letters or "reverends," as some call them, within a year from the day of the vacancy, to anyone who is not pressed for time by reason of an ecclesiastical benefice obtained or about to be obtained.[30] Otherwise, the contravening chapter shall be subject to ecclesiastical interdict, and those so ordained, if they are in minor orders, shall enjoy no clerical privilege, especially in criminal causes, while those in major orders shall be *ipso jure* suspended from the exercise thereof during the pleasure of the next prelate.

Chapter XI

AUTHORITY FOR PROMOTION WITHOUT A JUST CAUSE SHALL NOT AVAIL ANYONE

Authority for promotion by anyone shall be of no avail except to those who have a legitimate reason why they can-

---

28. Cc.10-12, C.X, q.1; Sess. XXI, chap. 8 de ref. and Sess. XXIV, chap. 9 de ref.
29. C.2, D.LXXV; c.1, D.C.
30. C.3, VI°, De temp. ord., I, 9; cf. Sess. XXIII, chap. 10 de ref.

not be ordained by their own bishops, which must be expressed in writing; and then they shall not be ordained except by the bishop who resides in his own diocese,[31] or by one who exercises the pontifical functions for him, and after a careful examination.

Chapter XII

PERMISSION GRANTED FOR NON-PROMOTION SHALL NOT EXCEED ONE YEAR

Permission granted for not being promoted shall be good for one year only, except in the cases provided by law.[32]

Chapter XIII

WITH CERTAIN EXCEPTIONS, PERSONS, BY WHOMSOEVER PRESENTED, SHALL NOT BE APPOINTED WITHOUT BEING FIRST EXAMINED AND APPROVED BY THE ORDINARY

Those presented, elected or nominated by any ecclesiastical persons whatsoever, even by nuncios of the Apostolic See, shall not be appointed to, confirmed in or admitted to any ecclesiastical benefice,[33] even under the pretext of some privilege or immemorial custom, unless they shall have been first examined and found competent by the local ordinaries. And no one shall by recourse to an appeal be able to escape from being bound to undergo that examination. Those, however, are excepted who are presented, elected or nominated by universities or by colleges for general studies.[34]

Chapter XIV

THE CIVIL CAUSES OF EXEMPT PERSONS WHICH MAY BE TAKEN COGNIZANCE OF BY BISHOPS

In the causes of exempt persons the constitution of Innocent IV, beginning with "Volentes," published in the General Council of Lyons,[35] shall be observed, which this holy council

---

31. Cf. Sess. VI, chap. 5 de ref. and Sess. XIV, chap. 2 de ref.
32. Cc.14, 34, VI°, De elect., I, 6
33. Cf. Sess. XXV, chap. 9 de ref.
34. Cf. Sess. XXIV, chap. 18 de ref.
35. C.1, VI°, De privil., V, 7

has thought ought to be renewed and does renew; adding moreover, that in civil causes relative to wages and to persons in distress, secular clerics and regulars living outside their monasteries, howsoever exempt, even though they have a special judge deputed by the Apostolic See, and in other causes if they have no such judge, may be brought before the local ordinaries as delegated in this matter by that See and be constrained and compelled by law to pay what they owe; no privileges, exemptions, appointment of conservators and their inhibitions, being of any avail whatever against the aforesaid.

Chapter XV

ORDINARIES SHALL SEE TO IT THAT ALL HOSPITALS, EVEN THOSE EXEMPT, ARE FAITHFULLY MANAGED BY THEIR ADMINISTRATORS

Ordinaries shall take care that all hospitals are faithfully and diligently managed by their administrators, by whatsoever name known and in whatsoever manner exempt,[36] observing the form of the constitution of the Council of Vienne, which begins, "Quia contingit,"[37] which this holy council has thought ought to be renewed and does renew together with the restrictions therein contained.

ANNOUNCEMENT OF THE NEXT SESSION

This holy council has also ordained and decreed that the next session be held and celebrated on Thursday, the fifth day after the coming Sunday *in Albis,* which will be the twenty-first of April of the present year, 1547.

BULL AUTHORIZING THE TRANSFER OF THE COUNCIL

Paul, Bishop, servant of the servants of God, to our venerable brother John Maria, Bishop of Praeneste, and our beloved sons, Marcellus, priest of the Holy Cross in Jerusalem, and Reginald of St. Mary in Cosmedin, deacon, cardinals, our legates *a latere* and of the Apostolic See, health and apostolic benediction.

We, by the providence of God, presiding over the government of the universal Church, though with merits unequal

---

36. Cf. Sess. XXV, chap. 8 de ref.
37. C.2, De relig. dom. in Clem., III, 11

thereto, consider it a part of our office that when something of more than ordinary importance must be decided concerning the Christian commonwealth, it be done not only at an opportune time but also in a place at once convenient and suitable. Wherefore, when we lately, with the advice and consent of our venerable brethren, the cardinals of the holy Roman Church, on hearing that peace had been made between our most dear sons in Christ, Charles, ever august Emperor of the Romans, and Francis, the most Christian King of the French, raised and removed the suspension of the celebration of the holy, ecumenical and general council, which we had on another occasion, for reasons then stated, convoked with the same advice and consent in the city of Trent, and which was, for certain other reasons at that time also stated, suspended upon the same advice and consent to another more opportune and suitable time to be made known by us, being ourselves unable, because at that time lawfully hindered, to proceed personally to the aforesaid city and to be present at the council, we, by the same advice, appointed and deputed you as legates *a latere* on our behalf and on that of the Apostolic See in that council, and we sent you to that city as angels of peace, as is set forth more fully in our various letters dealing with this matter. Wishing now to provide opportunely that so holy a work as the celebration of this council may not through the inconvenience of the place or in any other manner be hindered or unduly delayed, we, by our own action and certain knowledge, with the plenitude of Apostolic authority and with the same advice and consent, grant to you all together or to two of you, in case the other should be detained by a lawful impediment or perchance be absent therefrom, by the tenor of these presents with Apostolic authority, full and unrestricted power and authority to transfer and change, whenever you shall deem it expedient, the aforesaid council from the city of Trent to any other more convenient, suitable and safer city which you shall judge appropriate; also to prohibit, even by ecclesiastical censures and penalties, the prelates and other members of that council to proceed therein to any further measures in the said city of Trent; further, to continue, hold and celebrate the same council in the other city to which it shall have been transferred and changed, and to summon to it the prelates and other members of the

Council of Trent, even under penalty of perjury and other penalties named in the letters of the convocation of that council; also to preside and proceed in the council thus translated and changed in the name and by the authority aforesaid, and to perform, regulate, ordain and execute the other things mentioned above and the things necessary and suitable to it, in accordance with the contents and tenor of previous letters addressed to you on another occasion; declaring that we will hold as ratified and pleasing whatsoever shall be done, regulated and ordained by you in the aforesaid matters, and will, with God's help, see to it that it be inviolately observed; Apostolic constitutions and ordinances and other things whatsoever to the contrary notwithstanding. Therefore, let no one infringe this letter of our authorization or with foolhardy boldness go contrary to it. But if anyone shall presume to attempt this, let him know that he will incur the indignation of Almighty God and of the blessed Peter and Paul, His Apostles. Given at Rome at St. Peter's in the year of the Lord's incarnation 1547, on the twenty-fifth of February, in the eleventh year of our pontificate.

Fab. Bishop of Spol.

B. Motta

EIGHTH SESSION

Celebrated on the eleventh day of March, 1547

DECREE CONCERNING THE TRANSLATION OF THE COUNCIL

Does it please you to decree and declare that from the foregoing and other reports regarding that disease, it is so clearly and manifestly certain that the prelates cannot without danger to their lives remain in this city, and that therefore they cannot and ought not to be detained in it against their will? And considering, moreover, the withdrawal of many prelates since the last session, and the protests made in the general congregations by many other prelates wishing by all means to depart from here through fear of the disease, who cannot justly be detained and by whose departure the council would either be dissolved or, from the small number of prelates, its beneficial progress hindered; and considering also the imminent danger to life and the other manifestly true and legitimate reasons alleged in the congregations by some of the Fathers, does it please you likewise to decree and declare that for the preservation and prosecution of the council, and for the safety of the lives of the prelates, this council be transferred for a time to the city of Bologna as a place more suitable, more healthy and better adapted, and that the translation have effect from this day forth, that the session already announced for the twenty-first of April ought to be celebrated and be celebrated there on the day appointed; and that further matters be proceeded with in succession, till it shall seem expedient to our most holy Lord and to the holy council, with the advice of the most invincible Emperor, the most Christian King, and with the other Christian kings and princes, that this council may and ought to be brought back to this or to some other place?

They answered: It pleases us.

NINTH SESSION

Celebrated at Bologna on the twenty-firt day of April, 1547

This holy, ecumenical and general council, which lately was assembled in the city of Trent and is now lawfully assembled in the Holy Ghost in Bologna, the same most reverend Lords, John Maria de Monte, Bishop of Praeneste, and Marcellus, priest of the Holy Cross in Jerusalem, cardinals of the holy Roman Church and legates Apostolic *a latere,* presiding in the name of our most holy Father and Lord in Christ, Paul III, by the providence of God, Pope, considering that on the eleventh day of the month of March of the present year, in a general and public session celebrated in the city of Trent and in the accustomed place, all formalities being observed in the accustomed manner, for reasons then pressing, urgent and legitimate, and also with the authority of the holy Apostolic See, which was granted specially to the same most reverend presidents, ordained and decreed that the council was to be transferred, as it has transferred it, from that place to this city, and likewise that the session announced there for this twenty-first day of April in order that decrees with regard to the sacraments and reform, with which it had intended to deal, might be enacted and promulgated, ought to be celebrated in this city of Bologna; and considering that some of the Fathers who have been accustomed to be present at this council being engaged in their own churches during these higher festival days of the great week [of Lent] and of the paschal solemnity, and some also, detained by other hindrances, have not yet arrived here, but who nevertheless, it is to be hoped, will shortly be present, and that for this reason it has happened that the matters regarding the sacraments and reform could not be examined and discussed in an assembly of prelates as numerous as the holy council desired; therefore, that everything may be done with mature deliberation, with due dignity and earnestness, it has decided and does decide that it is good, beneficial and expedient that the aforesaid session, which, as has been said, was to have been celebrated on this day, be deferred and prorogued, as it is now deferred and prorogued, for expediting the aforesaid matter, to the Thursday within the approaching octave of Pentecost; which day it has deemed and deems to be most convenient for the business to be transacted and most suitable especially for the Fathers who are absent; adding, however, that this holy council may and can, even in private congregation, limit and abridge that term at its will and pleasure, as it shall deem expedient for the business of the council.

TENTH SESSION

Celebrated at Bologna on the second day of June, 1547

DECREE CONCERNING THE PROROGATION OF THE SESSION

Although this holy, ecumenical and general council has decreed that the session which was to have been celebrated in this illustrious city of Bologna on the twenty-first of the month of April last on the subject of the sacraments and reform, in accordance with the decree promulgated in public session in the city of Trent on the eleventh of March, should be deferred and prorogued to this present day for certain reasons, especially on account of the absence of some of the Fathers, who it was hoped would in a short time be present; wishing, however, even yet to deal kindly with those who have not come, the same holy council, lawfully assembled in the Holy Ghost, the same cardinals of the holy Roman Church and legates of the Apostolic See presiding, ordains and decrees that that session which it had decreed to celebrate on this the second day of the month of June of the present year 1547, be deferred and prorogued, as it does defer and prorogue it, to the Thursday after the feast of the Nativity of the Blessed Virgin Mary, which will be the fifteenth of the next month of September, for the disposition of the aforesaid and other matters; so, however, that the continuance of the discussion and examination of those things that relate to dogmas and reform shall not in the meantime be suspended, and that the holy council may and can freely, at its will and pleasure, even in private congregation, abridge and prorogue that term.

On the fourteenth day of September, 1547, in a general congregation held at Bologna, the session which was to have been held on the following day, was prorogued at the good pleasure of the holy council.

BULL OF THE RESUMPTION OF THE COUNCIL OF TRENT

Under the Supreme Pontiff, Julius III

Julius, Bishop, servant of the servants of God, for a perpetual remembrance hereof

In order to put an end to the religious dissensions which for a long time have prevailed in Germany to the disturbance and scandal of the entire Christian world, it appears good, opportune and expedient to us, as also to our most dearly beloved son in Christ, Charles, ever august Emperor of the Romans, who has made this known to us by his letters and ambassadors, to bring back to the city of Trent the holy ecumenical and general council convoked by our predecessor, Pope Paul III, of happy memory, and begun, conducted and continued by us, who then enjoyed the honor of the cardinalate and, conjointly with two other cardinals of the holy Roman Church, presided in the name of our predecessor in the council, in which several public and solemn sessions were held and several decrees promulgated on the subjects of faith and reform, and also many other things relating to both subjects were examined and discussed. We, therefore, to whom, as reigning sovereign pontiff, it belongs to convoke and direct general councils, that we may, to the praise and glory of Almighty God, procure the peace of the Church and the increase of the Christian faith and of the orthodox religion, and may, as far as we are able, consider with paternal solicitude the tranquillity of Germany, a province which in times past was second to none in Christendom in cultivating true religion and the teaching of the holy councils and the holy Fathers, and in exhibiting due obedience and reverence to the supreme pontiffs, the vicars on earth of Christ our Redeemer, hoping that by the grace and bounty of God it will come about that all Christian kings and princes will approve, favor and aid our just and pious wishes in this matter, by the bowels of the mercy of Our Lord Jesus Christ, exhort, command and admonish our venerable brethren the patriarchs, archbishops, bishops, our beloved sons the abbots and each and all of the others who by right, custom or privilege ought to be present at general councils, and whom our predecessor in his letters of convocation and in any others made and published with regard to this matter wished to be present at the council, to convene and assemble in the same city of Trent, since the lawful impediment no longer exists, and to apply themselves without delay to the continuation and prosecution of the council on the next first of May, which day we, after mature deliberation, of our own certain knowledge, with the plenitude of Apostolic authority, and with the advice and consent of our venerable brethren, the cardinals of the holy Roman Church, appoint and set aside for the resumption and continuation of the council in the state in which it now is. We shall make it our special care that our legates will be in the city at the same time, through whom, if on account of our age, state of health and the demands of the Apostolic See we shall be unable to be present personally, we shall under the guidance of the Holy Ghost preside over the council; any translation and suspension of the council and any other things whatsoever to the contrary notwithstanding, and especially those things which it was the will of our predecessor should not create any obstacles, as expressed in his letters aforesaid, which, with each and all of restrictions and decrees therein contained, we wish and decree to remain in force, and so far as there is need we hereby renew them; declaring, moreover, null and void whatever may be attempted knowingly or unknowingly by any person or by any authority to the contrary. Let no one, therefore, infringe this our letter of exhortation, summons, monition, ordinance, declaration, renewal, will and decrees, or with foolhardy boldness go contrary to it. But if anyone shall presume to attempt this, let him know that he will incur the indignation of Almighty God and of His blessed Apostles Peter and Paul. Given at Rome at St. Peter's in the year 1550 of Our Lord's incarnation, on the fourteenth of December, in the first year of our pontificate.

M. Cardinal Crescen
Rom. Amasaeus

ELEVENTH SESSION
OF THE COUNCIL OF TRENT

which is the first celebrated under the Supreme Pontiff,
Julius III, on the first day of May, 1551

DECREE CONCERNING THE RESUMPTION OF THE COUNCIL

Does it please you, for the praise and glory of the holy
and undivided Trinity, Father, and Son, and Holy Ghost, for
the increase and exaltation of the Christian faith and religion, that the holy, ecumenical and general Council of Trent
be, in accordance with the form and tenor of the letters of
our most holy Lord, resumed, and that further matters be
proceeded with?

They answered: It pleases us.

ANNOUNCEMENT OF THE NEXT SESSION

Does it please you that the next session be held and celebrated on the following first of September?

They answered: It pleases us.

TWELFTH SESSION

which is the second under the Supreme Pontiff, Julius III,
celebrated on the first day of September, 1551

DECREE CONCERNING THE PROROGATION OF THE SESSION

The holy, ecumenical and general Council of Trent, lawfully assembled in the Holy Ghost, the same legates and
nuncios of the holy Apostolic See presiding, which had in
the last session decreed that the following one was to be
celebrated today and further matters to be proceeded with,
yet by reason of the absence of the illustrious German nation,
whose interests are chiefly to be considered, and also on
account of the small attendance of the other Fathers, has
hitherto delayed to proceed, now rejoicing in the Lord and
giving due thanks to Almighty God for the recent arrival of
our venerable brethren and sons in Christ, the Archbishops
of Mainz and Trier, electoral princes of the Holy Roman
Empire, and of many bishops of that country and of other
provinces, and entertaining a firm hope that many other
prelates both of Germany and of other nations, moved by
the requirement of their office and by this example, will
arrive in a few days, announces the next session for the for-
tieth day, which will be the eleventh of next October, to continue the council from the point where it now is; and since
in the preceding sessions decrees were enacted concerning
the seven sacraments of the New Law in general and baptism and confirmation in particular, it ordains and decrees
that it will treat and discuss the sacrament of the most
Holy Eucharist, and also, as regards reform, of the other
matters which pertain to the easier and more convenient
residence of prelates. It also admonishes and exhorts all the
Fathers that, after the example of Our Lord Jesus Christ,
they in the meantime give themselves to fasting and prayer
so far as human weakness will permit, so that God, who be
praised forever, being at length appeased, may vouchsafe to
bring back the hearts of men to the acknowledgment of His
true faith, to the unity of holy mother Church and to the
rule of righteous living.

THIRTEENTH SESSION

which is the third under the Supreme Pontiff, Julius III,
celebrated on the eleventh day of October, 1551

DECREE CONCERNING THE MOST HOLY SACRAMENT
OF THE EUCHARIST

The holy, ecumenical and general Council of Trent, lawfully assembled in the Holy Ghost, the same legate and nuncios of the holy Apostolic See presiding, though convened,
not without the special guidance and direction of the Holy
Ghost, for the purpose of setting forth the true and ancient
doctrine concerning faith and the sacraments, and of applying a remedy to all the heresies and the other most grievous troubles by which the Church of God is now miserably
disturbed and rent into many and various parts, yet, even
from the outset, has especially desired that it might pull
up by the roots the cockles[1] of execrable errors and schisms
which the enemy has in these our troubled times disseminated regarding the doctrine, use and worship of the Sacred
Eucharist, which our Saviour left in His Church as a symbol of that unity and charity with which He wished all Christians to be mutually bound and united. Wherefore, this holy
council, stating that sound and genuine doctrine of the venerable and divine sacrament of the Eucharist, which the
Catholic Church, instructed by Our Lord Jesus Christ Himself and by His Apostles, and taught by the Holy Ghost who
always brings to her mind all truth,[2] has held and will preserve even to the end of the world, forbids all the faithful
of Christ to presume henceforth to believe, teach or preach
with regard to the most Holy Eucharist otherwise than is
explained and defined in this present decree.

---

1. *Matt.* 13:30
2. *Luke* 12:12; *John* 14:26; 16:13

Chapter I

THE REAL PRESENCE OF OUR LORD JESUS CHRIST IN THE MOST HOLY SACRAMENT OF THE EUCHARIST

First of all, the holy council teaches and openly and plainly professes that after the consecration of bread and wine, Our Lord Jesus Christ, true God and true man, is truly, really and substantially contained in the august sacrament of the Holy Eucharist under the appearance of those sensible things. For there is no repugnance in this that our Saviour sits always at the right hand of the Father in Heaven[3] according to the natural mode of existing, and yet is in many other places sacramentally present to us in His own substance by a manner of existence which, though we can scarcely express in words, yet with our understanding illumined by faith, we can conceive and ought most firmly to believe is possible to God.[4] For thus all our forefathers, as many as were in the true Church of Christ and who treated of this most holy sacrament, have most openly professed that our Redeemer instituted this wonderful sacrament at the last supper, when, after blessing the bread and wine, He testified in clear and definite words that He gives them His own body and His own blood. Since these words, recorded by the holy Evangelists[5] and afterwards repeated by St. Paul,[6] embody that proper and clearest meaning in which they were understood by the Fathers, it is a most contemptible action on the part of some contentious and wicked men to twist them into fictitious and imaginary tropes by which the truth of the flesh and blood of Christ is denied, contrary to the universal sense of the Church, which, as *the pillar and ground of truth,*[7] recognizing with a mind ever grateful and unforgetting this most excellent favor of Christ, has detested as satanical these untruths devised by impious men.

---

3. Cf. Sess. III, the Symbol.
4. *Matt.* 19:26; *Luke* 18:27
5. *Matt.* 26:26-28; *Mark* 14:22-24; *Luke* 22:19f.
6. See *1 Cor.* 11:24f.
7. See *1 Tim.* 3:15

Chapter II

THE REASON FOR THE INSTITUTION OF
THIS MOST HOLY SACRAMENT

Therefore, our Saviour, when about to depart from this world to the Father, instituted this sacrament, in which He poured forth, as it were, the riches of His divine love towards men, *making a remembrance of his wonderful works,*[8] and commanded us in the participation of it to reverence His memory and *to show forth his death until he comes*[9] to judge the world. But He wished that this sacrament should be received as the spiritual food of souls,[10] whereby they may be nourished and strengthened, living by the life of Him who said: *He that eateth me, the same also shall live by me,*[11] and as an antidote whereby we may be freed from daily faults and be preserved from mortal sins. He wished it furthermore to be a pledge of our future glory and everlasting happiness, and thus be a symbol of that one body of which He is the head[12] and to which He wished us to be united as members by the closest bond of faith, hope and charity, that we might *all speak the same thing and there might be no schisms among us.*[13]

Chapter III

THE EXCELLENCE OF THE MOST HOLY EUCHARIST
OVER THE OTHER SACRAMENTS

The most Holy Eucharist has indeed this in common with the other sacraments, that it is a symbol of a sacred thing and a visible form of an invisible grace;[14] but there is found in it this excellent and peculiar characteristic, that the other sacraments then first have the power of sanctifying when one uses them, while in the Eucharist there is the Author Himself of sanctity before it is used. For the Apostles had not yet received the Eucharist from the hands of the Lord, when He Himself told them that what He was giving them

---

8. *Psalms* 110:4
9. *Luke* 22:19; *1 Cor.* 11:24-26
10. *Matt.* 26:26f.
11. *John* 6:58
12. See *1 Cor.* 11:3; *Eph.* 5:23
13. See *1 Cor.* 1:10
14. C.32, D.II de cons.

is His own body.[15] This has always been the belief of the Church of God, that immediately after the consecration the true body and the true blood of Our Lord, together with His soul and divinity exist under the form of bread and wine, the body under the form of bread and the blood under the form of wine *ex vi verborum;*[16] but the same body also under the form of wine and the same blood under the form of bread and the soul under both, in virtue of that natural connection and concomitance whereby the parts of Christ the Lord, *who hath now risen from the dead, to die no more,*[17] are mutually united;[18] also the divinity on account of its admirable hypostatic union with His body and soul. Wherefore, it is very true that as much is contained under either form as under both.[19] For Christ is whole and entire under the form of bread and under any part of that form; likewise the whole Christ is present under the form of wine and under all its parts.

Chapter IV

TRANSUBSTANTIATION

But since Christ our Redeemer declared that to be truly His own body which He offered under the form of bread,[20] it has, therefore, always been a firm belief in the Church of God, and this holy council now declares it anew, that by the consecration of the bread and wine a change is brought about of the whole substance of the bread into the substance of the body of Christ Our Lord, and of the whole substance of the wine into the substance of His blood.[21] This change the holy Catholic Church properly and appropriately calls transubstantiation.

---

15. *Matt.* 26:26; *Mark* 14:22
16. Cf. *infra,* can. 1
17. *Romans* 6:9
18. Cc.58, 71, 78, D.II de cons.
19. Cf. *infra,* can. 3 and Sess. XXI, chap. 3
20. *Luke* 22:19; *John* 6:48ff.; *1 Cor.* 11:24
21. Cf. c.55, D.II de cons.; *infra,* can. 3

Chapter V

THE WORSHIP AND VENERATION TO BE SHOWN TO
THIS MOST HOLY SACRAMENT

There is, therefore, no room for doubt that all the faithful of Christ may, in accordance with a custom always received in the Catholic Church, give to this most holy sacrament in veneration the worship of *latria,* which is due to the true God.[22] Neither is it to be less adored for the reason that it was instituted by Christ the Lord in order to be received.[23] For we believe that in it the same God is present of whom the eternal Father, when introducing Him into the world, says: *And let all the angels of God adore him;*[24] whom the Magi, falling down, adored;[25] who, finally, as the Scriptures testify, was adored by the Apostles in Galilee.[26]

The holy council declares, moreover, that the custom that this sublime and venerable sacrament be celebrated with special veneration and solemnity every year on a fixed festival day,[27] and that it be borne reverently and with honor in processions through the streets and public places,[28] was very piously and religiously introduced into the Church of God. For it is most reasonable that some days be set aside as holy on which all Christians may with special and unusual demonstration testify that their minds are grateful to and mindful of their common Lord and Redeemer for so ineffable and truly divine a favor whereby the victory and triumph of His death are shown forth. And thus indeed did it behoove the victorious truth to celebrate a triumph over falsehood and heresy, that in the sight of so much splendor and in the midst of so great joy of the universal Church, her enemies may either vanish weakened and broken, or, overcome with shame and confounded, may at length repent.

---

22. Cf. *infra,* can. 6
23. *Matt.* 26:26
24. *Heb.* 1:6
25. *Matt.* 2:11
26. *Ibid.,* 28:17; *Luke* 24:52
27. Cf. c.un. in Clem. De reliq. et venerat. sanct., III, 16
28. Cf. *infra,* can. 6

Chapter VI

THE RESERVATION OF THE SACRAMENT OF THE HOLY EUCHARIST AND TAKING IT TO THE SICK

The custom of reserving the Holy Eucharist in a sacred place is so ancient[29] that even the period of the Nicene Council recognized that usage.[30] Moreover, the practice of carrying the Sacred Eucharist to the sick and of carefully reserving it for this purpose in churches, besides being exceedingly reasonable and appropriate, is also found enjoined in numerous councils[31] and is a very ancient observance of the Catholic Church. Wherefore, this holy council decrees that this salutary and necessary custom be by all means retained.

Chapter VII

THE PREPARATION TO BE EMPLOYED THAT ONE MAY RECEIVE THE SACRED EUCHARIST WORTHILY

If it is unbecoming for anyone to approach any of the sacred functions except in a spirit of piety, assuredly, the more the holiness and divinity of this heavenly sacrament are understood by a Christian, the more diligently ought he to give heed lest he receive it without great reverence and holiness, especially when we read those terrifying words of the Apostle: *He that eateth and drinketh unworthily, eateth and drinketh judgment to himself, not discerning the body of the Lord.*[32] Wherefore, he who would communicate, must recall to mind his precept: *Let a man prove himself.*[33] Now, ecclesiastical usage declares that such an examination is necessary in order that no one conscious to himself of mortal sin, however contrite he may feel, ought to receive the Sacred Eucharist without previous sacramental confession.[34] This the holy council has decreed to be invariably observed by all Christians, even by those priests on whom it may be incumbent by their office to celebrate, provided the opportunity of a confessor is not wanting to them. But if in an

---

29. C.93, D.II de cons.; c.6, C.XXVI, q.6; c.10, X, De celebr, miss., III, 41; *infra,* can. 7
30. Cf. I Council of Nicaea (325), c.13
31. Cf. c.63, D.L and C.I, X, De custod. eucharist., III, 44
32. See *1 Cor.* 11:29
33. *Ibid.,* 11:28
34. Cf. *infra,* can. 11

urgent necessity a priest should celebrate without previous confession, let him confess as soon as possible.

Chapter VIII

ON THE USE OF THIS ADMIRABLE SACRAMENT

As to the use of this holy sacrament, our Fathers have rightly and wisely distinguished three ways of receiving it. They have taught that some receive it sacramentally only, as sinners; others spiritually only, namely, those who eating in desire the heavenly bread set before them, are by a lively *faith which worketh by charity*[35] made sensible of its fruit and usefulness; while the third class receives it both sacramentally and spiritually,[36] and these are they who so prove and prepare themselves beforehand that they approach this divine table clothed with the wedding garment.[37] As regards the reception of the sacrament, it has always been the custom in the Church of God that laics receive communion from priests, but that priests when celebrating communicate themselves,[38] which custom ought with justice and reason to be retained as coming down from Apostolic tradition.[39] Finally, the holy council with paternal affection admonishes, exhorts, prays and beseeches through the bowels of the mercy of our God, that each and all who bear the Christian name will now at last agree and be of one mind in this sign of unity, in this bond of charity, in this symbol of concord, and that, mindful of so great a majesty and such boundless love of Our Lord Jesus Christ, who gave His own beloved soul as the price of our salvation and His own flesh to eat,[40] they may believe and venerate these sacred mysteries of His body and blood with such constancy and firmness of faith, with such devotion of mind, with such piety and worship, that they may be able to receive frequently that supersubstantial bread and that it may truly be to them the life of the soul and the perpetual health of their mind; that being invigorated by its strength, they may be able after the journey of this miserable pilgrimage to arrive in their heavenly coun-

35. *Gal.* 5:6
36. Cf. *infra,* can. 8
37. *Matt.* 22:11
38. Cf. c.11, D.II de cons. and *infra,* can. 10
39. *Heb.* 5:3; 7:27
40. *John* 6:56ff.

try, there to eat, without any veil, the same bread of angels[41] which they now eat under sacred veils.

But since it is not enough to declare the truth unless errors be exposed and repudiated, it has seemed good to the holy council to subjoin these canons, so that, the Catholic doctrine being already known, all may understand also what are the heresies which they ought to guard against and avoid.

CANONS ON THE MOST HOLY SACRAMENT OF THE EUCHARIST

Canon 1. If anyone denies that in the sacrament of the most Holy Eucharist are contained truly, really and substantially the body and blood together with the soul and divinity of Our Lord Jesus Christ, and consequently the whole Christ,[42] but says that He is in it only as in a sign, or figure or force, let him be anathema.

Canon 2. If anyone says that in the sacred and holy sacrament of the Eucharist the substance of the bread and wine remains conjointly with the body and blood of Our Lord Jesus Christ, and denies that wonderful and singular change of the whole substance of the bread into the body and the whole substance of the wine into the blood, the appearances only of bread and wine remaining, which change the Catholic Church most aptly calls transubstantiation,[43] let him be anathema.

Canon 3. If anyone denies that in the venerable sacrament of the Eucharist the whole Christ is contained under each form and under every part of each form when separated,[44] let him be anathema.

Canon 4. If anyone says that after the consecration is completed, the body and blood of Our Lord Jesus Christ are not in the admirable sacrament of the Eucharist,[45] but are there only *in usu,* while being taken and not before or after, and that in the hosts or consecrated particles which are reserved or which remain after communion, the true body of the Lord does not remain, let him be anathema.

Canon 5. If anyone says that the principal fruit of the most Holy Eucharist is the remission of sins, or that other

---

41. *Psalms* 77:25
42. Cf. *supra,* chap. 3
43. *Ibid.,* chap. 4
44. *Ibid.,* chap. 3 and Sess. XXI, chap. 3
45. *Supra,* chap. 3

effects do not result from it,[46] let him be anathema.

Canon 6. If anyone says that in the holy sacrament of the Eucharist, Christ, the only begotten Son of God, is not to be adored with the worship of *latria,*[47] also outwardly manifested, and is consequently neither to be venerated with a special festive solemnity, nor to be solemnly borne about in procession according to the laudable and universal rite and custom of holy Church, or is not to be set publicly before the people to be adored and that the adorers thereof are idolaters, let him be anathema.

Canon 7. If anyone says that it is not lawful that the Holy Eucharist be reserved in a sacred place, but immediately after consecration must necessarily be distributed among those present,[48] or that it is not lawful that it be carried with honor to the sick, let him be anathema.

Canon 8. If anyone says that Christ received in the Eucharist is received spiritually only and not also sacramentally and really,[49] let him be anathema.

Canon 9. If anyone denies that each and all of Christ's faithful of both sexes are bound, when they have reached the years of discretion, to communicate every year at least at Easter,[50] in accordance with the precept of holy mother Church, let him be anathema.

Canon 10. If anyone says that it is not lawful for the priest celebrating to communicate himself,[51] let him be anathema.

Canon 11. If anyone says that faith alone is a sufficient preparation for receiving the sacrament of the most Holy Eucharist,[52] let him be anathema. And lest so great a sacrament be received unworthily and hence unto death and condemnation, this holy council ordains and declares that sacramental confession, when a confessor can be had, must necessarily be made beforehand by those whose conscience is burdened with mortal sin, however contrite they may consider themselves. Moreover, if anyone shall presume to teach, preach or obstinately assert, or in public disputation defend the contrary, he shall be *eo ipso* excommunicated.

---

46. *Ibid.,* chap. 2
47. *Supra,* chap. 5
48. *Ibid.,* chap. 6
49. *Ibid.,* chap. 8
50. Sess. XIV, Penance, can. 8
51. *Supra,* chap. 8
52. *Ibid.,* chap. 7

DECREE CONCERNING REFORM

Chapter I

BISHOPS SHALL APPLY THEMSELVES WITH PRUDENCE TO
REFORM THE MORALS OF THEIR SUBJECTS; FROM THE
CORRECTION OF THE BISHOPS THERE SHALL BE NO APPEAL

The same holy Council of Trent, lawfully assembled in the
Holy Ghost, the same legate and nuncios of the Apostolic See
presiding, having in mind to decide some things that relate
to the jurisdiction of bishops, in order that, as was announced
in the last session, they may the more willingly reside in the
churches committed to them the more easily and conveniently
they may be able to rule and keep in uprightness of life and
of morals those subject to them, deems it appropriate in the
first place to admonish them to bear in mind that they are
shepherds and not oppressors and that they ought so to preside over those subject to them as not to lord it over them,[53]
but to love them as children and brethren and to strive by
exhortation and admonition to deter them from what is unlawful, that they may not be obliged, should they transgress, to
coerce them by due punishments. In regard to those, however, who should happen to sin through human frailty, that
command of the Apostle is to be observed, that they reprove,
entreat, rebuke them in all kindness and patience,[54] since
benevolence toward those to be corrected often effects more
than severity, exhortation more than threat, and charity more
than force.[55] But if on account of the gravity of the offense
there is need of the rod, then is rigor to be tempered with
gentleness, judgment with mercy, and severity with clemency,
that discipline, so salutary and necessary for the people, may
be preserved without harshness and they who are chastised
may be corrected, or, if they are unwilling to repent, that others may by the wholesome example of their punishment be
deterred from vices, since it is the duty of a shepherd, at once
diligent and kind, to apply first of all mild anodynes to the
disorders of his sheep, and afterwards, if the gravity of the
disorder should demand it, to proceed to sharper and severer
remedies; but if even these prove ineffective in removing the

---

53. See *1 Peter* 5:2f.; c.1-9, D.XLV
54. See *2 Tim.* 4:2
55. C.6, D.XLV

disorders, then he is to liberate the other sheep at least from the danger of contagion.[56] Since, therefore, those guilty of crimes, for the most part to avoid punishment and to evade the judgments of their bishops, pretend to have complaints and grievances and under the subterfuge of an appeal, impede the process of the judge, [this council] in order to prevent a remedy which was instituted for the protection of the innocent from being abused and utilized for the defense of wickedness,[57] and that their cunning and tergiversation may be thwarted, has ordained and decreed: That in causes relative to visitation and correction, or to competency and incompetency, as also in criminal causes, there shall before the definitive sentence be no appeal from the bishop or his vicar-general in spiritual matters by reason of an interlocutory judgment or any other grievance whatsoever; nor shall the bishop or his vicar be bound to take notice of an appeal of this kind since it is frivolous, but he may proceed to further measures notwithstanding that appeal or any inhibition emanating from the judge of appeal, as also every written statement and custom, even immemorial, to the contrary, unless a grievance of this kind cannot be repaired by the definitive sentence or there is no appeal from it,[58] in which cases the statutes of the ancient canons shall remain unimpaired.

Chapter II

WHEN AN APPEAL FROM THE BISHOP IN CRIMINAL CAUSES IS TO BE COMMITTED TO THE METROPOLITAN OR TO ONE OF THE NEAREST BISHOPS

An appeal in criminal causes from the sentence of the bishop or his vicar-general in spiritual matters, where there is room for appeal, shall, if it happens to be a case assigned by Apostolic authority locally, be committed to the metropolitan, or also to his vicar-general in spiritual matters; or if he be for some reason suspected, or be distant more than two legal days' journey, or if it be from him that the appeal is made,[59] the case shall be assigned to one of the nearest bishops or their vicars, but not to inferior judges.

56. Cc.16, 17, C.XXIV, q.3
57. C.3, X, De appell., II, 28
58. *Ibid.,* c.59
59. C.11, VI°, De rescrip., I, 3

Chapter III

THE ACTS OF THE FIRST INSTANCE SHALL WITHIN THIRTY DAYS BE GIVEN GRATUITOUSLY TO THE ACCUSED APPELLANT

The accused who in a criminal cause appeals from the bishop or his vicar-general in spiritual matters, shall by all means produce before the judge to whom he has appealed, the acts of the first instance, and the judge, unless he has seen them, shall not proceed to his absolution. He from whom the appeal has been made shall, on demand of the appellant, furnish those acts gratuitously within thirty days; otherwise the case of an appeal of this kind shall be terminated without them according as justice may demand.

Chapter IV

IN WHAT MANNER CLERICS ARE ON ACCOUNT OF GRAVE CRIMES TO BE DEGRADED FROM SACRED ORDERS

Since ecclesiastics are sometimes guilty of crimes so grave that on account of their shocking wickedness they have to be deposed from sacred orders and handed over to the secular court, in which, according to the sacred canons, a certain number of bishops is required,[60] and if it should be difficult to assemble them all the due execution of the law would be retarded, whereas even when they are able to be present their residence would be interrupted; therefore, it is ordained and decreed that it shall be lawful for a bishop by himself or by his vicar-general in spiritual matters, even without the presence of other bishops, to proceed against a cleric, even if constituted in the priesthood, both in regard to his condemnation and to his verbal deposition, and he may by himself proceed also to actual and solemn degradation from ecclesiastical orders and grades, in the cases in which the presence of a specified number of other bishops is required by the canons after convoking and being assisted in this by a like number of abbots who have the right of using the miter and crosier by Apostolic privilege, if they can be found in the city or diocese and can conveniently be present; otherwise he may be assisted by other persons constituted in ecclesiastical dignity, who are outstanding by

---

60. C.2, C.III, q.8; cc.1, 4-7, C.XV, q.7

reason of their age and recommendable by their knowledge of law.

Chapter V

THE BISHOP MAY TAKE SUMMARY COGNIZANCE OF FAVORS RELATIVE EITHER TO THE ABSOLUTION FROM CRIME OR THE REMISSION OF PUNISHMENT

And since it sometimes happens that under false pleas, which however appear probable enough, certain persons fraudulently obtain favors of the kind, whereby the punishments imposed on them by the just severity of their bishops are either wholly remitted or mitigated; and since it is a thing not to be tolerated that a lie, which is so exceedingly displeasing to God, should not only go unpunished, but should even obtain for him who tells it the pardon of another crime; it is therefore ordained and decreed as follows: a bishop residing in his own church may *per se ipsum,* as the delegate of the Apostolic See, and without judicial process, take cognizance of the cheating and stealing of a favor obtained under false pretences for the absolution of any public crime or delinquency, concerning which he himself had instituted an inquiry, or for the remission of a punishment to which he has himself condemned the criminal; and he shall not admit that favor after it shall have been lawfully established that it was obtained by the statement of what is false or by the suppression of what is true.[61]

Chapter VI

A BISHOP MAY NOT BE PERSONALLY CITED EXCEPT IN A CASE INVOLVING DEPOSITION OR DEPRIVATION

Since the subjects of a bishop, even though they may have been justly corrected, do nevertheless often bear toward him a violent hatred and, as if they had suffered some wrong at his hands, bring false accusations against him in order that they may annoy him by any means in their power,[62] the fear of which annoyance chiefly renders him more backward in inquiring into and punishing their delinquencies; therefore,

---

61. Cc.20, 22, X, De rescrip., I, 3
62. C.21, C.II, q.7

in order that he may not be compelled to his own great disadvantage and that of his church to abandon the flock entrusted to him, and not without detriment to the episcopal dignity to wander from place to place, it is ordained and decreed: a bishop, even though he be proceeded against *ex officio,* or by way of inquiry or denunciation or accusation or in any other way, shall not be cited or warned to appear in person except for a cause for which he may be deposed from or deprived of his office.[63]

Chapter VII

QUALIFICATIONS OF WITNESSES AGAINST A BISHOP

In the matter of examination or information in a criminal cause or in an otherwise grave cause against a bishop, no witnesses shall be accepted unless their testimony is confirmed and they are of good life, of good esteem and reputation; and if they shall have made any deposition through hatred, rashness or self-interest, they shall be subject to severe penalties.

Chapter VIII

GRAVE EPISCOPAL CAUSES SHALL BE TAKEN COGNIZANCE OF BY THE SUPREME PONTIFF

Causes of bishops, when by reason of the nature of the crime charged against them they have to appear [in person], shall be taken before the supreme pontiff and be decided by him.[64]

DECREE

postponing the Definition of four Articles concerning the Sacrament of the Eucharist and granting Letters of Safe-conduct to the Protestants

The same holy council, desiring to root up from the field of the Lord all errors which have like thorns sprung up relative to this most holy sacrament, and to provide for the

---

63. Cf. Sess. XXIV, chap. 5 de ref.
64. C.7, C. VI, q.4; Sess. XXIV, chap. cit.

salvation of all the faithful, having devoutly offered daily prayers to Almighty God, among other articles pertaining to this sacrament which have been considered with the most careful examination of the Catholic truth, after many and most thorough discussions according to the importance of the matters have been held and the views also of the most eminent theologians have been ascertained, has also considered the following: Whether it is necessary to salvation and prescribed by divine law that all the faithful of Christ receive that venerable sacrament under both species; then, whether he receives less who communicates under one than he who communicates under both; further, whether holy mother Church errs when she permits the laity and priests when not celebrating to communicate under the form of bread only; finally, whether children also must communicate. But since those of the glorious province of Germany, who call themselves Protestants, desire to be heard by the holy council in regard to these articles before they are defined, and for this reason have asked of it a pledge that they may be permitted to come here in safety, sojourn in this city, speak and express freely their views before the council and then depart when they please, this holy council, though it has for many months looked forward with great eagerness to their arrival, nevertheless, like an affectionate mother that groans and labors, desiring and laboring tirelessly to the end that among those who bear the Christian name there may be no schisms, but that as all acknowledge the same God and Redeemer, so also may they confess the same, believe the same, know the same, trusting in the mercy of God and hoping that they may be brought back to the most holy and salutary union of one faith, hope and charity, willingly yielding to them in this matter, has, so far as it concerns [the council], given and granted, in accordance with their request, assurance of safety and good faith, which they call a safe-conduct, the tenor of which will be set forth below, and for their sake it has postponed the definition of those articles to the second session, which, that they may conveniently be present thereat, it has announced for the feast of the Conversion of St. Paul, which is the twenty-fifth day of the month of January of the following year. It was furthermore decided that in the same session the sacrifice of the mass will be treated of because of the close connection between the two subjects; meanwhile it will discuss the sacraments of penance and extreme unction in the next session. This it has decided to be held on the feast of St. Catherine, virgin and martyr, which will be the twenty-fifth of November, and at the same time, in both sessions, the matter of reform will be continued.

SAFE-CONDUCT GRANTED TO PROTESTANTS

The holy and general Council of Trent, lawfully assembled in the Holy Ghost, the same legate and nuncios of the holy Apostolic See presiding, grants, so far as it pertains to the council itself, to each and all persons throughout the whole of Germany, whether ecclesiastics or seculars, of whatever rank, station, condition and circumstances they may be, who may wish to come to this ecumenical and general council, security and full protection, which they call a safe-conduct, with each and all of the necessary and suitable clauses and decisions, even though they ought to be expressed specifically and not in general terms, and it is its wish that they be understood as so expressed, so that they may and shall enjoy full liberty to confer, make proposals and discuss those things that are to be discussed in the council; to come freely and safely to the ecumenical council, to remain and sojourn there and to propose therein, in writing as well as orally, as many articles as may seem good to them, to deliberate with the Fathers or with those who may have been chosen by the council and without any abuse and contumely dispute with them; they may also depart whenever they please. It has moreover seemed expedient to the holy council, that if for their greater liberty and safety they wish that certain judges be deputed on their behalf in regard to crimes that either have been committed or may be committed by them, they may themselves choose such as are favorably disposed toward them, even though the crimes should be of a grave nature or even savor of heresy.

FOURTEENTH SESSION

which is the fourth under the Supreme Pontiff, Julius III, celebrated on the twenty-fifth day of November, 1551

THE MOST HOLY SACRAMENTS OF PENANCE
AND EXTREME UNCTION

Though the holy, ecumenical and general Council of Trent, lawfully assembled in the Holy Ghost, the same legate and nuncios of the holy Apostolic See presiding, has in the decree on justification,[1] by reason of a certain necessity induced by the affinity of the subjects, given much consideration to the sacrament of penance, yet so great is in our days the number of errors relative to this sacrament, that it will be of no little general benefit to give to it a more exact and complete definition, in which all errors having under the guidance of the Holy Ghost been pointed out and refuted, Catholic truth may be made clear and resplendent, which [truth] this holy council now sets before all Christians to be observed for all time.

Chapter I

THE NECESSITY AND INSTITUTION OF THE
SACRAMENT OF PENANCE

If in all those regenerated such gratitude were given to God that they constantly safeguarded the justice received in baptism by His bounty and grace, there would have been no need for another sacrament besides that of baptism to be instituted for the remission of sins.[2] But since God, *rich in mercy,*[3] *knoweth our frame,*[4] He has a remedy of life even to those who may after baptism have delivered themselves up to the servitude of sin and the power of the devil, namely, the sacrament of penance, by which the benefit of Christ's death is applied to those who have fallen after baptism. Penance was indeed necessary at all times for all men who had stained themselves by

---

1. Cf. Sess. VI, chap. 14
2. Cf. *infra,* chap. 5, Penance
3. *Eph.* 2:4
4. *Psalms* 102:14

mortal sin,[5] even for those who desired to be cleansed by the sacrament of baptism, in order to obtain grace and justice; so that their wickedness being renounced and amended, they might with a hatred of sin and a sincere sorrow of heart detest so great an offense against God. Wherefore the Prophet says: *Be converted and do penance for all your iniquities, and iniquity shall not be your ruin.*[6] The Lord also said: *Except you do penance, you shall all likewise perish;*[7] and Peter the Prince of the Apostles, recommending penance to sinners about to receive baptism, said: *Do penance and be baptized every one of you.*[8] Moreover, neither before the coming of Christ was penance a sacrament nor is it such since His coming to anyone before baptism. But the Lord then especially instituted the sacrament of penance when, after being risen from the dead, He breathed upon His disciples, and said: *Receive ye the Holy Ghost, whose sins you shall forgive, they are forgiven them, and whose sins you shall retain, they are retained.*[9] The consensus of all the Fathers has always acknowledged that by this action so sublime and words so clear the power of forgiving and retaining sins was given to the Apostles and their lawful successors for reconciling the faithful who have fallen after baptism, and the Catholic Church with good reason repudiated and condemned as heretics the Novatians, who of old stubbornly denied that power of forgiving.[10] Therefore, this holy council, approving and receiving that perfectly true meaning of the above words of the Lord, condemns the grotesque interpretations of those who, contrary to the institution of this sacrament, wrongly contort those words to refer to the power of preaching the word of God and of making known the Gospel of Christ.

Chapter II

THE DIFFERENCES BETWEEN THE SACRAMENT OF PENANCE AND THAT OF BAPTISM

Besides, it is clear that this sacrament is in many respects different from baptism.[11] For apart from the fact that in

---

5. Sess. and chap. cited.
6. *Ezech.* 18:30
7. *Luke* 13:5
8. *Acts* 2:38
9. *John* 20:22f.; *infra,* can. 3, Penance
10. Eusebius, *Hist. eccl.,* VI, c.43
11. Cf. *infra,* can. 2 and Sess. VI, chap. 14

matter and form, which constitute the essence of a sacrament, it differs very widely, it is beyond question that the minister of baptism need not be a judge, since the Church exercises judgment on no one who has not entered it through the gate of baptism. *For what have I to do,* says St. Paul, *to judge them that are without?*[12] It is otherwise with regard to those who are of the household of the faith, whom Christ the Lord has once by the layer of baptism made members of His own body.[13] For these, if they should afterward have defiled themselves by some crime, He wished not to have cleansed by the repetition of baptism, since that is in no manner lawful in the Catholic Church, but to be placed as culprits before this tribunal that by the sentence of the priests they may be absolved, not only once but as often as, repentant of the sins committed, they should turn themselves thereto. Moreover, the fruit of baptism is one thing, that of penance another. For by baptism *we put on Christ*[14] and are made in Him an entirely new creature, receiving a full and complete remission of all sins; to which newness and integrity, however, we are by no means able to arrive by the sacrament of penance without many tears and labors on our part, divine justice demanding this, so that penance has rightly been called by the holy Fathers a laborious kind of baptism. This sacrament of penance is for those who have fallen after baptism necessary for salvation, as baptism is for those who have not yet been regenerated.

Chapter III

THE PARTS AND FRUITS OF THIS SACRAMENT

The holy council teaches furthermore, that the form of the sacrament of penance, in which its efficacy chiefly consists, are those words of the minister: *I absolve thee,* etc., to which are indeed laudably added certain prayers according to the custom of holy Church, which, however, do not by any means belong to the essence of the form nor are they necessary for the administration of the sacrament. But the acts of the penitent himself, namely, contrition,[15] confession

---

12. See *1 Cor.* 5:12
13. *Ibid.,* 12:13
14. *Gal.* 3:27
15. Cf. *infra,* chap. 4; Sess. VI, chap. 14, and *infra,* can. 4

and satisfaction, constitute the matter of this sacrament, which acts, inasmuch as they are by God's institution required in the penitent for the integrity of the sacrament and for the full and complete remission of sins, are for this reason called the parts of penance. But that which is signified and produced by this sacrament is, so far as its force and efficacy are concerned, reconciliation with God, which sometimes, in persons who are pious and who receive this sacrament with devotion, is wont to be followed by peace and serenity of conscience with an exceedingly great consolation of spirit. The holy council, while declaring these things regarding the parts and effect of this sacrament, at the same time condemns the opinions of those who maintain that faith and the terrors that agitate conscience are parts of penance.

Chapter IV

CONTRITION

Contrition, which holds the first place among the aforesaid acts of the penitent, is a sorrow of mind and a detestation for sin committed with the purpose of not sinning in the future.[16] This feeling of contrition was at all times necessary for obtaining the forgiveness of sins and thus indeed it prepares one who has fallen after baptism for the remission of sins, if it is united with confidence in the divine mercy and with the desire to perform the other things that are required to receive this sacrament in the proper manner. The holy council declares therefore, that this contrition implies not only an abstention from sin and the resolution and beginning of a new life, but also a hatred of the old,[17] according to the statement: *Cast away from you all your transgressions by which you have transgressed, and make to yourselves a new heart and a new spirit.*[18] And certainly he who has pondered those lamentations of the saints: *To thee only have I sinned, and have done evil before thee;*[19] *I have labored in my groanings, every night I will wash my bed;*[20] *I will recount to thee all my years in the bitterness of my soul,*[21] and others of this kind, will easily understand

---

16. Cf. Sess. VI, chaps. 6, 14
17. *Infra,* can. 5
18. *Ezech.* 18:31
19. *Psalms* 50:6
20. *Psalms* 6:7
21. *Is.* 38:15

that they issued from an overwhelming hatred of their past
life and from a profound detestation of sins. The council teaches
furthermore, that though it happens sometimes that this contrition is perfect through charity and reconciles man to God
before this sacrament is actually received, this reconciliation,
nevertheless, is not to be ascribed to the contrition itself without a desire of the sacrament, which desire is included in it.
As to imperfect contrition, which is called attrition, since it
commonly arises either from the consideration of the heinous-
ness of sin or from the fear of hell and of punishment, the
council declares that if it renounces the desire to sin and hopes
for pardon, it not only does not make one a hypocrite and a
greater sinner, but is even a gift of God and an impulse of
the Holy Ghost, not indeed as already dwelling in the penitent, but only moving him, with which assistance the penitent prepares a way for himself unto justice. And though without
the sacrament of penance it cannot *per se* lead the sinner to
justification, it does, however, dispose him to obtain the grace
of God in the sacrament of penance. For, struck salutarily by
this fear, the Ninivites, moved by the dreadful preaching of
Jonas, did penance and obtained mercy from the Lord.[22] Falsely
therefore do some accuse Catholic writers, as if they maintain that the sacrament of penance confers grace without any
pious exertion on the part of those receiving it, something that
the Church of God has never taught or ever accepted. Falsely
also do they assert that contrition is extorted and forced, and
not free and voluntary.

Chapter V

CONFESSION

From the institution of the sacrament of penance as already
explained, the universal Church has always understood that
the complete confession of sins was also instituted by the Lord
and is by divine law necessary for all who have fallen after
baptism;[23] because Our Lord Jesus Christ, when about to ascend
from earth to heaven, left behind Him priests, His own vicars,[24] as rulers and judges,[25] to whom all the mortal sins into

22. *Jonas* 3:5; *Matt.* 12:41; *Luke* 11:32
23. *Luke* 5:14; 17:14; *1 John* 1:9. Cf. *infra,* can. 6
24. *Matt.* 16:19; *John* 20:23
25. Cf. c.51, D.I de poenit.

which the faithful of Christ may have fallen should be brought
in order that they may, in virtue of the power of the keys,
pronounce the sentence of remission or retention of sins. For
it is evident that priests could not have exercised this judgment without a knowledge of the matter, nor could they have
observed justice in imposing penalties, had the faithful
declared their sins in general only and not specifically and
one by one. From which it is clear that all mortal sins of
which they have knowledge after a diligent self-examination,
must be enumerated by the penitents in confession,[26] even
though they are most secret and have been committed only
against the two last precepts of the Decalogue;[27] which sins
sometimes injure the soul more grievously and are more dan-
gerous than those that are committed openly. Venial sins, on
the other hand, by which we are not excluded from the grace
of God and into which we fall more frequently,[28] though they
may be rightly and profitably and without any presumption
declared in confession, as the practice of pious people evinces,
may, nevertheless, be omitted without guilt and can be expiated by many other remedies. But since all mortal sins, even
those of thought, make men *children of wrath*[29] and enemies
of God, it is necessary to seek pardon of all of them from
God by an open and humble confession. While therefore the
faithful of Christ strive to confess all sins that come to their
memory, they no doubt lay all of them before the divine
mercy for forgiveness; while those who do otherwise and
knowingly conceal certain ones, lay nothing before the divine
goodness to be forgiven through the priest; for if one sick be
ashamed to make known his wound to the physician, the
latter does not remedy what he does not know. It is evident
furthermore, that those circumstances that change the species
of the sin are also to be explained in confession, for without
them the sins themselves are neither integrally set forth by
the penitent nor are they known to the judges, and it would
be impossible for them to estimate rightly the grievousness
of the crimes and to impose the punishment due to the penitents on account of them. Hence it is unreasonable to teach
that these circumstances have been devised by idle men, or

---

26. Cf. *infra,* can. 7
27. *Deut.* 5:21
28. Cf. Sess. VI, can. 23; c.20, D.III de poenit.
29. *Eph.* 2:3

that one circumstance only is to be confessed, namely, to have sinned against another. It is also malicious to say that confession, commanded to be made in this manner, is impossible, or to call it a torture of consciences; for it is known that in the Church nothing else is required of penitents than that each one, after he has diligently examined himself and searched all the folds and corners of his conscience, confess those sins by which he remembers to have mortally offended his Lord and God; while the other sins of which he has after diligent thought no recollection, are understood to be in a general way included in the same confession; for which sins we confidently say with the Prophet: *From my secret sins cleanse me, O Lord.*[30] But the difficulty of such a confession and the shame of disclosing the sins might indeed appear a burdensome matter, if it were not lightened by so many and so great advantages and consolations, which are most certainly bestowed by absolution upon all who approach this sacrament worthily. Moreover, as regards the manner of confessing secretly to a priest alone, although Christ has not forbidden that one may in expiation for his crimes and for his own humiliation, for an example to others as well as for the edification of the Church thus scandalized, confess his offenses publicly, yet this is not commanded by divine precept; nor would it be very prudent to enjoin by human law that offenses, especially secret ones, should be divulged by a public confession. Wherefore, since secret sacramental confession, which holy Church has used from the beginning and still uses, has always been recommended by the most holy and most ancient Fathers with great and unanimous agreement, the empty calumny of those who do not fear to teach that it is foreign to the divine command, is of human origin and owes its existence to the Fathers assembled in the Lateran Council,[31] is convincingly disproved. For the Church did not through the Lateran Council decree that the faithful of Christ should confess, a thing that she recognized as of divine law and necessary, but that the precept of confession should be complied with by each and all at least once a year when they have attained the age of discretion. Hence this salutary custom of confessing during that sacred and most accept-

---

30. *Psalms* 18:13
31. Cf. c.12, X, De poenit., V, 38

able period of Lent is now observed in the whole Church to the great benefit of the souls of the faithful, which custom this holy council completely indorses and sanctions as pious and worthy of retention.

Chapter VI

THE MINISTER OF THIS SACRAMENT AND ABSOLUTION

With regard to the minister of this sacrament, the holy council declares false and absolutely foreign to the truth of the Gospel all doctrines which perniciously extend the ministry of the keys to all other men besides bishops and priests,[32] in the belief that those words of the Lord: *Whatsoever you shall bind upon earth, shall be bound also in heaven, and whatsoever you shall loose upon earth, shall be loosed also in heaven;*[33] and, *Whose sins you shall forgive, they are forgiven them, and whose sins you shall retain, they are retained,*[34] were, contrary to the institution of this sacrament, addressed indifferently and indiscriminately to all the faithful of Christ in such manner that everyone has the power of forgiving sins, public ones by way of rebuke, if the one rebuked complies, and secret ones by way of a voluntary confession made to anyone.[35] It [the council] teaches furthermore that even priests who are in mortal sin exercise, through the power of the Holy Ghost conferred in ordination,[36] as ministers of Christ the office of forgiving sins, and that the opinion of those is erroneous who maintain that bad priests do not possess this power. But although the absolution of the priest is the dispensation of another's bounty, yet it is not a bare ministry only, either of proclaiming the Gospel or of declaring that sins are forgiven, but it is after the manner of a judicial act,[37] by which sentence is pronounced by him as by a judge. The penitent, therefore, ought not so flatter himself on his own faith as to think that even though he have no contrition and there be wanting on the part of the priest the intention to act

32. *Infra,* can. 10
33. *Matt.* 16:19; 18:18
34. *John* 20:23
35. Cf. Sess. VII, Sacraments, can. 10
36. C.8, D.XIX; c.89, C.I, q.1
37. *Infra,* can. 9

earnestly and absolve effectively, he is nevertheless really and in the sight of God absolved by reason of faith alone. For faith without penance effects no remission of sins, and he would be most negligent of his salvation who, knowing that a priest absolved him jokingly, would not diligently seek another who would act earnestly.

Chapter VII

THE RESERVATION OF CASES

Wherefore, since the nature of a judgment requires that sentence be imposed only on subjects, the Church of God has always maintained and this council confirms it as most true, that the absolution which a priest pronounces upon one over whom he has neither ordinary nor delegated jurisdiction ought to be invalid.[38] To our most holy Fathers it seemed to be a matter of great importance to the discipline of the Christian people, that certain more atrocious and grave crimes should be absolved not by all but only by the highest priests;[39] whence the sovereign pontiffs in virtue of the supreme authority given to them in the universal Church could with right reserve to their own exclusive judgment certain more grave cases of crimes.[40] And since all things that are from God are well ordered,[41] it is not to be doubted that the same may be lawfully done by all bishops, each in his own diocese,[42] unto edification however, not unto destruction, in virtue of the authority over their subjects that is given to them above other priests inferior in rank, especially in regard to those crimes that carry with them the censure of excommunication. That this reservation of crimes have effect not only in external administration but also in God's sight is in accord with divine authority. But that no one may on this account perish, it has always been very piously observed in the same Church of God that there be no reservation *in articulo mortis,*[43] and that all priests, there-

---

38. Cf. c. 2, VI°, De poenit., V, 10
39. Cf. c.52, C.XVI, q.1 c.29, C.XVII, q.4 *et al.*
40. Cf. cc.1, 3, 19, 22, 24, 32, X, De sent. excomm., V, 39; cc. 11, 18, h.t. in VI°, V, 11; c. 1, h.t. in Extrav. comm., V, 10 *et al.*
41. *Romans* 13:1
42. Cf. *infra*, Sess. XXIV, chap. 6 de ref.
43. Cf. c.29, C.XVII, q.4; c.5, VI°, De poenis, V, 9; c.3, h.t. in Clem., V, 8; c.3, Extrav. comm., De privil., V, 7

fore, may in that case absolve all penitents from all sins and censures; and since outside of this single instance priests have no power in reserved cases, let them strive to persuade penitents to do this one thing, betake themselves to superiors and lawful judges for the benefit of absolution.

Chapter VIII

THE NECESSITY AND FRUIT OF SATISFACTION

Finally, in regard to satisfaction, which, of all the parts of penance, just as it is that which has at all times been recommended to the Christian people by our Fathers, so it is the one which chiefly in our age is under the high-sounding pretext of piety assailed by those who *have an appearance of piety, but have denied the power thereof*,[44] the holy council declares that it is absolutely false and contrary to the word of God, that the guilt is never remitted by the Lord without the entire punishment being remitted also.[45] For clear and outstanding examples are found in the sacred writings,[46] by which, besides divine tradition, this error is refuted in the plainest manner. Indeed the nature of divine justice seems to demand that those who through ignorance have sinned before baptism be received into grace in one manner, and in another those who, after having been liberated from the servitude of sin and of the devil, and after having received the gift of the Holy Ghost, have not feared knowingly to violate the temple of God[47] and to grieve the Holy Spirit.[48] And it is in keeping with divine clemency that sins be not thus pardoned us without any satisfaction, lest seizing the occasion and considering sins as trivial and offering insult and affront to the Holy Spirit,[49] we should fall into graver ones, *treasuring up to ourselves wrath against the day of wrath*.[50] For without doubt, these satisfactions greatly restrain from sin, check as it were with a bit, and make penitents more cautious and vigilant in the future; they also remove remnants of sin, and by acts of the oppo-

---

44. See *2 Tim.* 3:5
45. Cf. Sess. VI, chap. 14, can. 30 and *infra,* can. 12
46. Gen. 3:16ff.; *Num.* 12:14f.; 20:11f.; *2 Kings* 12:13f., etc.
47. See *1 Cor.* 3:17
48. *Eph.* 4:30
49. *Heb.* 10:29
50. *Romans* 2:5; *James* 5:3

site virtues destroy habits acquired by evil living. Neither
was there ever in the Church of God any way held more
certain to ward off impending chastisement by the Lord
than that men perform with true sorrow of mind these works
of penance.[51] Add to this, that while we by making satisfaction suffer for our sins, we are made conformable to Christ
Jesus who satisfied for our sins,[52] from whom is all our sufficiency,[53] having thence also a most certain pledge, that *if
we suffer with him, we shall also be glorified with him.*[54]
Neither is this satisfaction which we discharge for our sins
so our own as not to be through Christ Jesus; for we who
can do nothing of ourselves as of ourselves, can do all things
with the cooperation of Him who strengthens us.[55] Thus man
has not wherein to glory, but all our glorying is in Christ,[56]
in whom we live,[57] in whom we merit, in whom we make
satisfaction, *bringing forth fruits worthy of penance,*[58] which
have their efficacy from Him, by Him are offered to the
Father, and through Him are accepted by the Father. The
priests of the Lord must therefore, so far as reason and prudence suggest, impose salutary and suitable satisfactions,
in keeping with the nature of the crimes and the ability of
the penitents; otherwise, if they should connive at sins and
deal too leniently with penitents, imposing certain very light
works for very grave offenses, they might become partakers in the sins of others. But let them bear in mind that
the satisfaction they impose be not only for the protection
of a new life and a remedy against infirmity, but also for
the atonement and punishment of past sins; for the early
Fathers also believed and taught that the keys of the priests
were bestowed not to loose only but also to bind.[59] It was
not their understanding, moreover, that the sacrament of
penance is a tribunal of wrath or of punishments, as no
Catholic ever understood that through our satisfactions the
efficacy of the merit and satisfaction of Our Lord Jesus

51. *Matt.* 3:2, 8; 4:17; 11:21
52. *Romans* 5:10
53. See *2 Cor.* 3:5
54. *Romans* 8:17
55. See *1 Cor.* 3:5; *Phil.* 4:13
56. See *1 Cor.* 1:31; *2 Cor.* 10:17; *Gal.* 6:14
57. *Acts* 17:28
58. *Matt.* 3:8; *Luke* 3:8
59. *Matt.* 16:19; *John* 20:23; *infra,* can. 15

Christ is either obscured or in any way diminished;[60] but since the innovators wish to understand it so, they teach, in order to destroy the efficacy and use of satisfaction, that a new life is the best penance.

Chapter IX

THE WORKS OF SATISFACTION

It [the council] teaches furthermore that the liberality of the divine munificence is so great that we are able through Jesus Christ to make satisfaction to God the Father not only by punishments voluntarily undertaken by ourselves to atone for sins, or by those imposed by the judgment of the priest according to the measure of our offense, but also, and this is the greatest proof of love, by the temporal afflictions imposed by God and borne patiently by us.

THE DOCTRINE OF THE SACRAMENT OF EXTREME UNCTION

It has seemed good to the holy council to add to the preceding doctrine on penance the following concerning the sacrament of extreme unction, which was considered by the Fathers as the completion not only of penance but also of the whole Christian life, which ought to be a continual penance. First therefore, with regard to its institution it declares and teaches that our most benevolent Redeemer, who wished to have His servants at all times provided with salutary remedies against all the weapons of all enemies,[61] as in the other sacraments He provided the greatest aids by means of which Christians may during life keep themselves free from every graver spiritual evil, so did He fortify the end of life by the sacrament of extreme unction as with the strongest defense. For though our adversary seeks and seizes occasions throughout our whole life to devour our souls in any manner,[62] yet there is no time when he strains more vehemently all the powers of his cunning to ruin us utterly, and if possible to make us even lose faith in the divine mercy, than when he perceives that the end of our life is near.

---

60. Cf. *infra, can.* 14
61. *Eph.* 6:10ff.
62. See *1 Peter* 5:8

Chapter I

THE INSTITUTION OF THE SACRAMENT OF EXTREME UNCTION

This sacred unction of the sick was instituted by Christ Our Lord as truly and properly a sacrament of the New Law, alluded to indeed by Mark[63] but recommended and announced to the faithful by James the Apostle and brother of the Lord. *Is any man,* he says, *sick among you? Let him bring in the priests of the Church and let them pray over him, anointing him with oil in the name of the Lord; and the prayer of faith shall save the sick man, and the Lord shall raise him up; and if he be in sins, they shall be forgiven him.*[64] In which words, as the Church has learned from Apostolic tradition received from hand to hand, he teaches the matter, form, proper administration and effect of this salutary sacrament. For the Church has understood that the matter is the oil blessed by the bishop, because the anointing very aptly represents the grace of the Holy Ghost with which the soul of the sick person is invisibly anointed. The form, furthermore, are those words: "By this unction, etc."

Chapter II

THE EFFECT OF THIS SACRAMENT

Moreover, the significance and effect of this sacrament are explained in these words: *And the prayer of faith shall save the sick man, and the Lord shall raise him up, and if he be in sins they shall be forgiven him.*[65] For the thing signified is the grace of the Holy Ghost whose anointing takes away the sins if there be any still to be expiated, and also the remains of sin and raises up and strengthens the soul of the sick person by exciting in him great confidence in the divine mercy, supported by which the sick one bears more lightly the miseries and pains of his illness and resists more easily the temptations of the devil who lies in wait for his heel;[66] and at times when expedient for the welfare of the soul restores bodily health.

63. *Mark* 6:13
64. *James* 5:14f.
65. *Ibid.,* 5:15
66. *Gen.* 3:15

Chapter III

THE MINISTER OF THIS SACRAMENT AND THE TIME
WHEN IT OUGHT TO BE ADMINISTERED

And now, with regard to prescribing who ought to receive and administer this sacrament, this also was not obscurely expressed in the words cited above. For there it is also pointed out that the proper ministers of this sacrament are the priests of the Church; by which name in that place are to be understood not the elders by age or the highest in rank among the people, but either bishops or priests[67] rightly ordained by bishops with *the imposition of the hands of the priesthood.*[68] It is also declared that this anointing is to be applied to the sick, but especially to those who are in such danger as to appear to be at the end of life, whence it is also called the sacrament of the dying. If the sick should after the reception of this sacrament recover, they may again be strengthened with the aid of this sacrament when they fall into another similar danger of death. Wherefore, they are under no condition to be listened to who against so manifest and clear a statement of the Apostle James[69] teach that this anointing is either a human contrivance or is a rite received from the Fathers, having neither a command from God nor a promise of grace; nor those who declare that this has already ceased, as though it were to be understood only as referring to the grace of healing in the primitive Church; nor those who maintain that the rite and usage which the holy Roman Church observes in the administration of this sacrament are opposed to the expression of the Apostle James,[70] and therefore must be changed into some other; nor finally those who assert that this last anointing may without sin be despised by the faithful; for all these things are most clearly at variance with the manifest words of so great an Apostle. Assuredly, in reference to those things that constitute the substance of this sacrament, the Roman Church, the mother and mistress of all other churches, does not observe anything in administering this unction that has not been prescribed by the blessed James. Nor indeed can

---

67. C.3, D.XCV and *infra,* Extr. Unct., can. 4
68. See *1 Tim.* 4:14
69. *James* 5:14f.
70. *Infra,* Extr. Unct., can. 3

there be contempt for so great a sacrament without a grievous sin and offense to the Holy Ghost.

These things regarding the sacraments of penance and
extreme unction this holy ecumenical council professes and
teaches and proposes to all the faithful of Christ to be believed
and held. And it submits the following canons to be inviolately observed, and forever anathematizes those who maintain the contrary.

CANONS CONCERNING THE MOST HOLY SACRAMENT OF PENANCE

Canon 1. If anyone says that in the Catholic Church penance
is not truly and properly a sacrament instituted by Christ
the Lord for reconciling the faithful of God as often as they
fall into sin after baptism,[71] let him be anathema.

Canon 2. If anyone, confounding the sacraments, says that
baptism is itself the sacrament of penance,[72] as though these
two sacraments were not distinct, and that penance therefore is not rightly called a second plank after shipwreck,[73]
let him be anathema.

Canon 3. If anyone says that those words of the Lord Saviour, *Receive ye the Holy Ghost, whose sins you shall forgive,
they are forgiven them, and whose sins you shall retain, they
are retained,*[74] are not to be understood of the power of forgiving and retaining sins in the sacrament of penance, as
the Catholic Church has always understood them from the
beginning, but distorts them, contrary to the institution of
this sacrament, as applying to the authority of preaching
the Gospel, let him be anathema.

Canon 4. If anyone denies that for the full and perfect
remission of sins three acts are required on the part of the
penitent, constituting as it were the matter of the sacrament of penance, namely, contrition, confession and satisfaction, which are called the three parts of penance;[75] or
says that there are only two parts of penance, namely, the
terrors of a smitten conscience convinced of sin and the faith
received from the Gospel or from absolution, by which one
believes that his sins are forgiven him through Christ, let

71. Cf. *supra,* chap. 1
72. *Ibid.*
73. C.72, D.I de poenit.
74. *Matt.* 16:19; *John* 20: 23f.; cf. Sess. VI, chap. 14 and *supra,* chap. 1
75. *Supra,* chap. 3

him be anathema.

Canon 5. If anyone says that the contrition which is evoked by examination, recollection and hatred of sins,[76] whereby one recounts his years in the bitterness of his soul,[77] by reflecting on the grievousness, the multitude, the baseness of his sins, the loss of eternal happiness and the incurring of eternal damnation, with a purpose of amendment, is not a true and beneficial sorrow, does not prepare for grace, but makes a man a hypocrite and a greater sinner; finally, that this sorrow is forced and not free and voluntary, let him be anathema.

Canon 6. If anyone denies that sacramental confession was instituted by divine law or is necessary to salvation;[78] or says that the manner of confessing secretly to a priest alone, which the Catholic Church has always observed from the beginning and still observes, is at variance with the institution and command of Christ and is a human contrivance, let him be anathema.

Canon 7. If anyone says that in the sacrament of penance it is not required by divine law for the remission of sins to confess each and all mortal sins which are recalled after a due and diligent examination,[79] also secret ones and those that are a violation of the two last commandments of the Decalogue,[80] as also the circumstances that change the nature of a sin, but that this confession is useful only to instruct and console the penitent and in olden times was observed only to impose a canonical satisfaction; or says that they who strive to confess all sins wish to leave nothing to the divine mercy to pardon; or finally, that it is not lawful to confess venial sins, let him be anathema.

Canon 8. If anyone says that the confession of all sins as it is observed in the Church is impossible and is a human tradition to be abolished by pious people;[81] or that each and all of the faithful of Christ of either sex are not bound thereto once a year in accordance with the constitution of the great Lateran Council,[82] and that for this reason the faithful of Christ are to be persuaded not to confess dur-

---

76. *Ibid.*, chap. 4
77. *Is.* 38:15
78. *Supra,* chap. 5
79. *Supra,* chap. 5.
80. *Deut.* 5:21
81. *Supra,* chap. 5
82. *Ibid.*, chap. 5 at the end

ing Lent, let him be anathema.

Canon 9. If anyone says that the sacramental absolution of the priest is not a judicial act but a mere service of pronouncing and declaring to him who confesses that the sins are forgiven, provided only he believes himself to be absolved, even though the priest absolves not in earnest but only in jest;[83] or says that the confession of the penitent is not necessary in order that the priest may be able to absolve him, let him be anathema.

Canon 10. If anyone says that priests who are in mortal sin have not the power of binding and loosing,[84] or that not only priests are the ministers of absolution but that to each and all of the faithful of Christ was it said: *Whatsoever you shall bind upon earth, shall be bound also in heaven; and whatsoever you shall loose upon earth, shall be loosed in heaven;*[85] and *whose sins you shall forgive, they are forgiven them, and whose sins you shall retain, they are retained;*[86] by virtue of which words everyone can absolve from sins, from public sins by reproof only, provided the one reproved accept correction, and from secret sins by voluntary confession, let him be anathema.

Canon 11. If anyone says that bishops have not the right to reserve cases to themselves except such as pertain to external administration, and that therefore the reservation of cases does not hinder a priest from absolving from reserved cases,[87] let him be anathema.

Canon 12. If anyone says that God always pardons the whole penalty together with the guilt and that the satisfaction of penitents is nothing else than the faith by which they perceive that Christ has satisfied for them,[88] let him be anathema.

Canon 13. If anyone says that satisfaction for sins, as to their temporal punishment, is in no way made to God through the merits of Christ by the punishments inflicted by Him and patiently borne, or by those imposed by the priest, or even those voluntarily undertaken, as by fasts, prayers, almsgiving or other works of piety, and that therefore the best

---

83. *Ibid.,* chap. 6
84. *Ibid.,* chaps. 5-6
85. *Matt.* 16:19; 18:18
86. *John* 20:23
87. *Supra,* chap. 7
88. *Ibid.,* chap. 8

penance is merely a new life,[89] let him be anathema.

Canon 14. If anyone says that the satisfactions by which penitents atone for their sins through Christ are not a worship of God but traditions of men, which obscure the doctrine of grace and the true worship of God and the beneficence itself of the death of Christ,[90] let him be anathema.

Canon 15. If anyone says that the keys have been given to the Church only to loose and not also to bind, and that therefore priests, when imposing penalties on those who confess, act contrary to the purpose of the keys and to the institution of Christ, and that it is a fiction that there remains often a temporal punishment to be discharged after the eternal punishment has by virtue of the keys been removed,[91] let him be anathema.

CANONS CONCERNING THE SACRAMENT OF EXTREME UNCTION

Canon 1. If anyone says that extreme unction is not truly and properly a sacrament instituted by Christ Our Lord and announced by the blessed Apostle James,[92] but is only a rite received from the Fathers or a human invention, let him be anathema.

Canon 2. If anyone says that the anointing of the sick neither confers any grace nor remits sins nor comforts the sick, but that it has already ceased, as if it had been a healing grace only in the olden days,[93] let him be anathema.

Canon 3. If anyone says that the rite and usage of extreme unction which the holy Roman Church observes is at variance with the statement of the blessed Apostle James,[94] and is therefore to be changed and may without sin be despised by Christians, let him be anathema.

Canon 4. If anyone says that the priests of the Church, whom blessed James exhorts to be brought to anoint the sick, are not the priests who have been ordained by a bishop, but the elders in each community, and that for this reason a priest only is not the proper minister of extreme unction,[95] let him be anathema.

---

89. *Ibid.*, chaps. 8-9
90. *Ibid.*, chap. 8
91. *Ibid.*, chaps. 1, 8
92. *James* 5:14f.
93. Cf. *supra*, Extr. Unct., chap. 2
94. *James* 5:14f.
95. *Ibid.; supra,* Extr. Unct., chap. 3

DECREE CONCERNING REFORM

Introduction

It is the office of the bishops to admonish their subjects of their duty, especially those appointed to the cura animarum

Since it is properly the office of bishops to reprove the transgressions of all their subjects, this especially must claim their attention, that clerics, particularly those appointed to the *cura animarum,* be not wicked, nor lead a disorderly life with their connivance.[96] For if they permit them to be given to evil and corrupt morals, how shall they reprove the lay people for their transgressions when these can by one word repulse them for permitting clerics to be worse than they?[97] And with what freedom shall priests be able to correct laics when they must answer silently to themselves that they have committed the same things that they censure?[98] Wherefore, bishops shall admonish their clergy, of whatever rank they may be, that in conduct, speech and knowledge they be a guide to the people of God committed to them;[99] being mindful of what is written: *Be holy, for I also am holy.*[100] And in accordance with the word of the Apostle, let them not give offense to any man, that their ministry may not be blamed; but in all things let them exhibit themselves as the ministers of God,[101] lest the saying of the prophet be fulfilled in them: *The priests of God defile the sanctuaries and despise the law.*[102] But that the bishops may be able to execute this more freely, and may not be hindered therein by any pretext whatsoever, the same holy, ecumenical and general Council of Trent, the same legate and nuncios of the Apostolic See presiding therein, has thought it proper that the following canons be established and decreed.

---

96. C.13, X, De off. jud. ord., I, 31; *supra,* Sess. VI, chap. 3 de ref.
97. See *1 Cor.* 9:27
98. C.6, D. XXV
99. Cf. Sess. XXII, chap. 1 de ref.
100. *Lev.* 11:44; 19:2; 20:7; *1 Peter* 1:16
101. See *2 Cor.* 6:3f.
102. *Ezech.* 22:26; *Soph.* 3:4

Chapter I

IF ANY, FORBIDDEN TO ADVANCE TO ORDERS, DO SO ADVANCE, IF INTERDICTED OR SUSPENDED, THEY ARE TO BE PUNISHED

Since it is more honorable and safe for a subject to serve in an inferior ministry and render due obedience to those placed over him than to the scandal of the superiors seek the dignity of a higher rank, to him to whom the advance to sacred orders has, for any reason whatsoever, even on account of secret crime, or in whatsoever manner, even extra-judicially, been denied by his own prelate, or who has been suspended from his orders or ecclesiastical rank or dignities, no permission granted against the will of that prelate to bring about his promotion or restoration to former orders, rank, dignities or honors, shall be of any avail.

Chapter II

IF A BISHOP SHALL CONFER ANY ORDERS WHATSOEVER ON ONE NOT SUBJECT TO HIM, EVEN IF HE BE HIS OWN DOMESTIC, WITHOUT THE EXPRESSED CONSENT OF THAT PERSON'S PRELATE, BOTH SHALL BE SUBJECT TO THE PENALTY PRESCRIBED

Since some bishops of churches located *in partibus infidelium,* having neither clergy nor Christian people, being well-nigh wanderers and without a fixed residence, seeking not the things of Jesus Christ, but other sheep without the knowledge of their pastor,[103] and finding themselves forbidden by this holy council to exercise episcopal functions in the diocese of another without the expressed permission of the local ordinary,[104] and then only in regard to persons who are subject to that ordinary, do in their boldness, by evasion and in contempt of the law, choose as it were an episcopal see in a place which belongs to no diocese, and presume to mark with the clerical character and even promote to the sacred order of the priesthood any who come to them, even though they have no commendatory letters from their bishops or prelates, whence it happens very often that persons are ordained who are but little qualified, who are

---

103. Cf. *infra,* chap. 8 de ref.
104. Cf. Sess. VI, chap. 5 de ref.

untrained and ignorant, and have been rejected by their
own bishops as incompetent and unworthy, neither able to
perform the divine offices nor to administer rightly the sacraments of the Church; none of the bishops, therefore, who
are called titular, even though they reside or sojourn in a
place within no diocese, even if it be exempt, or in a monastery
of whatsoever order, may, by virtue of any privilege granted
them for a time, promote those who come to them, or promote or ordain to any sacred or minor orders, or even to
the first tonsure, the subject of another bishop, even under
the pretext that he is his domestic and companion at table,
without the expressed consent of or dimissory letters from
that person's own bishop.[105] Those acting contrary to this
shall be *ipso jure* suspended for one year from the exercise
of pontifical functions, and the one so promoted shall likewise be suspended from the exercise of the orders as long
as his own prelate shall see fit.

Chapter III

A BISHOP MAY SUSPEND HIS CLERICS WHO HAVE BEEN IMPROPERLY PROMOTED BY ANOTHER, IF HE SHOULD FIND THEM INCOMPETENT

A bishop may suspend for as long a time as he may see
fit from the exercise of the orders received, and may prohibit from ministering or from exercising the functions of
any order, any of his clerics, especially those who are in
sacred orders, who have been promoted by any authority
whatsoever without his previous examination and commendatory letters, even though they shall have been approved
as competent by him who ordained them, but whom he himself shall find unfit and incapable to celebrate the divine
offices or to administer the sacraments of the Church.[106]

---

105. *Ibid.* and Sess. XXIII, chaps. 3, 8, 10 de ref.
106. Cf. Sess. XXIII, chap. 8 de ref.

Chapter IV

NO CLERIC SHALL BE EXEMPT FROM THE CORRECTION OF THE BISHOP, EVEN OUTSIDE THE TIME OF VISITATION

All prelates of churches who ought to apply themselves diligently to correct the excesses of their subjects,[107] and against whom no cleric is by the statutes of this council under pretext of any privilege whatsoever considered secure that he may not be visited, punished and corrected in accordance with the canons, shall, if they reside in their own churches, have the power, delegated for this purpose by the Apostolic See, to correct and punish, even outside the time of visitation, all secular clerics in whatever manner exempt, who would otherwise be subject to their jurisdiction, for their excesses, crimes and delinquencies as often as and whenever there shall be need;[108] no exemptions, declarations, customs, sentences, oaths, agreements, which bind only their authors, shall be of any avail to said clerics and their relations, chaplains, domestics, agents, or to any others whatsoever in view and in consideration of said exempt clerics.

Chapter V

THE JURISDICTION OF CONSERVATORS IS RESTRICTED WITHIN CERTAIN LIMITS

Moreover, since some who, under the pretext that divers wrongs and annoyances are inflicted on them in their goods, possessions and rights, obtain certain judges to be appointed by means of conservatory letters to protect and defend them against such annoyances and wrongs and to maintain and keep them in the real or quasi possession of their goods, property and rights without suffering them to be molested therein, in most cases wrest from such letters a meaning that is contrary to the intention of the donor, therefore, conservatory letters, whatever may be their clauses and decrees, whatever judges may be appointed, or under whatever other sort of pretext or color they may have been granted, shall avail absolutely no one, of whatever dignity and condition,

---

107. Sess. VI, chap. 3 de ref.; c.13, X, De off. jud. ord., I, 31
108. Sess. cit., chap. 4 de ref.

even though a chapter, from being in criminal and mixed causes accused and summoned, examined and proceeded against before his own bishop or other ordinary superior, or from being freely summoned before the ordinary judge in those matters, even if any rights should come to him from a concession made to him. In civil causes also, if he be the plaintiff, it shall under no condition be lawful for him to bring anyone for judgment before his own conservatory judges. And if in those cases in which he shall be defendant, it should happen that the conservator chosen by him should be declared by the plaintiff to be suspected by him, or if any dispute shall have arisen between the judges themselves, the conservator and the ordinary, with regard to the competency of jurisdiction, the cause shall not be proceeded with until a decision shall have been made relative to said suspicion or competency of jurisdiction by arbiters legally chosen. Nor shall such conservatory letters be of any avail to the said party's domestics, who are in the habit of shielding themselves thereby, except to two only and then provided they live at his own cost. No one, moreover, shall enjoy the benefit of such letters more than five years. It shall also not be lawful for conservatory judges to have any fixed tribunal. With regard to causes that relate to wages and to destitute persons, the decree of this holy council shall remain in its full force.[109] General universities, however, colleges of doctors or scholars, places belonging to regulars, also hospitals in which hospitality is actually exercised, and persons belonging to such universities, colleges, places and hospitals, are not to be considered included in the present decree, but are and are to be understood as wholly exempt.

Chapter VI

A PENALTY IS DECREED AGAINST CLERICS WHO, CONSTITUTED IN SACRED ORDERS OR HOLDING BENEFICES, DO NOT WEAR CLOTHES CONFORMING TO THEIR ORDER

And since, though the habit does not make the monk,[110] it is necessary nevertheless that clerics always wear a dress conformable to their order, that by the propriety of their

---

109. Cf. Sess. VII, chap. 14 de ref.
110. C. 13, X, De regular., III, 31

outward apparel they may show forth the inward upright-ness of their morals, yet to such a degree have the contempt of religion and the boldness of some grown in these days, that esteeming but little their own dignity and the clerical honor, they even wear in public the dress of laymen, set-ting their feet in different paths, one of things divine, the other of the flesh. Wherefore, all ecclesiastical persons, how-soever exempt, who are either in sacred orders or in pos-session of dignities with or without jurisdiction, offices or whatsoever ecclesiastical benefices, if, after having been admonished by their bishops, even by a public edict, they do not wear a becoming clerical dress conformable to their order and dignity and in conformity with the ordinance and mandate of their bishop, may and ought to be compelled thereto by suspension from their orders, office, benefice and from the fruits, revenues and proceeds of those benefices; and also, if, after having been once rebuked, they offend again in the matter, even by deprivation of those offices and benefices; the constitution of Clement V published in the Council of Vienne, beginning "Quoniam," being hereby renewed and amplified.[111]

Chapter VII

THE ORDINATION OF VOLUNTARY HOMICIDES IS FORBIDDEN; HOW INVOLUNTARY HOMICIDES ARE TO BE ORDAINED

Since also he who has killed his neighbor on set purpose and by lying in wait for him, is to be taken away from the altar,[112] he who has voluntarily committed a homicide, even though that crime has neither been proved by ordinary judi-cial process nor is otherwise public, but is secret, can never be promoted to sacred orders; nor shall it be lawful to con-fer on him any ecclesiastical benefices, even though they have not annexed the *cura animarum;* but he shall be for-ever excluded from every ecclesiastical order, benefice and office. But if it be declared that the homicide was not com-mitted intentionally but accidentally, or when repelling force with force that one might defend himself from death (in which case indeed a dispensation for the ministry of sacred

---

111. C.2, in Clem., De vit. et hon. cler., III, 1
112. *Exodus* 21:14; c. 1, X, De homicid., V, 12

orders and of the altar and for all benefices and dignities
is in some manner due by right), the matter shall be referred
to the local ordinary, or if need be to the metropolitan or to
the nearest bishop, who may dispense only after having
taken cognizance of the case and after the entreaties and
allegations have been proved, and not otherwise.

Chapter VIII

NO ONE SHALL BY VIRTUE OF ANY PRIVILEGE
PUNISH THE CLERICS OF ANOTHER

Furthermore, since there are persons, some of whom are
true pastors and have their own sheep, who seek to rule
over the sheep of others also,[113] and at times give their
attention to the subjects of others to such an extent as to
neglect the care of their own; no one, even though he enjoy
the episcopal dignity, who may have the privilege of punishing the subjects of another, shall under any circumstances
proceed against clerics not subject to him, especially such
as are in sacred orders, even if guilty of crimes ever so
atrocious, except with the intervention of the bishop of those
clerics, if that bishop resides in his own church, or of the
person that may be deputed by that bishop; otherwise the
proceedings and all their consequences shall be entirely
without effect.

Chapter IX

THE BENEFICES OF ONE DIOCESE SHALL NOT UNDER ANY
PRETEXT BE UNITED TO THE BENEFICES OF ANOTHER

And since it is by a very good law that dioceses and
parishes have been made distinct,[114] and to each flock has
been assigned its proper pastor and to inferior churches
their rectors, each to take care of his own sheep, so that
ecclesiastical order may not be disturbed or one and the
same church belong in some way to two dioceses, not without grave disadvantage to those subject thereto; the benefices
of one diocese, even if they be parochial churches, perpetual vicariates, simple benefices, prestimonies or prestimonial

---

113. Cf. *supra*, chap. 2 de ref. and Sess. VI, chap. 5 de ref.
114. Cf. c.9, X, De his, quae fiunt a prael., III, 10 and Sess. XXIV, chap. 13 de ref.

portions, shall not be united *in perpetuum* to a benefice, monastery, college or even to a pious place of another diocese, not even for the purpose of augmenting divine worship or the number of beneficiaries, or for any other reason whatsoever; hereby explaining the decree of this holy council on the subject of unions of this kind.[115]

Chapter X

REGULAR BENEFICES SHALL BE CONFERRED ON REGULARS

Benefices of regulars that have been accustomed to be granted in title to professed regulars, shall, when they happen to become vacant by the death of the titular incumbent, or by his resignation or otherwise, be conferred on religious of the same order only[116] or on persons who shall be absolutely bound to take the habit and make profession, and on no others, that they may *not wear a garment that is woven of woolen and linen together.*[117]

Chapter XI

THOSE TRANSFERRED TO ANOTHER ORDER SHALL REMAIN IN THE ENCLOSURE UNDER OBEDIENCE, AND SHALL BE DISQUALIFIED TO HOLD SECULAR BENEFICES

Since regulars, transferred from one order to another, usually obtain permission easily from their superior to remain out of the monastery, whereby occasion is given to wandering about and apostatizing, no prelate or superior of any order shall by virtue of any authority whatsoever, admit anyone to the habit and to profession, unless he remain in the order to which he was transferred and perpetually in the cloister under obedience to his superior,[118] and one so transferred, even though he be a canon regular, shall be wholly disqualified to hold secular benefices, even with the *cura* annexed.

---

115. Cf. Sess. VII, chaps. 6 and 7 de ref.; Sess. XXIV, chaps. 13 and 15 de ref.
116. Cf. Sess. XXV, chap. 21 de regular.; c.5, VI°, De praeb., III, 4; c.27, X, De elect., I, 6
117. *Deut.* 22:11
118. Cf. Sess. XXV, chap. 4 de regular

Chapter XII

NO ONE SHALL OBTAIN A RIGHT OF PATRONAGE
EXCEPT BY MEANS OF A FOUNDATION
OR AN ENDOWMENT

Moreover, no one, of whatever ecclesiastical or secular dignity, may or ought to procure or have a right of patronage for any reason whatever, except that he has founded and erected *de novo* a church, benefice or chapel; or has adequately endowed out of his own patrimonial resources one already erected but insufficiently endowed.[119] But in case of such foundation or endowment, appointments thereto shall be reserved to the bishop and not to some other inferior person.

Chapter XIII

THE PRESENTATION MUST BE MADE TO THE ORDINARY,
OTHERWISE IT AND THE APPOINTMENT ARE NULL

Furthermore, it shall not be lawful for a patron, under pretext of any privilege, to present anyone in any way to the benefices that are under his right of patronage except to the ordinary bishop of the locality, to whom the provision for or appointment to that benefice would by right belong if the privilege ceased;[120] otherwise the presentation and the appointment perchance following shall be null and shall be understood as such.

Chapter XIV

The holy council declares, moreover, that in the next session, which it has already decreed to be held on the twenty-fifth day of January of the following year, 1552, it will, besides treating of the sacrifice of the mass, also apply itself to and treat of the sacrament of order and continue the subject of reform.

---

119. Cf. Sess. cit., chap. 9 de ref.
120. Cf. Sess. and chap. cited, and cc.8, 21, X, De jur. patr., III, 38

FIFTEENTH SESSION

which is the fifth under the Supreme Pontiff, Julius III,
celebrated on the twenty-fifth day of January, 1552

DECREE FOR PROROGUING THE SESSION

Since this holy and general council has during these days,
in accordance with the decrees enacted in the last sessions,
most accurately and diligently considered the things that
relate to the most holy sacrifice of the mass and to the
sacrament of order, in order that in the present session it
might publish, as the Holy Ghost would have prompted,
decrees on these matters and on the four articles concerning the most holy sacrament of the Eucharist, which had
been finally deferred to this session; and since it was thought
that those who call themselves Protestants, for whose sake
it had deferred the publication of those articles, and to whom
it had given the public faith or a safe-conduct that they
might come here freely and without any delay,[1] would in
the meantime have presented themselves at this holy council; seeing, however, that they have not yet come, and the
holy council having been petitioned in their name that the
publication which was to have been made on this day be
deferred to the following session, an assured hope being
expressed that they will doubtlessly be present long before
that session upon receipt in the meantime of a safe-conduct
in a more amplified form, the same holy council, lawfully
assembled in the Holy Ghost, the same legate and nuncios
presiding, desiring nothing more than to remove from among
the illustrious German nation all dissensions and schisms
regarding religion, and to provide for its tranquillity, peace
and concord; being prepared, should they come, to receive
them kindly and to listen to them favorably, and trusting
that they will come not with the intention of obstinately
assailing the Catholic faith but of learning the truth, and
that they will at last, as becomes those zealous for evangelical truth, acquiesce in the decrees and discipline of holy
mother Church, has deferred the next session for the pub-

---

1. *Supra,* Sess. XIII at the end.

lication and promulgation of the aforesaid matters to the
feast of St. Joseph, which will be the nineteenth day of the
month of March, in order that they may have sufficient time
and leisure not only to come but also to propose before that
day arrives whatever they may wish. And that all cause for
further delay on their part may be removed, it freely gives
and grants them the public faith or a safe-conduct, the contents and tenor of which is given below. But it ordains and
decrees that in the meantime the sacrament of matrimony
is to be considered, and it will give in the same session its
decisions thereon, in addition to the publication of the above-
mentioned decrees, also continuing the matter of reform.

SAFE-CONDUCT GIVEN TO THE PROTESTANTS

The holy, ecumenical and general Council of Trent, lawfully assembled in the Holy Ghost, the same legate and
nuncios of the Apostolic See presiding, adhering to the safe-
conduct given in the session before the last and amplifying
it in the manner following, certifies to all men that by the
tenor of these presents, it grants and fully concedes the public faith and the fullest and truest security, which they call
a safe-conduct, to each and all priests, electors, princes,
dukes, marquises, counts, barons, soldiers, the common people, and to all other persons of whatever state, condition or
character they may be, of the German province and nation,
to the cities and other places thereof, and to all other ecclesiastical and secular persons, especially those of the Confession of Augsburg, who shall come or be sent with them to
this general Council of Trent, and to those who are going
to come or have already come, by whatever name they are
or may be designated, to come freely to this city of Trent,
to remain, abide and sojourn here and to propose, speak
and consider, examine and discuss any matters whatever
with the council, and to present freely whatever they may
think suitable, to set forth any articles whatever either in
writing or orally, and to explain, establish and prove them
by the Sacred Scriptures and by the words, decisions and
arguments of the blessed Fathers, and also to reply, if need
be, to the objections of the general council, and to dispute
and confer charitably and respectfully and without hindrance
with those who have been selected by the council, reproachful, vexatious and offensive language being absolutely put

aside; and particularly, that the controverted matters shall be treated in this Council of Trent in accordance with Sacred Scripture and the traditions of the Apostles, the approved councils, the consensus of the Catholic Church and the authority of the holy Fathers; with this further addition, that they shall under no condition be punished by reason of religion or of offenses committed or that may be committed in regard thereto; and also that the divine offices shall not by reason of their presence, either upon the road or in any place of their journey, their stay or their return, or in the city of Trent itself, be in any way interrupted; and that on the conclusion of these matters or before their conclusion, whensoever it shall please them, if they should wish by the command and permission of their superiors to return to their homes, or if any one of them should so wish, they may at their pleasure return freely and securely, without restraint, formality or delay, without injury to their property and to the honor and persons of their attendants and vice versa; making known, however, their intention of withdrawing to those to be deputed by the council, so that at a convenient time, without deceit or fraud, provision may be made for their security. The holy council wishes also that all clauses whatsoever, which may be necessary and suitable for a complete, effective and sufficient security for coming, sojourning and returning, be included and contained, and to be considered as included, in this public faith and safe-conduct. For their greater security and for the sake of peace and reconciliation, it declares also that if, which God forbid, any one or several of them should, either on the way to Trent or while sojourning there or returning therefrom, perpetrate or commit an atrocious act, by which the benefit of this public faith and assurance granted to them might be annulled and cassated, it wishes and concedes that those discovered in such crime shall be forthwith punished by their own countrymen and not by others, with a condign chastisement and proper reparation, which the council on its part may justly approve and commend, the form, conditions and terms of the safe-conduct remaining entirely intact thereby. In like manner it wishes also that if, which God forbid, any one or several of this council should, either on the road or while sojourning or returning, perpetrate or commit an atrocious act by which the benefit of this public faith

or assurance may be violated or in any manner annulled,
those discovered in any such crime shall be forthwith punished by the council itself and not by others, with a condign
chastisement and proper reparation, which the Germans of
the Augsburg Confession here present may on their part
approve and commend, the present form, conditions and
terms of the safe-conduct remaining entirely intact thereby.
The council wishes furthermore, that each and all of their
ambassadors shall be allowed to go out of the city of Trent
to take the fresh air as often as it shall be convenient or
necessary and to return here; also freely to send or dispatch
their messenger or messengers to any place whatsoever to
attend to their necessary affairs and to receive those sent
or dispatched or the one sent or dispatched as often as they
may deem fit; so however that several or one of those
appointed by the council may accompany them or him in
order to provide for their safety. This safe-conduct and security shall be good and extend from and during the time that
they shall have been taken under the protection of this council and its agents to their arrival at Trent, and during the
entire time of their sojourn here; and further, after a sufficient hearing has been had, a period of twenty days having
expired, when they themselves should desire, or the council on the conclusion of such hearing should give them notice
to return, it will, all deceit and fraud being wholly excluded,
reconduct them with the help of God from Trent to that
place of safety which each may choose for himself. All of
which it promises and pledges in good faith to be inviolately
observed toward each and all of the faithful of Christ, toward
all ecclesiastical and secular princes and all ecclesiastical
and secular persons, of whatsoever state and condition they
may be or by whatsoever name they may be known. Moreover, it promises in sincere and good faith, to the exclusion
of fraud and deceit, that the council will neither openly nor
secretly seek any occasion, nor make use of, nor permit anyone else to make use of, any authority, power, right or statute,
privilege of laws or canons, or of any councils in whatever
form of words expressed, especially those of Constance and
Siena, in any way prejudicial to this public faith and the
fullest security, and of the public and free hearing granted
by this council to the above-named; these it abrogates in
this respect and for this occasion. And if the holy council

or any member thereof, or any of its adherents, of whatever condition, state or pre-eminence, shall violate, which may the Almighty prevent, in any point or clause whatever, the form and terms of the security and safe-conduct as set forth above, and a satisfactory reparation that in their judgment may be justly approved and commended shall not have forthwith followed, they may consider the council to have incurred all those penalties which by human and divine law or by custom the violators of such safe-conducts can incur, without any excuse or contrary allegation in this respect.

SIXTEENTH SESSION

which is the sixth under the Supreme Pontiff, Julius III, celebrated on the twenty-eighth day of April, 1552

DECREE SUSPENDING THE COUNCIL

The holy, ecumenical and general Council of Trent, lawfully assembled in the Holy Ghost, the most reverent Lords, Sebastian, Archbishop of Sipontum, and Aloysius, Bishop of Verona, Apostolic nuncios, presiding in their own names as well as in that of the most reverend and illustrious Lord, the legate Marcellus Crescentius, Cardinal of the holy Roman Church with the title of St. Marcellus, who is absent by reason of a very grave illness, doubts not that it is known to all Christians that this ecumenical Council of Trent was first convoked and assembled by Paul, of happy memory. Afterward at the instance of the most august Emperor, Charles V, reconvened by our most holy Lord Julius III, chiefly for the reason that it might restore religion, which was deplorably divided into various opinions in many parts of the world, especially in Germany, to its former state, and correct the abuses and most corrupt morals of the Christians. And since very many Fathers from different countries, regardless of personal hardships and dangers, had for this purpose willingly assembled, and the business progressed earnestly and happily in the midst of a great concourse of the faithful, and there was great hope that those Germans who had inaugurated those innovations would come to the council so disposed as to accept unanimously the true foundations of the Church, some light seemed at last to have dawned upon affairs, and the Christian commonwealth, before so depressed and afflicted, began to lift up its head. Then suddenly such tumults and wars were enkindled by the craftiness of the enemy of the human race, that the council was at much inconvenience compelled to pause as it were and to interrupt its course, so that all hope for further progress at that time was dissipated; and so far was the council from remedying the evils and troubles existing among the Christians, that, contrary to its intentions, it irritated rather than calmed the minds of many. Since, therefore, the holy council saw that all places, and especially Germany, were ablaze with arms and discords, that almost all the German bishops, especially the electoral princes, solicitous for their churches, had withdrawn from the council, it decided not to resist so great a necessity and to await better times, so that the Fathers who now could achieve nothing might return to their churches to take care of their sheep and no longer spend their time in useless inactivity. Hence, since the conditions of the times so require, it decrees that the progress of this ecumenical Council of Trent shall be suspended for two years, as it does suspend it by the present decree; with this understanding, however, that if peace is brought about sooner and the former tranquillity restored, which it trusts will, with the help of the all-good and great God, come about soon, the progress of the council shall be regarded as resumed from that time and as having its full validity, stability and authority. But if, which may God prevent, the aforesaid lawful impediments shall at the expiration of the time specified not have been removed, the suspension shall immediately upon their removal thereafter be considered *eo ipso* revoked, and the council shall be and shall be understood to be restored to its full power and authority without any new convocation thereof, provided the consent and authority of His Holiness and of the Apostolic See has been given to this decree.

In the meantime, however, this holy council exhorts all Christian princes and prelates to observe, and so far as it pertains to them, to cause to be observed in their kingdoms, dominions and churches each and all the things which have so far been ordained and decreed by this holy ecumenical council.

BULL
FOR THE CELEBRATION OF THE COUNCIL OF TRENT

under the Supreme Pontiff, Pius IV

Pius, Bishop, servant of the servants of God, for a perpetual remembrance hereof

Called by the divine providence of God to the government of the Church, though unequal to so great a burden, and immediately casting the eyes of our mind over every part of the Christian commonwealth, and beholding, not without great horror, how far and wide the pest of heresy and schism have penetrated and how much the morals of the Christian people

are in need of reform, we began in accordance with the duty
of our office to devote our care and thought to the means
whereby we should be able to exterminate those heresies,
destroy so great and pernicious a schism, and reform the
morals so much corrupted and depraved. And since we understand that for the correction of these evils that remedy is the
most suitable which this Holy See has been accustomed to
apply, namely, an ecumenical and general council, we formed
the resolution to assemble and with the help of God to celebrate one. The same had indeed already been summoned by
our predecessor, Paul III, of happy memory, and Julius, his
successor, but due to frequent hindrance and interruption by
various causes, it could not be brought to a conclusion. For
Paul, having convoked it at first in the city of Mantua, then
in Vicenza, for reasons expressed in his letters first suspended
it and afterwards transferred it to Trent; then, when for certain reasons the time of its celebration was postponed here
also, it was at length, after the removal of the suspension,
begun in the city of Trent. After a few sessions had been held,
however, and some decrees enacted, the council for certain
reasons and with the concurrence of Apostolic authority, transferred itself to Bologna.[1] But Julius, who succeeded him, recalled
it to the city of Trent,[2] at which time some more decrees were
enacted. But since new disturbances were stirred up in the
neighboring parts of Germany, and a very grave war enkindled in Italy and France, the council was again suspended
and postponed; the enemy of the human race exerting himself exceedingly and throwing hindrances and difficulties in
the way to retard at least as long as possible, since he could
not entirely prevent, such a great advantage to the Church.
But how greatly the heresies in the meantime increased, mul-
tiplied and propagated, how widely the schism spread, we can
neither ponder nor relate without the greatest sorrow of mind.
But at length the good and merciful Lord, who is never so
angry that He forgets mercy,[3] deigned to grant peace and unanimity to the Christian kings and princes. By this proffered
opportunity we, relying on His mercy, entertained the strongest
hope that by the same means of a council an end may be put
to these grave evils in the Church. That therefore schisms

---

1. *Supra,* Sess. VIII
2. *Ibid.,* Sess. XI
3. *Heb.* 3:2

and heresies may be destroyed, morals corrected and reformed, and peace among the Christian princes preserved, we have judged that its celebration should no longer be deferred. Wherefore, after mature deliberation with our venerable brethren, the cardinals of the holy Roman Church, and having also made known our intention to our most dear sons in Christ, Ferdinand, Emperor-elect of the Romans, and other kings and princes, whom, as we expected from their great piety and wisdom, we found very well disposed to aid in the celebration of the council, we, to the praise, honor and glory of the Almighty God, for the benefit of the universal Church, with the advice and consent of the same venerable brethren, and relying on and supported by the authority of God Himself and of the blessed Apostles Peter and Paul, which we also exercise on earth, summon a holy, ecumenical and general council to the city of Trent for the next following most holy day of the Lord's resurrection, and ordain and decree that, all suspension being removed, it be celebrated there. Wherefore, we urgently exhort and admonish in the Lord and also strictly command in virtue of holy obedience, and in virtue also of the oath which they have taken, and under the penalties which they know are prescribed by the sacred canons against those who neglect to attend general councils, our venerable brethren wherever located, patriarchs, archbishops, bishops, and our beloved sons the abbots, and others who by common law, privilege or ancient custom are allowed to sit and express their opinion in a general council, unless they happen to be prevented by a legitimate impediment, which they must prove to the council by lawful procurators. We furthermore admonish each and all whom it does or may concern that they do not neglect to attend the council. Our most dear sons in Christ, the Emperor-elect of the Romans and other Christian kings and princes, whose presence at the council would be earnestly desired, we exhort and beseech that if they themselves should not be able to be present at the council, they at least send as their deputies prudent, reputable and pious men to be present in their name, who, animated by their piety, will see to it that the prelates of their kingdoms and dominions perform without refusal and delay their duty to God and the Church at this so urgent a time; neither do we doubt in the least that they will also see to it that a safe and free road through their kingdoms and dominions is open to the prelates, their attendants, followers

and all others who are proceeding to or returning from the
council, and that they will be received and treated in all places
kindly and courteously, as we also will provide so far as it
concerns us, for we have resolved to omit absolutely nothing
that we, who have been placed in this position, can do toward
the completion of so pious and salutary a work, seeking nothing else, as God knows, and in the celebration of the council
having no other desire but the honor of God, the recovery and
salvation of the scattered sheep, and the lasting peace and
tranquillity of the Christian commonwealth. And that this
document and its contents may come to the knowledge of all
whom it concerns, and that no one may offer the excuse that
he was ignorant of it, especially since there may not perhaps
be safe access to all who ought to have knowledge of this letter, we wish and command that it be read publicly and in a
loud voice by messengers of our court or by some public notaries
in the Vatican Basilica of the Prince of the Apostles and in
the Church of the Lateran, at a time when the people are
accustomed to assemble there for the celebration of the masses;
and that, after having been read, it be affixed to the doors of
those churches, also to the Apostolic Chancery, and at the
usual place in the Campo di Fiore, where it shall be left for
some time that it may be read and made known to all. When
it is removed, copies thereof shall remain affixed in the same
places. For we wish that by this reading, publication and affixture each and all of those whom it includes, shall after two
months from the day of publication and affixture be so obligated and bound as if it had been published and read in their
presence. We also ordain and decree that unshaken faith be
given to the transcripts thereof, written or subscribed by the
hand of a public notary and provided with the seal and signature of some person constituted in ecclesiastical dignity.
Therefore, let no one infringe this letter of our summons,
statute, decree, admonition and exhortation, or with foolhardy
boldness oppose it. But if anyone shall presume to attempt
this, let him know that he will incur the indignation of Almighty
God and of His blessed Apostles Peter and Paul. Given at
Rome at Saint Peter's on the thirtieth of November in the
year 1560 of the Lord's incarnation and in the first year of
our pontificate.

Antonius Florebellus Lavellinus.
Barengus.

SEVENTEENTH SESSION

COUNCIL OF TRENT

which is the first under the Supreme Pontiff, Pius IV,
celebrated on the eighteenth day of January, 1562

DECREE CONCERNING THE CELEBRATION OF THE COUNCIL

Does it please you, for the praise and glory of the holy
and undivided Trinity, Father, Son, and Holy Ghost, for the
increase and exaltation of the faith and of the Christian
religion, that the holy, ecumenical and general Council of
Trent, lawfully assembled in the Holy Ghost, all suspension
being removed, be celebrated from this day on, which is the
eighteenth of the month of January of the year 1562 after
the Nativity of the Lord, consecrated to the chair at Rome
of blessed Peter, the Prince of the Apostles, according to the
form and tenor of the letter of our most holy Lord, the sovereign pontiff, Pius IV, and that, due order being observed,
those things be considered therein which at the suggestion
and under the presidency of the legates shall appear suitable and proper to the council for alleviating the calamities
of these times, adjusting religious controversies, restraining
deceitful tongues, correcting the abuses of depraved morals,
and to bring about true and Christian peace in the Church?

They answered: It pleases us.

SUMMONING OF THE NEXT SESSION

Does it please you that the next following session be held
and celebrated on the Thursday after the second Sunday of
Lent, which will be on the twenty-sixth day of the month
of February?

They answered: It pleases us.

EIGHTEENTH SESSION

which is the second under the Supreme Pontiff, Pius IV,
celebrated on the twenty-sixth day of February, 1562

DECREE CONCERNING THE CHOICE OF BOOKS AND
THE INVITATION OF ALL TO THE COUNCIL UNDER
PUBLIC PROTECTION

The holy, ecumenical and general Council of Trent, lawfully assembled in the Holy Ghost, the same legates of the
Apostolic See presiding, not confiding in human strength
but relying on the power and support of Our Lord Jesus
Christ, who has promised to give to His Church a mouth
and wisdom,[1] has in view above all to restore to its purity
and splendor the doctrine of the Catholic faith, which in
many places has become defiled and obscured by the opinions of many differing among themselves, and to bring back
to a better mode of life morals which have deviated from
ancient usage, and to *turn the heart of the fathers unto the
children,*[2] and the heart of the children unto the fathers.
Since therefore it has first of all observed that the number
of suspected and pernicious books in which an impure doctrine is contained and disseminated far and wide has in
these days exceedingly increased, for which reason indeed
many censures have with pious zeal been issued in various
provinces and especially in the fair city of Rome, and that
as yet no salutary remedy has been of avail against so great
and pernicious a disease; it has thought it proper that the
Fathers chosen for this inquiry should consider carefully
what ought to be done with regard to censures and books
and at an opportune time report thereon to the council, so
that it may more easily separate the various and strange
doctrines as cockle from the wheat of Christian truth,[3] and
may more conveniently deliberate and determine what seems
better adapted to remove anxiety from the minds of many
and to put an end to causes of complaints. It wishes, moreover, that all this be brought to the knowledge of all per-

1. *Luke* 21:15
2. *Ibid.,* 1:17
3. *Matt.* 13:30

sons, as it also does by the present decree bring it, so that if anyone should consider himself in any manner concerned either in the matter of books and censures or in other things which it has declared beforehand are to be treated in this general council, he may not doubt that he will be courteously listened to by the holy council.

And since the same holy council heartily desires and earnestly beseeches God for the things that are for the peace of the Church,[4] so that all acknowledging our common mother on earth, who cannot forget those whom she has begotten,[5] we *may with one mind and one mouth glorify God and the Father of Our Lord Jesus Christ,*[6] it invites and exhorts, by the bowels of the mercy of our same God and Lord, to concord and reconciliation all who do not hold communion with us, and to come to this holy council, to embrace *charity, which is the bond of perfection,* and to show forth the peace of Christ rejoicing in their hearts, wherein they are called in one body.[7] Wherefore, *hearing this voice,* not of man but of the Holy Ghost, let them not *harden their hearts,*[8] but, walking not after their own sense,[9] nor pleasing themselves,[10] let them be moved and converted by this so pious and salutary admonition of their own mother. For as the holy council invites them with all the kindness of charity, so will it receive them.

Moreover, the same holy council has decreed that the public faith can be granted in a general congregation, and that it shall have the same force, authority and obligation as if it had been given and decreed in public session.

SUMMONS FOR THE NEXT SESSION

The same holy Council of Trent, lawfully assembled in the Holy Ghost, the same legates of the Apostolic See presiding, ordains and decrees that the next following session be held and celebrated on the Thursday after the most sacred feast of the Ascension of the Lord, which will be on the fourteenth day of the month of May.

---

4. *Psalms* 121:6
5. *Is*. 49:15
6. *Romans* 15:6
7. *Col.* 3:14f.
8. *Psalms* 94:8; *Heb.* 3:8
9. *Eph.* 4:17
10. *Romans* 15:1ff.

SAFE-CONDUCT GRANTED TO THE GERMAN NATION IN A
GENERAL CONGREGATION ON THE FOURTH DAY
OF MARCH, 1562

The holy, ecumenical and general Council of Trent, lawfully assembled in the Holy Ghost, the same legates of the
Apostolic See presiding, certifies to all men that by the tenor
of these presents it grants and fully concedes the public faith
and the fullest and truest security, which they call a safe-
conduct, to each and all priests, electors, princes, dukes, marquises, counts, barons, soldiers, the common people, and to
all other persons, of whatever state, condition or character
they may be, the German province and nation, to the cities
and other places thereof, and to all other ecclesiastical and
secular persons, especially those of the Confession of Augsburg, who shall come or shall be sent with them to this general Council of Trent, and to those who are going to come or
have already come, by whatever name they are or may be
designated, to come freely to this city of Trent, to remain,
abide and sojourn here, and to propose, speak and consider,
examine and discuss any matters whatever with the council,
to present freely whatever they may think suitable, to set
forth any articles whatever either in writing or orally, and to
explain, establish and prove them by the Sacred Scriptures
and by the words, decisions, and arguments of the blessed
Fathers, and also to reply, if need be, to the objections of the
general council, and to dispute and confer charitably and
respectfully and without hindrance with those who have been
selected by the council, putting aside absolutely reproachful,
vexatious and offensive language; and particularly, it certifies that the controverted matters shall be treated in this
Council of Trent in accordance with Sacred Scriptures and
the traditions of the Apostles, the approved councils, the consensus of the Catholic Church and the authority of the holy
Fathers; with this further provision, it grants and entirely
concedes that they shall under no condition be punished by
reason of religion or of offenses committed or that may be
committed in regard thereto; provided also that the divine
offices shall not by reason of their presence, either upon the
road or in any place of their journey, their stay or their return,
or in the city of Trent itself, be in any way interrupted; and
that on the conclusion of these matters or before their conclusion, whensoever it shall please them, if they should wish

by the command and permission of their superiors to return to their homes, or if any one of them should so wish, they may at their pleasure return freely and securely, without restraint, formality or delay, without injury to their property and to the honor and persons of their attendants and vice versa; making known, however, their intention of withdrawing to those to be deputed by the council, so that at a convenient time, without deceit or fraud, provision may be made for their security. The holy council wishes also that all clauses whatsoever, which may be necessary and suitable for a complete, effective and sufficient security for coming, sojourning and returning, be included and contained, and to be considered as included, in this public faith and safe-conduct. For their greater security and for the sake of peace and reconciliation, it declares also that if, which God forbid, any one or several of them should either on the way to Trent or while sojourning in or returning therefrom, perpetrate or commit an atrocious act, by which the benefit of this public faith and assurance granted to them might be annulled and cassated, it wishes and concedes that those discovered in any such crime shall be forthwith punished by their own countrymen and not by others, with a condign chastisement and proper reparation, which the council on its part may justly approve and commend, the form, conditions and terms of the safe-conduct remaining entirely intact thereby. In like manner it wishes also that if, which God forbid, any one or several of this council should, either on the road or while sojourning or returning, perpetrate or commit an atrocious act by which the benefit of this public faith or assurance may be violated or in any manner annulled, those discovered in any such crime shall be forthwith punished by the council itself and not by others, with a condign chastisement and proper reparation, which the Germans of the Augsburg Confession here present may on their part approve and commend, the present form, conditions and terms of the safe-conduct remaining entirely intact thereby. The council wishes furthermore, that each and all of their ambassadors shall be allowed to go out of the city of Trent to take the fresh air as often as it shall be convenient or necessary and to return here; also freely to send or dispatch their messenger or messengers to any place whatsoever to attend to their necessary affairs and to receive those sent or dispatched or the one sent or dispatched as often as they may deem fit; so however that several or one of those appointed by the council may accompany them or him in order to provide for their safety. This safe-conduct and security shall be good and extend from and during the time that they shall have been taken under the protection of this council and its agents to their arrival at Trent, and during the entire time of their sojourn here; and further, after a sufficient hearing has been had, a period of twenty days having expired, when they themselves should desire, or the council on the conclusion of such hearing should give them notice to return, it will, all deceit and fraud being wholly excluded, reconduct them with the help of God from Trent to that place of safety which each may choose for himself. All of which it promises and pledges in good faith to be inviolately observed toward each and all of the faithful of Christ, toward all ecclesiastical and secular princes and all ecclesiastical and secular persons, of whatsoever state and condition they may be or by whatsoever name they may be known. Moreover, it promises in sincere and good faith, to the exclusion of fraud and deceit, that the council will neither openly nor secretly seek any occasion, nor make use of, nor permit anyone else to make use of, any authority, power, right or statute, privilege of laws or canons, or of any councils in whatever form of words expressed, especially those of Constance and Siena, in any way prejudicial to this public faith and the fullest security, and of the public and free hearing granted by this council to the above-named; these it abrogates in this respect and for this occasion. And if the holy council or any member thereof, or any of its adherents, of whatever condition, state or pre-eminence, shall violate, which may the Almighty prevent, in any point or clause whatever, the form and terms of the security and safe-conduct as set forth above, and a satisfactory reparation that in their judgment may be justly approved and commended shall not have forthwith followed, they may consider the council to have incurred all those penalties which by human and divine law or by custom the violators of such safe-conducts can incur, without any excuse or contrary allegation in this respect.

THE EXTENSION OF THE ABOVE TO OTHER NATIONS

The same holy council, lawfully assembled in the Holy Ghost, the same legates *de latere* of the Apostolic See presiding, grants the public faith or a safe-conduct under the same form and terms in which it is granted to the Germans, to each and all others who do not hold communion with us in matters of faith, of whatever kingdoms, nations, provinces, cities and places they may be, in which the contrary to that which the holy Roman Church holds is publicly and with impunity preached, taught or believed.

NINETEENTH SESSION

which is the third under the Supreme Pontiff, Pius IV,
celebrated on the fourteenth day of May, 1562

DECREE FOR THE PROROGATION OF THE SESSION

The holy, ecumenical and general Council of Trent, lawfully assembled in the Holy Ghost, the same legates of the
Apostolic See presiding, has for good and just reasons
thought it fit to prorogue and does hereby prorogue to the
Thursday after the next feast of Corpus Christi, which will
be the fourth day of June, those decrees which were to have
been drawn up and sanctioned today in the present session,
and announces to all that the session will be held and celebrated on that day. In the meantime, supplication is to be
made to God and the Father of Our Lord Jesus Christ, the
author of peace, that He may sanctify the hearts of all; that
by His help the holy council may now and always be able
to counsel and accomplish those things that will be for His
praise and glory.

TWENTIETH SESSION

which is the fourth under the Supreme Pontiff, Pius IV,
celebrated on the fourth day of June, 1562

DECREE FOR THE PROROGATION OF THE SESSION

The holy, ecumenical and general Council of Trent, lawfully assembled in the Holy Ghost, the same legates of the Apostolic See presiding, has, by reason of various difficulties arising from various causes, and also to the end that all things may proceed in a more befitting manner and with greater deliberation, namely, that dogmas may be dealt with and ratified conjointly with what relates to reform, decreed that whatever seems good to be enacted, concerning both reform and dogma, shall be defined in the next session, which it announces to all for the sixteenth day of the following month of July; adding however, that this holy council may and can freely, at its will and pleasure, as it may judge expedient for the affairs of the council, shorten or extend that term also in a general congregation.

TWENTY-FIRST SESSION

which is the fifth under the Supreme Pontiff, Pius IV,
celebrated on the sixteenth day of July, 1562

THE DOCTRINE OF COMMUNION UNDER BOTH KINDS AND THE COMMUNION OF LITTLE CHILDREN

The holy, ecumenical and general Council of Trent, lawfully assembled in the Holy Ghost, the same legates of the
Apostolic See presiding, has thought fit that, since relative
to the awe-inspiring and most holy sacrament of the
Eucharist various monstrous errors are in different places
circulated by the wiles of the evil spirit, by reason of which,
in some provinces, many are seen to have fallen away from
the faith and obedience of the Catholic Church, those things
which relate to communion under both forms and to that
of little children be explained in this place. Wherefore, it
forbids all the faithful of Christ to presume henceforth to
believe, teach or preach on these matters otherwise than is
explained and defined in these decrees.

Chapter I

LAYMEN AND CLERICS WHEN NOT OFFERING THE SACRIFICE ARE NOT BOUND BY DIVINE LAW TO COMMUNION UNDER BOTH SPECIES

This holy council instructed by the Holy Ghost, who is *the
spirit of wisdom and understanding, the spirit of counsel and
godliness,*[1] and following the judgment and custom of the
Church,[2] declares and teaches that laymen and clerics when
not offering the sacrifice are bound by no divine precept to
receive the sacrament of the Eucharist under both forms, and
that there can be no doubt at all, *salva fide,* that communion
under either form is sufficient for them to salvation. For
though Christ the Lord at the last supper instituted and
delivered to the Apostles this venerable sacrament under the
forms of bread and wine,[3] yet that institution and adminis-

---

1. *Is.* 11:2
2. Council of Constance, Sess. XIII (Denzinger, no. 626); cf. *infra,* can. 2.
3. *Matt.* 26:26-28; *Mark* 14:22-24; *Luke* 22:19f.; *1 Cor.* 11:24f.

tration do not signify that all the faithful are by an enactment of the Lord to receive under both forms. Neither is it rightly inferred from that discourse contained in the sixth chapter of John that communion under both forms was enjoined by the Lord, notwithstanding the various interpretations of it by the holy Fathers and Doctors. For He who said: *Except you eat the flesh of the Son of man and drink his blood, you shall not have life in you,*[4] also said: *He that eateth this bread shall live forever;*[5] and He who said: *He that eateth my flesh and drinketh my blood hath life everlasting,*[6] also said: *The bread that I will give is my flesh for the life of the world;*[7] and lastly, He who said: *He that eateth my flesh and drinketh my blood, abideth in me and I in him,*[8] said, nevertheless: *He that eateth this bread shall live forever.*[9]

Chapter II

THE POWER OF THE CHURCH CONCERNING THE DISPENSATION OF THE SACRAMENT OF THE EUCHARIST

It declares furthermore, that in the dispensation of the sacraments, *salva illorum substantia,* the Church may, according to circumstances, times and places, determine or change whatever she may judge most expedient for the benefit of those receiving them or for the veneration of the sacraments; and this power has always been hers. The Apostle seems to have clearly intimated this when he said: *Let a man so account of us as of the ministers of Christ, and the dispensers of the mysteries of God;*[10] and that he himself exercised this power, as in many other things so in this sacrament, is sufficiently manifest, for after having given some instructions regarding its use, he says: *The rest I will set in order when I come.*[11] Wherefore, though from the beginning of the Christian religion the use of both forms has not been infrequent, yet since that custom has been already very widely changed, holy mother Church, cognizant of her

---

4. *John* 6:54
5. *Ibid.,* 6:52
6. *Ibid.,* 6:55
7. *Ibid.,* 6:52.
8. *Ibid.,* 6:57
9. *Ibid.,* 6:59.
10. See *1 Cor.* 4:1.
11. *Ibid.,* 11:34.

authority in the administration of the sacraments, has, induced by just and weighty reasons, approved this custom of communicating under either species and has decreed that it be considered the law, which may not be repudiated or changed at pleasure without the authority of the Church.

Chapter III

CHRIST, WHOLE AND ENTIRE, AND A TRUE SACRAMENT ARE RECEIVED UNDER EITHER SPECIES

It declares, moreover, that though our Redeemer at the last supper instituted and administered this sacrament to the Apostles under two forms, as has already been said, yet it must be acknowledged that Christ, whole and entire, and a true sacrament are received under either form alone,[12] and therefore, as regards its fruits, those who receive one species only are not deprived of any grace necessary to salvation.

Chapter IV

LITTLE CHILDREN ARE NOT BOUND TO SACRAMENTAL COMMUNION

Finally, the same holy council teaches that little children who have not attained the use of reason are not by any necessity bound to the sacramental communion of the Eucharist; for having been regenerated by the laver of baptism and thereby incorporated with Christ,[13] they cannot at that age lose the grace of the sons of God already acquired. Antiquity is not therefore to be condemned, however, if in some places it at one time observed that custom. For just as those most holy Fathers had acceptable ground for what they did under the circumstances, so it is certainly to be accepted without controversy that they regarded it as not necessary to salvation.

CANONS ON COMMUNION UNDER BOTH SPECIES AND THAT OF LITTLE CHILDREN

Canon 1. If anyone says that each and all the faithful of Christ are by a precept of God or by the necessity of sal-

---

12. Cf. Sess. XIII, chap. 3 and can. 3
13. Titus 3:5

vation bound to receive both species of the most holy sacrament of the Eucharist,[14] let him be anathema.

Canon 2. If anyone says that the holy Catholic Church was not moved by just causes and reasons that laymen and clerics when not consecrating should communicate under the form of bread only,[15] or has erred in this, let him be anathema.

Canon 3. If anyone denies that Christ, the fountain and author of all graces, is received whole and entire under the one species of bread, because, as some falsely assert, He is not received in accordance with the institution of Christ under both species,[16] let him be anathema.

Canon 4. If anyone says that communion of the Eucharist is necessary for little children before they have attained the years of discretion,[17] let him be anathema.

The two articles proposed on another occasion but not yet discussed,[18] namely, whether the reasons which moved the holy Catholic Church to decree that laymen and priests not celebrating are to communicate under the one species of bread only, are so stringent that under no circumstances is the use of the chalice to be permitted to anyone; and whether, in case it appears advisable and consonant with Christian charity that the use of the chalice be conceded to a person, nation or kingdom, it is to be conceded under certain conditions, and what are those conditions, the same holy council reserves for examination and definition to another time, at the earliest opportunity that shall present itself.

DECREE CONCERNING REFORM

The same holy, ecumenical and general Council of Trent, lawfully assembled in the Holy Ghost, the same legates of the Apostolic See presiding, has judged it proper, to the praise of Almighty God and to the glory of holy Church, that what follows, relative to the matter of reform, be at present enacted.

14. Cf. *supra,* chap. 1
15. *Ibid.,* chap. 2
16. *Ibid.,* chap. 3; Sess. XIII, chap. 3 and can. 3
17. *Supra,* chap. 4
18. Cf. pp. 85f.

Chapter I

BISHOPS SHALL CONFER ORDERS AND GIVE DIMISSORY AND
TESTIMONIAL LETTERS *GRATIS;* THEIR MINISTERS SHALL
RECEIVE ABSOLUTELY NOTHING THEREFOR AND NOTARIES
THAT WHICH IS PRESCRIBED IN THIS DECREE

Since the ecclesiastical order must be free from every suspicion of avarice, neither bishops nor others who confer orders,
or their ministers, shall under any pretext whatever receive
anything for the collation of any orders, not even for the
clerical tonsure, or for dimissory or testimonial letters, or
for the seal or for any other reason whatsoever, even though
it should be offered voluntarily. Notaries, except in those
places only where the laudable custom of receiving nothing
does not prevail, may receive only the tenth part of a gold
florin for each dimissory or testimonial letter, provided no
salary is paid them for the discharge of the office. Further,
no emolument from the income of the notary shall accrue
either directly or indirectly to the bishop from the collation
of orders, for in that case the council decrees that they are
bound to give their labor wholly *gratis;* annulling and pro-
hibiting absolutely in all localities taxes, statutes and customs to the contrary, even though immemorial, which might
preferably be called abuses and corruptions tending to simoniacal depravity. Those who act otherwise, givers as well as
receivers, shall, apart from the divine punishment, incur
ipso facto the penalties prescribed by law.[19]

Chapter II

THOSE WHO HAVE NOT THE MEANS OF LIVELIHOOD ARE TO
BE EXCLUDED FROM SACRED ORDERS

Since it is not becoming that those who are enrolled in
the sacred ministry should, to the dishonor of the order, beg
or engage in some improper business; and since it is known
that very many in different localities are admitted to sacred
orders with almost no selection, who by various methods of
fraud and deception pretend to have an ecclesiastical benefice
or sufficient means, the holy council decrees that henceforth

---

19. Cc. 6, 8, 101, 107, 113, C.I, q. 1; C.14, C.II, q.5; cc.4, 5, 11, 13, 30, X, De simonia,
   V, 3, etc.

no secular cleric, though otherwise qualified as regards morals, knowledge and age, shall be promoted to sacred orders unless it be first legitimately established that he is in peaceful possession of an ecclesiastical benefice sufficient for a decent livelihood; and he may not resign that benefice without mentioning the fact that he was promoted by reason of the title thereof; neither shall that resignation be accepted unless it is certain that he can live suitably from other sources; a resignation made otherwise shall be void. As to those who have a patrimony or pension, only those may hereafter be ordained whom the bishop judges ought to be received in consideration of the need or benefit of his churches, having first informed himself that they really possess that patrimony or pension and that there are means sufficient for their subsistence. The same, moreover, may not under any condition be alienated, canceled or remitted without the permission of the bishop, until they have obtained a sufficient ecclesiastical benefice or have some other means whereby to live; the penalties of the ancient canons in respect hereto being renewed.[20]

Chapter III

THE MANNER OF INCREASING THE DAILY DISTRIBUTIONS IS PRESCRIBED; TO WHOM THEY SHALL BE DUE; THE CONTUMACY OF THOSE WHO DO NOT SERVE IS PUNISHED

Since benefices have been established for divine worship and for administering the ecclesiastical offices, to the end that divine worship may not be in any part curtailed, but may in all things receive due attention,[21] the holy council decrees that in churches, cathedral as well as collegiate, in which there are no daily distributions, or so meager that they are probably disregarded, a third part of the fruits and of all proceeds and revenues of dignities with and without jurisdiction as well as of canonries, portions and offices, shall be set apart and used for daily distributions, to be divided proportionately among those who possess dignities and others who are present at divine service in accordance with the proportion to be decided by the bishop, also as del-

---

20. Cc.2, 4, 16, 23, X, De praeb., III, 5; c.37, h.t. in VI°, III, 4
21. C.15, VI°, De rescrip., I, 3

egate of the Apostolic See, at the first distribution of the fruits;[22] with the retention, however, of the customs of those churches in which those who do not reside therein or do not serve receive nothing or less than a third; exemptions and other customs, even though immemorial, and appeals whatsoever notwithstanding. In case the contumacy of those who do not serve should increase, they may be proceeded against according to the provision of the law and the sacred canons.[23]

Chapter IV

WHEN ASSISTANTS ARE TO BE EMPLOYED IN THE *CURA ANIMARUM*. THE MANNER OF ERECTING NEW PARISHES IS SPECIFIED

In all parochial or baptismal churches in which the people are so numerous that one rector does not suffice to attend to the administration of the sacraments of the Church and divine worship, the bishops shall, also as delegates of the Apostolic See, compel the rectors, or those to whom it pertains, to associate with themselves in this office as many priests as are necessary to administer the sacraments and carry on divine worship. In those, moreover, to which, by reason of distance and hardship, the parishioners cannot come without great inconvenience to receive the sacraments and hear the divine offices, they may, even against the will of the rectors, establish new parishes, pursuant to the form of the constitution of Alexander III, which begins, "Ad audientiam."[24] To those priests who are first to be appointed to the newly erected churches, a suitable portion, decided by the bishop, shall be assigned from the fruits in whatever way belonging to the mother-church, and if it be necessary, he may compel the people to contribute what may be sufficient for the sustenance of those priests; every general or special reservation or attachment respecting the aforesaid churches notwithstanding. Neither can such ordinances and erections be invalidated or hindered by any provisions, even by virtue of resignation or by any other restrictions or hindrances.

---

22. Cf. Sess. XXII, chap. 3 de ref. and Sess. XXIV, chap. 12 de ref.
23. Cc.16, 17, X, De cler. non resid., III, 4; Sess. XXIII, chap. 1 de ref.
24. C.3, X. De eccl. aedif., III, 48

Chapter V

BISHOPS MAY FORM PERPETUAL UNIONS IN CASES PERMITTED BY LAW

Likewise, in order that the state of the churches in which the divine services are offered to God may be maintained in accordance with their dignity, the bishops may, also as delegates of the Apostolic See, according to the prescription of the law, form perpetual unions,[25] without detriment, however, to the incumbents, of any parochial and baptismal churches and of other benefices with or without the *cura* with those to which a *cura* is annexed, by reason of their poverty or in other cases permitted by law, even if those churches or benefices be generally or specially reserved or in any way attached. These unions shall not be revoked or suppressed by virtue of any provision whatever or by reason of resignation, restriction or hindrance.

Chapter VI

TO ILLITERATE RECTORS VICARS SHALL BE GIVEN WITH THE ASSIGNMENT OF A PORTION OF THE FRUITS; THOSE CONTINUING TO GIVE SCANDAL MAY BE DEPRIVED OF THEIR BENEFICES

Since illiterate and incompetent rectors of parochial churches are but little suited for sacred offices,[26] and others by the depravity of their lives corrupt rather than edify, the bishops may, also as delegates of the Apostolic See, give temporarily to such illiterate and incompetent rectors, if otherwise blameless, assistants or vicars, with a portion of the fruits sufficient for their maintenance or provide for them in some other manner, every appeal and exemption being set aside. But those who live a disgraceful and scandalous life, they shall, after admonishing them, restrain and punish; and if they should continue to be incorrigible in their wickedness, they shall have the authority to deprive them of their benefices in accordance with the prescriptions of the sacred canons,[27] every exemption and appeal being rejected.

---

25. C.8, X, De excess. prael., V, 31; Sess. XIV, chap. 9 de ref. and Sess. XXIV, chap. 13 de ref.
26. C.1, D.XXXVI; c.1, D.XXXVIII; c.10, X, Dc renunc., I, 9
27. Cc.13-15, X, De vit. et hon. cler., III, 1

Chapter VII

BISHOPS SHALL TRANSFER BENEFICES FROM CHURCHES
WHICH CANNOT BE RESTORED; OTHERS THEY SHALL HAVE
REPAIRED; WHAT IS TO BE OBSERVED IN THIS MATTER

Since great care is to be taken also lest those things which
have been dedicated to sacred services may through the
injury of time decay and pass away from the memory of
men, the bishops may, also as delegates of the Apostolic See,
after having summoned those who are interested, transfer
simple benefices, even those having the right of patronage,
from churches which have fallen into ruin by reason of age
or otherwise and which cannot by reason of their poverty
be restored, to the mother-churches or to others of the same
or neighboring places as they shall judge suitable; and in
these churches they shall erect altars or chapels under the
same invocations, or transfer them with all the emoluments
and obligations imposed on the former churches to altars
or chapels already erected. Parochial churches, however, thus
fallen into decay, they shall, even if they enjoy the right of
patronage, have repaired and restored from the fruits and
revenues in any way belonging to those churches.[28] If these
are not sufficient, they shall compel by all suitable means
the patrons and others who receive any revenues from the
said churches, or, in their default, the parishioners, to provide for the repairs; every appeal, exemption and objection
being set aside. But if they should all be too poor, then they
are to be transferred to the mother-church or neighboring
churches, with authority to convert both the said parochial
churches and others that are in ruins to profane, though
not to sordid uses, nevertheless erecting a cross there.

Chapter VIII

MONASTERIES HELD *IN COMMENDAM* IN WHICH REGULAR
OBSERVANCE DOES NOT EXIST, AS WELL AS ALL BENEFICES
SHALL BE VISITED BY THE BISHOPS ANNUALLY

It is proper that all things in a diocese pertaining to the
worship of God be diligently watched over by the ordinary
and, where necessary, set in order by him. Wherefore, monas-

---

28. Cc.1,4, X, De eccl. aedif., III, 48. Cf. Sess. VII, chap. 8 de ref.

teries held *in conmendam,* also abbeys, priories and those called provostries, in which regular observance does not exist, also benefices with or without the *cura,* secular and regular, in whatever manner held *in commendam,* even if exempt, shall be visited annually by the bishops, also as delegates of the Apostolic See;[29] and the same bishops shall provide by suitable measures, even by the sequestration of revenues, that whatever needs to be renewed or repaired, be done, and that the care of souls, if those places or those annexed to them be charged therewith, and other services due to them be properly exercised; appeals, privileges, customs, even though prescribed from time immemorial, conservators, commissions of judges and their inhibitions notwithstanding. But if regular observance is therein maintained, the bishops shall by fatherly admonitions see to it that the superiors of those regulars observe and cause to be observed the manner of life required by the rules of their order and that they keep and govern those subject to them in their duty. If however, after having been admonished, they shall not within six months have visited or corrected them, then the bishops, also as delegates of the Apostolic See, may visit and correct them, just as the superiors themselves should do in accordance with their rules; all appeals, privileges and exemptions being absolutely set aside.

---

29. Cf. Sess. VII, chap. 8 de ref.; Sess. XXIV, chap. 9 de ref. and Sess. XXV, chap. 20 de regular.

Chapter IX

THE NAME AND SERVICES OF QUESTORS OF ALMS IS
ABOLISHED. THE ORDINARIES SHALL PUBLISH INDULGENCES
AND SPIRITUAL GRACES. TWO OF THE CHAPTER SHALL
WITHOUT FEE RECEIVE THE ALMS

Since many remedies heretofore applied by different councils, those of the Lateran[30] and Lyons as well as that of Vienne,[31] against the pernicious abuses of questors of alms,[32] have in later times become useless, and since their depravity is, to the great scandal and complaint of the faithful, found to be daily so much on the increase that there seems to be no longer any hope of their amendment left, it is decreed that in all parts of Christendom their name and service be henceforth absolutely abolished and in no wise shall they be permitted to exercise such an office; any privileges granted to churches, monasteries, hospitals, pious places, and to any persons of whatever rank, state and dignity, or any customs, even though immemorial, notwithstanding. With regard to indulgences or other spiritual graces of which the faithful of Christ ought not on this account to be deprived, it is decreed that they are in the future to be announced to the people at suitable times by the local ordinaries aided by two members of the chapter. To these also the authority is given to collect faithfully and without fee the alms and charitable contributions offered them, so that all may understand that these heavenly treasures of the Church are administered not for gain but for piety.

ANNOUNCEMENT OF THE NEXT SESSION

The holy, ecumenical and general Council of Trent, lawfully assembled in the Holy Ghost, the same legates of the Apostolic See presiding, has ordained and decreed that the next following session be held and celebrated on the Thursday after the octave of the feast of the Nativity of the Blessed Virgin Mary, which will be on the seventeenth of the month of September next; with the addition, however, that the same

---

30. C.14, X, De poenit., V, 38
31. C.2, in Clem., h.t. V, 9
32. Cf. Sess. V, chap. 2 de ref. and Sess. XXV, Decree on Indulgences.

holy council freely may and can, according to its will and pleasure, as it shall judge expedient for the affairs of the council, limit or extend, even in a general congregation, the said term and also everyone that is hereafter set for any session.

TWENTY-SECOND SESSION

which is the sixth under the Supreme Pontiff, Pius IV,
celebrated on the sixteenth day of September, 1562

DOCTRINE CONCERNING THE SACRIFICE OF THE MASS

That the ancient, complete and in every way perfect faith
and teaching regarding the great mystery of the Eucharist
in the Catholic Church may be retained, and with the removal
of errors and heresies may be preserved in its purity, the
holy, ecumenical and general Council of Trent, lawfully
assembled in the Holy Ghost, the same legates of the Apostolic See presiding, instructed by the light of the Holy Ghost,
teaches, declares and orders to be preached to the faithful
the following concerning it, since it is the true and only
sacrifice.

Chapter I

THE INSTITUTION OF THE MOST HOLY SACRIFICE OF THE MASS

Since under the former Testament, according to the testimony of the Apostle Paul, there was no perfection because of
the weakness of the Levitical priesthood, there was need, God
the Father of mercies so ordaining, *that another priest should
rise according to the order of Melchisedech,*[1] Our Lord Jesus
Christ, who might perfect and lead to perfection as many as
were to be sanctified. He, therefore, our God and Lord, though
He was by His death about to offer Himself once upon the
altar of the cross to God the Father that He might there
accomplish an eternal redemption, nevertheless, that His
priesthood might not come to an end with His death,[2] at the
last supper, on the night He was betrayed, that He might
leave to His beloved spouse the Church a visible sacrifice,
such as the nature of man requires, whereby that bloody sacrifice once to be accomplished on the cross might be represented, the memory thereof remain even to the end of the
world, and its salutary effects applied to the remission of

---

1. *Heb.* 7:11
2. *Ibid.,* 7:24

those sins which we daily commit, declaring Himself constituted *a priest forever according to the order of Melchisedech,*[3]
offered up to God the Father His own body and blood under
the form of bread and wine, and under the forms of those
same things gave to the Apostles, whom He then made priests
of the New Testament, that they might partake, commanding
them and their successors in the priesthood by these words
to do likewise: *Do this in commemoration of me,*[4] as the Catholic
Church has always understood and taught. For having celebrated the ancient Passover which the multitude of the children of Israel sacrificed in memory of their departure from
Egypt,[5] He instituted a new Passover, namely, Himself, to be
immolated under visible signs by the Church through the
priests in memory of His own passage from this world to the
Father, when by the shedding of His blood He redeemed and
*delivered us from the power of darkness and translated us
into his kingdom.*[6] And this is indeed that clean oblation
which cannot be defiled by any unworthiness or malice on
the part of those who offer it; which the Lord foretold by
Malachias was to be great among the Gentiles,[7] and which
the Apostle Paul has clearly indicated when he says, that
they who are defiled by partaking of the table of devils cannot be partakers of the table of the Lord,[8] understanding by
table in each case the altar. It is, finally, that [sacrifice] which
was prefigured by various types of sacrifices during the period
of nature and of the law,[9] which, namely, comprises all the
good things signified by them, as being the consummation
and perfection of them all.

Chapter II

THE SACRIFICE OF THE MASS IS PROPITIATORY BOTH FOR
THE LIVING AND THE DEAD

And inasmuch as in this divine sacrifice which is celebrated
in the mass is contained and immolated in an unbloody manner the same Christ who once offered Himself in a bloody

3. *Psalms* 109:4
4. *Luke* 22:19; *1 Cor.* 11:24f.
5. *Exodus* 13.6
6. *Col.* 1:13
7. *Mal.* 1:11
8. Cf. *1 Cor.* 10:21.
9. *Gen.* 4:4; 12:8, etc.

manner on the altar of the cross, the holy council teaches
that this is truly propitiatory and has this effect, that if we,
contrite and penitent, with sincere heart and upright faith,
with fear and reverence, draw nigh to God, *we obtain mercy
and find grace in seasonable aid.*[10] For, appeased by this sacrifice, the Lord grants the grace and gift of penitence and
pardons even the gravest crimes and sins. For the victim is
one and the same, the same now offering by the ministry of
priests who then offered Himself on the cross, the manner
alone of offering being different. The fruits of that bloody sacrifice, it is well understood, are received most abundantly
through this unbloody one, so far is the latter from derogat-
ing in any way from the former. Wherefore, according to the
tradition of the Apostles,[11] it is rightly offered not only for
the sins, punishments, satisfactions and other necessities of
the faithful who are living, but also for those departed in
Christ but not yet fully purified.

Chapter III

MASSES IN HONOR OF THE SAINTS

And though the Church has been accustomed to celebrate
at times certain masses in honor and memory of the saints,
she does not teach that sacrifice is offered to them but to
God alone who crowned them;[12] whence, the priest does not
say: "To thee, Peter or Paul, I offer sacrifice,"[13] but, giving
thanks to God for their victories, he implores their favor
that they may vouchsafe to intercede for us in heaven whose
memory we celebrate on earth.

Chapter IV

THE CANON OF THE MASS

And since it is becoming that holy things be administered
in a holy manner, and of all things this sacrifice is the most
holy, the Catholic Church, to the end that it might be worthily
and reverently offered and received, instituted many cen-

---

10. *Heb.* 4:16
11. Cf. *infra,* can. 3, and Sess. XXV, decr. on Purgatory
12. *Ibid.,* can. 5, and Sess. XXV, Invocation of the Saints
13. St. Aug., *De civitate Dei,* VIII, c.27

turies ago the holy canon,[14] which is so free from error that it contains nothing that does not in the highest degree savor of a certain holiness and piety and raise up to God the minds of those who offer. For it consists partly of the very words of the Lord, partly of the traditions of the Apostles, and also of pious regulations of holy pontiffs.

Chapter V

THE CEREMONIES AND RITES OF THE MASS

And since the nature of man is such that he cannot without external means be raised easily to meditation on divine things, holy mother Church has instituted certain rites, namely, that some things in the mass be pronounced in a low tone and others in a louder tone. She has likewise, in accordance with apostolic discipline and tradition, made use of ceremonies,[15] such as mystical blessings, lights, incense, vestments, and many other things of this kind, whereby both the majesty of so great a sacrifice might be emphasized and the minds of the faithful excited by those visible signs of religion and piety to the contemplation of those most sublime things which are hidden in this sacrifice.

Chapter VI

THE MASS IN WHICH THE PRIEST ALONE COMMUNICATES

The holy council wishes indeed that at each mass the faithful who are present should communicate, not only in spiritual desire but also by the sacramental partaking of the Eucharist, that thereby they may derive from this most holy sacrifice a more abundant fruit; if, however, that is not always done, it does not on that account condemn as private and illicit those masses in which the priest alone communicates sacramentally, but rather approves and commends them, since these masses also ought to be considered as truly common, partly because at them the people communicate spiritually and partly also because they are celebrated by a public minister of the Church, not for himself only but for all the faithful who belong to the body of Christ.

---

14. C.6, X, De celebr. miss., III, 41
15. Cf. *infra*, can. 7

Chapter VII

THE MIXTURE OF WATER WITH WINE IN THE OFFERING
OF THE CHALICE

The holy council in the next place calls to mind that the Church has instructed priests to mix water with the wine that is to be offered in the chalice;[16] because it is believed that Christ the Lord did this, and also because from His side there came blood and water;[17] the memory of this mystery is renewed by this mixture, and since in the Apocalypse of St. John the "people" are called "waters,"[18] the union of the faithful people with Christ their head is represented.

Chapter VIII

THE MASS MAY NOT BE CELEBRATED IN THE VERNACULAR.
ITS MYSTERIES TO BE EXPLAINED TO THE PEOPLE

Though the mass contains much instruction for the faithful, it has, nevertheless, not been deemed advisable by the Fathers that it should be celebrated everywhere in the vernacular tongue. Wherefore, the ancient rite of each Church, approved by the holy Roman Church, the mother and mistress of all churches, being everywhere retained, that the sheep of Christ may not suffer hunger, or *the little ones ask for bread and there is none to break it unto them,*[19] the holy council commands pastors and all who have the *cura animarum* that they, either themselves or through others, explain frequently during the celebration of the mass some of the things read during the mass, and that among other things they explain some mystery of this most holy sacrifice, especially on Sundays and festival days.[20]

---

16. Cc.4, 5, 7, D.II de cons.; c.6, X, De celebr. miss., III, 41. Cf. Denzinger, nos. 416, 698, 945
17. *John* 19:34
18. *Apoc.* 17:1, 15
19. *Lam.* 4:4
20. Cf. Sess. V, chap. 2 de ref., and Sess. XXIV, chap. 7 de ref.

Chapter IX

PRELIMINARY REMARKS ON THE FOLLOWING CANONS

Since many errors are at this time disseminated and many things taught and discussed by many persons that are in opposition to this ancient faith, which is founded on the holy Gospel, the traditions of the Apostles, and the teaching of the holy Fathers, the holy council, after many and grave deliberations concerning these matters, has resolved with the unanimous consent of all to condemn and eliminate from holy Church by means of the following canons whatever is opposed to this most pure faith and sacred doctrine.

CANONS ON THE SACRIFICE OF THE MASS

Canon 1. If anyone says that in the mass a true and real sacrifice is not offered to God; or that to be offered is nothing else than that Christ is given to us to eat, let him be anathema.

Canon 2. If anyone says that by those words, *Do this for a commemoration of me,*[21] Christ did not institute the Apostles priests;[22] or did not ordain that they and other priests should offer His own body and blood, let him be anathema.

Canon 3. If anyone says that the sacrifice of the mass is one only of praise and thanksgiving; or that it is a mere commemoration of the sacrifice consummated on the cross but not a propitiatory one;[23] or that it profits him only who receives, and ought not to be offered for the living and the dead, for sins, punishments, satisfactions, and other necessities, let him be anathema.

Canon 4. If anyone says that by the sacrifice of the mass a blasphemy is cast upon the most holy sacrifice of Christ consummated on the cross; or that the former derogates from the latter, let him be anathema.

Canon 5. If anyone says that it is a deception to celebrate masses in honor of the saints and in order to obtain their intercession with God, as the Church intends,[24] let him be anathema.

---

21. *Luke* 22:19; *1 Cor.* 11:25
22. Cf. *supra,* chap. 1
23. *Ibid.,* chap. 2
24. *Ibid.,* chap. 3

Canon 6. If anyone says that the canon of the mass contains errors and is therefore to be abrogated,[25] let him be anathema.

Canon 7. If anyone says that the ceremonies, vestments, and outward signs which the Catholic Church uses in the celebration of masses, are incentives to impiety rather than stimulants to piety,[26] let him be anathema.

Canon 8. If anyone says that masses in which the priest alone communicates sacramentally are illicit and are therefore to be abrogated,[27] let him be anathema.

Canon 9. If anyone says that the rite of the Roman Church, according to which a part of the canon and the words of consecration are pronounced in a low tone, is to be condemned; or that the mass ought to be celebrated in the vernacular tongue only;[28] or that water ought not to be mixed with the wine that is to be offered in the chalice because it is contrary to the institution of Christ,[29] let him be anathema.

DECREE CONCERNING THE THINGS TO BE OBSERVED AND AVOIDED IN THE CELEBRATION OF MASS

What great care is to be taken that the holy sacrifice of the mass be celebrated with all religious devotion and reverence, each one may easily conceive who considers that in the sacred writings he is called accursed who does the work of God negligently.[30] And since we must confess that no other work can be performed by the faithful that is so holy and divine as this awe-inspiring mystery, wherein that life-giving victim by which we are reconciled to the Father is daily immolated on the altar by priests, it is also sufficiently clear that all effort and attention must be directed to the end that it be performed with the greatest possible interior cleanness and purity of heart and exterior evidence of devotion and piety.[31] Therefore, since either through the depravity of the times or through the indifference and corruption of men many things seem already to have crept in that are foreign to the dignity of so great a sacrifice, in order that the honor

---

25. *Supra,* chap. 4
26. *Ibid.,* chap. 5
27. *Ibid.,* chap. 6
28. *Ibid.,* chap. 8
29. *Ibid.,* chap. 7
30. *Jer.* 48:10
31. Cf. Sess. XIII, chap. 7

and worship due to it may for the glory of God and the edification of the faithful be restored, the holy council decrees that the local ordinaries shall be zealously concerned and be bound to prohibit and abolish all those things which either *covetousness, which is a serving of idols,*[32] or irreverence, which can scarcely be separated from ungodliness, or superstition, a false imitation of true piety, have introduced.

And that many things may be summed up in a few, they shall in the first place, as regards avarice, absolutely forbid conditions of compensations of whatever kind, bargains, and whatever is given for the celebration of new masses; also those importunate and unbecoming demands, rather than requests, for alms and other things of this kind which border on simoniacal taint or certainly savor of filthy lucre.

In the second place, that irreverence may be avoided, each in his own diocese shall forbid that any wandering or unknown priest be permitted to celebrate mass. Furthermore, they shall permit no one who is publicly and notoriously wicked either to minister at the altar or to be present at the sacred services; nor suffer the holy sacrifice to be celebrated by any seculars and regulars whatsoever in private houses or entirely outside the church and the oratories dedicated solely to divine worship and to be designated and visited by the same ordinaries;[33] or unless those present have first shown by their outward disposition and appearance that they are there not in body only but also in mind and devout affection of heart. They shall also banish from the churches all such music which, whether by the organ or in the singing, contains things that are lascivious or impure; likewise all worldly conduct, vain and profane conversations, wandering around, noise and clamor, so that the house of God may be seen to be and may be truly called a house of prayer.[34]

Finally, that no room may be given to superstition, they shall by ordinance and prescribed penalties provide that priests do not celebrate at other than proper hours; or make use of rites or ceremonies and prayers in the celebration of masses other than those that have been approved by the Church and have been received through frequent and praise-

32. *Eph.* 5:5
33. Cc.12, 34, D.I de cons.
34. *Is.* 56:7; *Matt.* 21:13

worthy usage. They shall completely banish from the Church the practice of any fixed number of masses and candles, which has its origin in superstitious worship rather than in true religion; and they shall instruct the people as to what the very precious and heavenly fruit of this most holy sacrifice is and whence especially it is derived. They shall also admonish their people to go frequently to their own parish churches, at least on Sundays and the greater feast days.[35] All these things, therefore, which have been summarily enumerated, are in such wise set before all local ordinaries, that by the authority given them by this holy council, and also as delegates of the Apostolic See, they may prohibit, command, reform and establish not only the things aforesaid but also whatsoever else shall seem to them to be connected therewith; and they may by ecclesiastical censures and other penalties, which in their judgment they may impose, compel the faithful to observe them inviolately; any privileges, exemptions, appeals and customs to the contrary notwithstanding.

DECREE CONCERNING REFORM

The same holy, ecumenical and general Council of Trent, lawfully assembled in the Holy Ghost, the same legates of the Apostolic See presiding, that the work of reform may be continued, has deemed it well that the following things be established in the present session.

Chapter I

DECREES CONCERNING THE LIFE AND CONDUCT OF CLERICS ARE RENEWED

There is nothing that leads others to piety and to the service of God more than the life and example of those who have dedicated themselves to the divine ministry.[36] For since they are observed to be raised from the things of this world to a higher position, others fix their eyes upon them as upon a mirror and derive from them what they are to imitate. Wherefore, clerics, called to have the Lord for their portion,[37] ought by all means so to regulate their life and con-

---

35. C.35, D.I de cons.; cc.4., 5, C.IX, q.2; c.2, X, De paroch., III, 29
36. Cf. Sess. XXV, chap. 1 de ref.
37. C.1, D.XXI

duct that in dress, behavior, gait, speech, and all other things nothing may appear but what is dignified, moderated, and permeated with piety; avoiding also minor offenses which in them would be grievous, so that their actions may inspire reverence. Since therefore the more these things contribute to usefulness and honor in the Church of God, so the more zealously must they be observed, the holy council ordains that those things which have in the past been frequently and wholesomely enacted by the supreme pontiffs and holy councils concerning adherence to the life, conduct, dress, and learning of clerics, as also the avoidance of luxury, feastings, dances, gambling, sports, and all sorts of crime and secular pursuits, shall in the future be observed under the same or greater penalties to be imposed at the discretion of the ordinary;[38] nor shall appeal suspend the execution of that which pertains to the correction of morals. If any of these things shall be found to have fallen into desuetude, the ordinaries shall make it their duty to restore their practice as soon as possible and enforce the careful observance by all, any customs to the contrary notwithstanding; lest they themselves, God being the avenger, may have to pay the penalty deserved by their neglect of the correction of their subjects.

Chapter II

WHO ARE TO BE PROMOTED TO CATHEDRAL CHURCHES

Everyone who is hereafter to be promoted to a cathedral church shall not only be qualified by birth, age, morals, and life, and in other respects as required by the sacred canons,[39] but shall also for the space of at least six months previously have been constituted in sacred orders. Information covering these points, in case the (Roman) Curia has no knowledge or only recent knowledge of the person, shall be obtained from the legates of the Apostolic See or from the nuncios of the provinces or from his ordinary, and in his default, from the nearest ordinaries. In addition, he shall possess such learning as will enable him to discharge the

---

38. Cf. tot. tit. de vit. et hon. cler. apud Greg., in VI° et in Clem. (III, 1)
39. Cf. c.5, D.LI; cc.7, 19, X, De elect., I, 6; Sess. VII, chap. 1 de ref., and Sess. XXIV, chaps. 1, 12 de ref.

obligations of the office that is to be conferred on him. He shall, therefore, have been previously promoted by merit in a university of learning to the rank of master or doctor or licentiate in sacred theology or canon law, or shall be declared by the public testimony of some academy competent to teach others. If he be a regular he shall have a similar attestation from the superiors of his order. All the aforesaid persons from whom the information or testimony is to be obtained, shall be bound to report on these matters faithfully and *gratis;* otherwise let them know that their consciences will be grievously burdened and that they will have God and their superiors as avengers.

Chapter III

DAILY DISTRIBUTIONS ARE TO BE MADE FROM THE THIRD PART OF ALL REVENUES; ON WHOM THE PORTION OF ABSENTEES FALLS; CERTAIN CASES EXCEPTED

Bishops, also as delegates of the Apostolic See, have the authority to divide the third part of the fruits and revenues of all dignities with and without jurisdiction and offices existing in cathedral and collegiate churches into distributions, to be assigned as they shall judge advisable;[40] so namely, that if their recipients should fail on any day to discharge personally the duty that devolves upon them in accordance with the form to be prescribed by the bishops, they shall forfeit the distribution of that day and in no manner acquire proprietorship thereof; but it should be applied to the administration of the church so far as there is need, or, in the judgment of the ordinary, to some other pious purpose. If, however, their contumacy should increase, they shall proceed against them according to the prescriptions of the sacred canons.[41] If anyone of the aforesaid dignitaries possesses neither by right nor by custom any jurisdiction, administration or office in cathedral or collegiate churches, but should there be outside the city in the diocese a *cura animarum* which he is willing to take upon himself, then he shall during the time that he resides in and administers the church with such *cura* be considered as though he were

---

40. Cf. Sess. XXI, chap. 3 de ref.
41. *Ibid.*

present and assisted at the divine offices in those cathedral and collegiate churches. These things are to be understood as applying to those churches only in which there is no custom or statute whereby the said dignitaries who do not serve, lose something which amounts to the third part of the fruits and revenues; any customs, even though immemorial, exemptions and constitutions, even though confirmed by oath or by any authority whatsoever, to the contrary notwithstanding.

Chapter IV

THOSE NOT IN SACRED ORDER SHALL NOT HAVE A VOICE IN THE CHAPTER OF A CATHEDRAL OR COLLEGIATE CHURCH. THE QUALIFICATIONS AND DUTIES OF THOSE WHO HOLD BENEFICES THEREIN

Anyone engaged in the divine offices in a cathedral or collegiate church, whether secular or regular, who is not constituted at least in the subdiaconal order, shall not have a voice in the chapter of those churches, even though this may have been freely conceded to him by the others. Those who hold or shall hereafter hold in the said churches dignities with or without jurisdiction, offices, prebends, portions, or any other benefices whatsoever, to which are attached various obligations, namely, that some say or sing the masses, others the Gospel, others the Epistles, shall be bound, in the absence of a just impediment, to receive the required orders within a year, whatever privilege, exemption, prerogative or nobility of birth they may possess; otherwise they shall incur the penalties provided by the constitution of the Council of Vienne, which begins, "Ut ii qui,"[42] which is by the present decree renewed. The bishops shall compel them to exercise personally the aforesaid orders on the days specified, and to discharge all other duties required of them in the divine service under the same and even other more severe penalties which may be imposed at their discretion.[43] In the future such offices shall not be assigned except to those who are known to have attained the required age and the other qualifications; otherwise such assignments shall be null.

---

42. C.2, De aet. et qual. et ord. praef., in Clem., I, 6
43. Cf. Sess. XXIV, chap. 12 de ref.

Chapter V

DISPENSATIONS OUTSIDE THE CURIA SHALL BE COMMITTED TO THE BISHOP AND EXAMINED BY HIM

Dispensations, by whatever authority to be granted, if they are to be sent outside the Roman Curia, shall be committed to the ordinaries of those who have obtained them. Those, however, which are granted as a favor shall not have effect until the ordinaries, as delegates of the Apostolic See, have established summarily only and extra-judicially that the terms of the petition are free from fraud and deception.

Chapter VI

LAST TESTAMENTS ARE TO BE ALTERED WITH CAUTION

In alterations of last testaments, which ought not to be made except for a just and necessary cause,[44] the bishops, as delegates of the Apostolic See, shall, before the alterations are put into execution, ascertain summarily and extrajudicially that nothing has been stated in the petition which suppresses what is true or suggests what is false.

Chapter VII

THE CHAPTER "ROMANA" IN *SEXTO,* CONCERNING APPEALS, IS RENEWED

Apostolic legates and nuncios, patriarchs, primates and metropolitans, in appeals brought before them, shall in all causes, both in admitting the appeals and in granting inhibitions after an appeal, be bound to observe the form and tenor of the sacred constitutions and particularly that of Innocent IV, which begins, "Romana";[45] any custom, even though immemorial, usage or privilege to the contrary notwithstanding. Otherwise the inhibitions and proceedings and all consequences thereof shall be *ipso jure* null.

---

44. Cf. Sess. XXV, chap. 4 de ref.
45. C.3, VI°, De appell., II, 15

Chapter VIII

BISHOPS SHALL EXECUTE THE PIOUS DISPOSITIONS OF ALL PERSONS; SHALL VISIT PIOUS PLACES IF NOT UNDER THE IMMEDIATE PROTECTION OF KINGS

The bishops, also as delegates of the Apostolic See, shall in the cases conceded by law be the executors of all pious dispositions, whether made by last will or among the living; they shall have the right to visit hospitals and all colleges and confraternities of laymen,[46] even those that are called schools or are known by some other name (not, however, those that are under the immediate protection of kings, except with their permission); also eleemosynary institutions known as loan or charity foundations, and all pious places by whatever name designated, even though the care of the aforesaid institutions be in the hands of laymen and the said pious places protected by the privilege of exemption; by virtue of their office they shall, moreover, take cognizance of and execute in accordance with the ordinances of the sacred canons all things that have been instituted for the worship of God or for the salvation of souls or for the support of the poor;[47] any custom, even though immemorial, privilege or statute whatsoever to the contrary notwithstanding.

Chapter IX

ADMINISTRATORS OF ALL PIOUS PLACES SHALL RENDER AN ACCOUNT TO THE ORDINARY, UNLESS IT IS OTHERWISE PROVIDED IN THE FOUNDATION

Administrators, whether ecclesiastical or lay, of the revenues of any church, also of cathedrals, hospitals,[48] confraternities, eleemosynary institutions known as loan foundations, and of all pious places, shall be bound to render to the ordinary each year an account of their administration, all customs and privileges to the contrary being set aside, unless perchance it be expressly provided otherwise in the institution and regulation of such a church or fund. But if by reason of custom, privilege or some local regulation their

---

46. C.2, in Clem., De relig. dom., III, 11
47. Cf. cc.3, 6, 17, 19, X, De test. et ult. volunt., III, 26
48. Cf. Sess. VII, chap. 15 de ref., and Sess. XXV, chap. 8 de ref.

account has to be rendered to others deputed thereto, then the ordinary shall also be employed conjointly with them, and releases made otherwise shall be of no avail to the said administrators.

Chapter X

NOTARIES SHALL BE SUBJECT TO THE EXAMINATION AND JUDGMENT OF THE BISHOPS

Since the incompetency of notaries causes very much harm and is the occasion of many lawsuits, the bishop, also as delegate of the Apostolic See, may by examination inquire into the fitness of all notaries, even though appointed by Apostolic, imperial or royal authority; and if found incompetent or at any time delinquent in office, he may forbid them either altogether or for a time to exercise the office in ecclesiastical and spiritual affairs, lawsuits and causes. No appeal on their part shall suspend the prohibition of the ordinary.

Chapter XI

USURPERS OF THE PROPERTY OF ANY CHURCH OR PIOUS PLACES ARE PUNISHED

If any cleric or laic, of whatever rank, even imperial or royal, should be so possessed by avarice, the root of all evil,[49] as to presume to convert to his own use and to usurp *per se vel alios,* by force or fear, or even by means of supposititious persons, whether clerical or lay, or by any fraud or colored pretext whatsoever, the prerogatives, properties, rents and rights, even those held in fee or under lease, revenues, profits, or any incomes whatsoever, belonging to any church or benefices, secular or regular, eleemosynary institutions or any other pious places, which ought to be used for the needs of the ministers and the poor, or to hinder them from being received by those to whom they by right belong, he shall be anathematized till he shall have restored integrally to the church and to its administrator or beneficiary the prerogatives, properties, effects, rights, fruits and revenues which he has seized or in whatever way they have come to him, even by way of gift from a supposititious person, and furthermore,

---

49. Cf. *1 Tim.* 6:10

till he shall have obtained absolution from the Roman pontiff. If he be a patron of that church, he shall, in addition to the aforesaid penalties, be *eo ipso* deprived of the right of patronage. The cleric who instigates or consents to an execrable fraud and usurpation of this kind, shall be subject to the same penalties, and he shall be deprived of all benefices and be rendered unqualified to hold others; and even after complete satisfaction and absolution, he shall be suspended, at the discretion of his ordinary, from the exercise of his orders.

DECREE CONCERNING THE PETITION FOR THE CONCESSION OF THE CHALICE

Moreover, since the same holy council in the preceding session reserved to another and more convenient time the examination and definition of two articles which had been proposed on another occasion[50] and had then not yet been discussed, namely, whether the reasons which induced the holy Catholic Church to decide that lay people and also priests when not celebrating are to communicate under the one species of bread, are so to be retained that under no condition is the use of the chalice to be permitted to anyone; and whether in case, for reasons befitting and consonant with Christian charity, it appears that the use of the chalice is to be conceded to any nation or kingdom, it is to be conceded under certain conditions, and what are those conditions; it has now, in its desire to provide for the salvation of those on whose behalf the petition is made, decreed that the entire matter be referred to our most holy Lord [the Pope], as in the present decree it does refer it, who in accordance with his singular prudence will do what he shall judge beneficial for the Christian commonwealth and salutary for those who petition for the use of the chalice.

ANNOUNCEMENT OF THE NEXT SESSION

Moreover, the same holy Council of Trent announces the day of the next session to be the Thursday after the octave of All Saints, which will be the twelfth day of the month of November, and in it will deal with the sacrament of order and the sacrament of matrimony, etc.

The session was prorogued till the fifteenth day of July, 1563.

---

50. Cf. Sess. XIII in the decree of prorogation and Sess. XXI, following can. 4

TWENTY-THIRD SESSION

which is the seventh under the Supreme Pontiff, Pius IV,
celebrated on the fifteenth day of July, 1563

THE TRUE AND CATHOLIC DOCTRINE CONCERNING THE
SACRAMENT OF ORDER, DEFINED AND PUBLISHED BY THE
HOLY COUNCIL OF TRENT IN THE SEVENTH SESSION IN
CONDEMNATION OF CURRENT ERRORS

Chapter I

THE INSTITUTION OF THE PRIESTHOOD OF THE NEW LAW

Sacrifice and priesthood are by the ordinance of God so
united that both have existed in every law. Since therefore
in the New Testament the Catholic Church has received
from the institution of Christ the holy, visible sacrifice of
the Eucharist, it must also be confessed that there is in
that Church a new, visible and external priesthood, into
which the old has been translated.[1] That this was instituted
by the same Lord Our Saviour, and that to the Apostles and
their successors in the priesthood was given the power of
consecrating, offering and administering His body and blood,
as also of forgiving and retaining sins, is shown by the
Sacred Scriptures and has always been taught by the tradition of the Catholic Church.

Chapter II

THE SEVEN ORDERS

But since the ministry of so holy a priesthood is something divine, that it might be exercised in a more worthy
manner and with greater veneration, it was consistent that
in the most well-ordered arrangement of the Church there
should be several distinct orders of ministers, who by virtue of their office should minister to the priesthood, so distributed that those already having the clerical tonsure should

---

1. *Heb.* 7:12

162

ascend through the minor to the major orders.[2] For the Sacred Scriptures mention unmistakably not only the priests but also the deacons,[3] and teach in the most definite words what is especially to be observed in their ordination; and from the very beginning of the Church the names of the following orders and the duties proper to each one are known to have been in use, namely, those of the subdeacon, acolyte, exorcist, lector and porter, though these were not of equal rank; for the subdiaconate is classed among the major orders by the Fathers and holy councils,[4] in which we also read very often of other inferior orders.[5]

Chapter III

THE ORDER OF THE PRIESTHOOD IS TRULY A SACRAMENT

Since from the testimony of Scripture, Apostolic tradition and the unanimous agreement of the Fathers it is clear that grace is conferred by sacred ordination, which is performed by words and outward signs, no one ought to doubt that order is truly and properly one of the seven sacraments of holy Church. For the Apostle says: *I admonish thee that thou stir up the grace of God which is in thee by the imposition of my hands. For God has not given us the spirit of fear, but of power and of love and of sobriety.*[6]

Chapter IV

THE ECCLESIASTICAL HIERARCHY AND ORDINATION

But since in the sacrament of order, as also in baptism and confirmation, a character is imprinted which can neither be effaced nor taken away,[7] the holy council justly condemns the opinion of those who say that the priests of the New Testament have only a temporary power, and that those who have once been rightly ordained can again become laymen if they do not exercise the ministry of the word of God. And if any-

---

2. Cf. *infra,* can. 2 and chap. 17 de ref.
3. *Acts* 6:5; 21:8; *1 Tim.* 3:8, 12
4. Cc.11-13, D.XXXII; c.4, D.LX; c.9, X, De aet. et qual. et ord. praef., I, 14.
5. Cf. Synods of Elvira (*ca.*305), c.33; Antioch (341), c.10; cc.14, 16, D.XXXII; Denzinger, *Enchiridion,* nos. 45, 153-158.
6. See *2 Tim.* 1:6f.
7. Cf. Sess. VII, Sacraments, can. q and *infra,* can. 4.

one should assert that all Christians without distinction are priests of the New Testament, or that they are all *inter se* endowed with an equal spiritual power, he seems to do nothing else than derange the ecclesiastical hierarchy,[8] which is *an army set in array;*[9] as if, contrary to the teaching of St. Paul, all are apostles, all prophets, all evangelists, all pastors, all doctors.[10] Wherefore, the holy council declares that, besides the other ecclesiastical grades, the bishops, who have succeeded the Apostles, principally belong to this hierarchial order, and have been placed, as the same Apostle says, by the Holy Ghost to rule the Church of God;[11] that they are superior to priests, administer the sacrament of confirmation,[12] ordain ministers of the Church, and can perform many other functions over which those of an inferior order have no power. The council teaches furthermore, that in the ordination of bishops, priests and the other orders, the consent, call or authority, whether of the people or of any civil power or magistrate is not required in such wise that without this the ordination is invalid;[13] rather does it decree that all those who, called and instituted only by the people or by the civil power or magistrate, ascend to the exercise of these offices, and those who by their rashness assume them, are not ministers of the Church, but are to be regarded as thieves and robbers, who have not entered by the door.[14] These are the things which in general it has seemed good to the holy council to teach to the faithful of Christ regarding the sacrament of order. The contrary, however, it has resolved to condemn in definite and appropriate canons in the following manner, in order that all, making use with the help of Christ of the rule of faith, may in the midst of the darkness of so many errors recognize more easily the Catholic truth and adhere to it.

CANONS ON THE SACRAMENT OF ORDER

Canon 1. If anyone says that there is not in the New Testament a visible and external priesthood,[15] or that there is

---

8. Cf. *infra,* can. 6
9. *Cant.* 6:3, 9
10. See *1 Cor.* 12:28ff.; *Eph.* 4:11
11. *Acts* 20:28
12. Cf. Sess. VII, Confirmation, can. 3
13. Cf. Synod of Laodicea, can. 13
14. *John* 10:1
15. Cf. *supra,* chap. 1

no power of consecrating and offering the true body and blood of the Lord and of forgiving and retaining sins,[16] but only the office and bare ministry of preaching the Gospel; or that those who do not preach are not priests at all, let him be anathema.

Canon 2. If anyone says that besides the priesthood there are not in the Catholic Church other orders, both major and minor,[17] by which, as by certain steps, advance is made to the priesthood,[18] let him be anathema.

Canon 3. If anyone says that order or sacred ordination is not truly and properly a sacrament instituted by Christ the Lord,[19] or that it is some human contrivance devised by men unskilled in ecclesiastical matters, or that it is only a certain rite for choosing ministers of the word of God and of the sacraments, let him be anathema.

Canon 4. If anyone says that by sacred ordination the Holy Ghost is not imparted and that therefore the bishops say in vain: *Receive ye the Holy Ghost,* or that by it a character is not imprinted, or that he who has once been a priest can again become a layman, let him be anathema.

Canon 5. If anyone says that the holy unction which the Church uses in ordination is not only not required but is detestable and pernicious, as also are the other ceremonies of order, let him be anathema.

Canon 6. If anyone says that in the Catholic Church there is not instituted a hierarchy by divine ordinance, which consists of bishops, priests and ministers, let him be anathema.

Canon 7. If anyone says that bishops are not superior to priests, or that they have not the power to confirm and ordain, or that the power which they have is common to them and to priests, or that orders conferred by them without the consent or call of the people or of the secular power are invalid, or that those who have been neither rightly ordained nor sent by ecclesiastical and canonical authority, but come from elsewhere, are lawful ministers of the word and of the sacraments, let him be anathema.

Canon 8. If anyone says that the bishops who are chosen by the authority of the Roman pontiff are not true and

---

16. *Matt.* 16:19; *Luke* 22:19f.; cc.5, 6, C.XXIV, q.1
17. Cf. *supra,* chap. 2
18. Cc.2, 3, D.LXXVII; and *infra,* chap. 13 de ref.
19. Cf. *supra,* chap. 3

legitimate bishops, but merely human deception, let him be anathema.

DECREE CONCERNING REFORM

The same holy Council of Trent, continuing the matter of reform, resolves and ordains that the things following be at present decreed.

Chapter I

THE NEGLIGENCE OF PASTORS OF CHURCHES IN THE MATTER OF RESIDENCE IS IN VARIOUS WAYS RESTRAINED. THE *CURA ANIMARUM* IS PROVIDED FOR

Since by divine precept it is enjoined on all to whom is entrusted the *cura animarum* to know their sheep,[20] to offer sacrifice for them, and to feed them by the preaching of the divine word, the administration of the sacraments, and the example of all good works, to exercise a fatherly care in behalf of the poor and other distressed persons and to apply themselves to all other pastoral duties, all of which cannot be rendered and fulfilled by those who do not watch over and are not with their flock, but desert it after the manner of hirelings,[21] the holy council admonishes and exhorts them that, mindful of the divine precepts and *made a pattern of the flock,*[22] they in judgment and in truth be shepherds and leaders. And lest those things that concern residence which have already been piously and with profit decreed under Paul III,[23] of happy memory, be understood in a sense foreign to the mind of the holy council, as if in virtue of that decree it were lawful to be absent during five continuous months, the holy council, adhering to that decree, declares that all who, under whatever name or title, even though they be cardinals of the holy Roman Church, preside over patriarchal, primatial, metropolitan and cathedral churches, are bound to personal residence in their church or diocese, where they are obligated to discharge the office committed to them and from which they may not absent themselves except for the reasons and in the manner subjoined. Since Christian charity,

20. *John* 10: 1-16; 21:15-17; *Acts* 20:28
21. *John* 10:12f.
22. See *1 Peter* 5:3
23. Cf. Sess. VI, chaps. 1, 2 de ref.

urgent necessity, due obedience, and manifest advantage to the Church or the commonwealth require and demand that some at times be absent, the same holy council decrees that these reasons for lawful absence must be approved in writing by the most blessed Roman pontiff, or by the metropolitan, or, in his absence, by the oldest resident suffragan bishop, whose duty it shall also be to approve the absence of the metropolitan; except when the absence is necessitated by some function or office of the state attached to the episcopal dignity, in which cases the absence being a matter of public knowledge and at times unexpected, it will not be necessary to make known to the metropolitan the reasons therefor. To him, however, in conjunction with the provincial council, it shall pertain to decide concerning the permissions granted by himself or by his suffragans and to see that no one abuses that right and that transgressors are punished in accordance with canonical prescriptions. Moreover, those who are about to depart should remember so to provide for their sheep that as far as possible they may not suffer any injury through their absence.[24] But since those who are absent only for a brief period appear in the sense of the ancient canons not to be absent, because they are soon to return, the holy council wishes that that period of absence in a single year, whether continuous or interrupted, ought, except for the reasons mentioned above, in no case to exceed two or at most three months, and that consideration be taken that it be made from a just cause and without any detriment to the flock. Whether this be the case, the council leaves to the conscience of those who depart, which it hopes will be religious and delicate, for hearts are open to God,[25] whose work they are bound at their peril not to do deceitfully.[26] Meanwhile it admonishes and exhorts them in the Lord, that unless their episcopal duties call them elsewhere in their diocese, they are on no account to absent themselves from their cathedral church during the periods of the Advent of the Lord, Quadragesima, the Nativity, Easter, Pentecost and Corpus Christi, on which days especially the sheep ought to be refreshed and to rejoice in the Lord at the presence of the shepherd.[27]

---

24. Cf. c.34, VI°, De elect., I, 6; Sess. VI, chap. 2 de ref. at the end.
25. *Psalms* 7:10; *Acts* 1:24
26. *Jer.* 48:10
27. C.29, C.VII, q. 1

But if anyone, which it is hoped will never happen, shall have been absent in violation of the provision of this decree, the holy council ordains that in addition to the other penalties imposed upon and renewed against non-residents under Paul III,[28] and the guilt of mortal sin which he incurs, he can acquire no proprietorship of any fruits in proportion to the time of his absence, and cannot, even though no other declaration follows the present one, retain them with a safe conscience, but is bound, even in his default, through his ecclesiastical superior, to apply them to the treasury of the churches or to the poor of the locality; every agreement or arrangement to which appeal is made for ill-gotten fruits, whereby the aforesaid fruits might be restored to him in whole or in part, being forbidden; any privileges whatsoever granted to any college or treasury to the contrary notwithstanding.

Absolutely the same, as regards the guilt, the loss of fruits, and the penalties, does the holy council declare and decree with reference to inferior pastors and to all others who hold any ecclesiastical benefice having the *cura animarum;*[29] so however, that should it happen that they are absent for a reason that has first been made known to and approved by the bishop, they shall leave a due allowance of the stipend to a competent vicar to be approved by the ordinary. The permission to go away, which is to be granted in writing and gratuitously, they shall not obtain for a period longer than two months except for a grave reason. In case they shall be summoned, even though not personally, by an edict, and should be contumacious, the ordinaries shall be at liberty to constrain them by ecclesiastical censures, by the sequestration and withdrawal of fruits and other legal means, even deprivation; and no privilege whatsoever, no concession, domestic position, exemption, not even by reason of some benefice, no contract or statute, even though confirmed by oath or by any authority whatsoever, no custom, even though immemorial, which is to be regarded rather as a corruption, no appeal or inhibition, even in the Roman Curia or by virtue of the constitution of Eugene,[30] shall be able to suspend the execution hereof.

Finally, the holy council commands that both the decree

---

28. Cf. Sess. VI, chap. 1 de ref.
29. Sess. VI, chap. 2 de ref.
30. Cf. c.3, Extrav. comm., De privil., V, 7

under Paul III[31] and this present one be published in the provincial and episcopal councils; for it desires that things which so intimately concern the office of pastors and the salvation of souls, be frequently impressed on the ears and mind of all, so that with the help of God they may not hereafter fall into decay either through the corrosive action of time, the forgetfulness of men or by desuetude.

Chapter II

THOSE PLACED OVER CHURCHES SHALL RECEIVE CONSECRATION WITHIN THREE MONTHS; WHERE THE CONSECRATION IS TO TAKE PLACE

If those who, under whatever name or title, even though they be cardinals of the holy Roman Church, have been placed over cathedral or superior churches, shall not within three months have received consecration,[32] they shall be bound to restore the fruits received; if for three more months they shall have neglected to do this, they shall be *ipso jure* deprived of their churches. Their consecration, if performed outside the Roman Curia, shall take place in the church to which they have been promoted, or in the province if it can be conveniently done.

Chapter III

BISHOPS, EXCEPT IN CASE OF ILLNESS, SHALL CONFER ORDERS IN PERSON

Bishops shall confer orders themselves; but should they be prevented by illness, they shall not send their subjects to another bishop to be ordained unless they have first been examined and approved.[33]

Chapter IV

WHO MAY RECEIVE THE FIRST TONSURE

No one shall be admitted to the first tonsure who has not received the sacrament of confirmation; who has not been

---

31. Cf. Sess. VI, chap. 1 de ref.
32. C.2, D.LXXV; c.1, D.C.; Sess. VII, chap. 9 de ref.
33. Cf. *infra,* chaps. 8, 10; III Synod of Carthage (397), c.22

taught the rudiments of the faith; who does not know how to read and write,[34] and concerning whom there is not a probable conjecture that he has chosen this manner of life that he may render to God a faithful service and not to escape fraudulently from civil justice.

Chapter V

WHEREWITH THOSE TO BE ORDAINED ARE TO BE PROVIDED

Those who are to be promoted to minor orders shall have a good testimonial from their pastor and from the master of the school in which they are educated. Those, however, who are to be raised to any one of the major orders, shall a month before the ordination repair to the bishop, who shall commission the pastor or another person whom he may deem more suitable, to make known publicly in the church the names and desire of those who wish to be promoted, to inform himself diligently from trustworthy sources regarding the birth, age, morals and life of those to be ordained,[35] and to transmit to the bishop as soon as possible testimonial letters containing the results of the inquiry.[36]

Chapter VI

THE AGE OF FOURTEEN YEARS IS REQUIRED FOR AN ECCLESI-ASTICAL BENEFICE; WHO IS TO ENJOY THE *PRIVILEGIUM FORI*

No one who has received the first tonsure or is constituted in minor orders shall be able to hold a benefice before his fourteenth year.[37] Furthermore, he shall not enjoy the *privilegium fori* unless he has an ecclesiastical benefice, or, wearing the clerical garb and tonsure, serves in some church by order of the bishop, or is in an ecclesiastical seminary or with the permission of the bishop in some school or university on the way, as it were, to the reception of major orders.[38] As regards married clerics, the constitution of Boniface VIII, which begins, "Clerici, qui cum unicis,"[39] shall be observed, provided

---

34. Cf. c.4, VI°, De temp. ord., I, 9
35. Cf. c.5, D.XXIV
36. Cf. *infra*, chap. 7
37. C.3, X, De aet. et qual. et ord. praef., I, 14
38. C.7, X, de cler. conjug., III, 3
39. C. un h.t. in VI°, III, 2

these clerics, being assigned by the bishop to the service or ministry of some church, serve or minister in that church and wear the clerical garb and tonsure; privilege or custom, even immemorial, shall avail no one in this matter.

Chapter VII

THOSE TO BE ORDAINED ARE TO BE EXAMINED BY MEN SKILLED IN DIVINE AND HUMAN LAW

The holy council, following the footsteps of the ancient canons, decrees that when the bishop has arranged to hold an ordination, all who wish to dedicate themselves to the sacred ministry shall be summoned to the city for the Wednesday before the ordination, or any other day which the bishop may deem convenient.[40] And calling to his assistance priests and other prudent men skilled in the divine law and experienced in the laws of the Church, the bishop shall carefully investigate and examine the parentage, person, age, education, morals, learning and faith of those who are to be ordained.[41]

Chapter VIII

HOW AND BY WHOM EACH ONE OUGHT TO BE ORDAINED

The conferring of sacred orders shall be celebrated publicly, at the times specified by law,[42] and in the cathedral church in the presence of the canons of the church, who are to be summoned for that purpose; but if celebrated in another place of the diocese, in the presence of the local clergy, the church holding the highest rank should always, so far as possible, be chosen. Each one shall be ordained by his own bishop.[43] But if anyone should ask to be promoted by another, this shall under no condition, even under the pretext of any general or special rescript or privilege, even at the times specified, be permitted him unless his probity and morals be recommended by the testimony of his ordinary.[44] Otherwise the one ordaining shall be suspended for a year from

---

40. C.5, D.XXIV
41. Cf. *supra,* chap. 5 de ref.
42. Cf. c.7, D.LXXV; cc.1-3, X, De temp. ord., I, 11
43. Cc.1-4, D.LXXI; c.2, D.LXXII; cc.6, 7, 9, 10, C.IX, q.2; cc. 1, 2, VI°, De temp, ord., I, 9
44. Cf. Sess. XIV, chaps. 2, 3 de ref.

conferring orders, and the one ordained shall be suspended
from exercising the orders received for as long a period as
his ordinary shall see fit.

Chapter IX

A BISHOP ORDAINING ONE OF HIS OWN HOUSEHOLD SHALL AT
ONCE AND IN REALITY CONFER ON HIM A BENEFICE

A bishop may not ordain one of his household who is not
his subject, unless he has lived with him for a period of
three years and to the exclusion of fraud confers on him at
once a benefice;[45] any custom, even though immemorial, to
the contrary notwithstanding.

Chapter X

PRELATES INFERIOR TO BISHOPS SHALL NOT CONFER THE
TONSURE OR MINOR ORDERS EXCEPT ON RELIGIOUS SUBJECT
TO THEM; NEITHER THEY NOR ANY CHAPTER WHATSOEVER
SHALL GRANT DIMISSORY LETTERS; A SEVERER PENALTY IS
PRESCRIBED AGAINST THOSE WHO TRANSGRESS THE DECREE

It shall not be lawful in the future for abbots and any
other persons, however exempt, residing within the limits of
a diocese, even in case they are said to be of no diocese or
exempt, to confer the tonsure or minor orders on anyone who
is not a religious subject to them; nor shall abbots themselves and other exempt persons, or any colleges or chapters, even those of cathedral churches, grant dimissory letters
to any secular clerics that they may be ordained by others.
But the ordination of all these persons, when everything contained in the decrees of this holy council has been observed,[46]
shall pertain to the bishops within the limits of whose diocese they are; any privileges, prescriptions or customs, even
though immemorial, notwithstanding. It commands also that
the penalty imposed on those who, contrary to the decree of
this holy council under Paul III,[47] procure dimissory letters
from the chapter during the vacancy of the episcopal see, be
extended to those who shall obtain the said letters not from

---

45. C.2, X, De praeb., III, 5
46. Cf. *supra*, chaps. 5, 6 and *infra*, chaps. 11, 12 de ref.
47. Cf. Sess. VII, chap. 10 de ref.

the chapter but from any other persons who during the vacancy of the see succeed to the jurisdiction of the bishop in lieu of the chapter. Those who issue dimissory letters contrary to the form of this decree, shall be *ipso jure* suspended from their office and benefices for one year.

Chapter XI

THE INTERSTICES AND CERTAIN OTHER REGULATIONS TO BE OBSERVED IN THE RECEPTION OF MINOR ORDERS

The minor orders shall be conferred on those who understand at least the Latin language, observing the prescribed interstices,[48] unless the bishop should deem it more expedient to act otherwise, that they may be taught more accurately how great is the burden of this vocation and may in accordance with the direction of the bishop exercise themselves in each office,[49] and this in the church to which they will be assigned (unless they happen to be absent *causa studiorum);* and thus they shall ascend step by step, that with increasing age they may grow in worthiness of life and in learning, which especially the example of their good conduct, their assiduous service in the Church, their greater reverence toward priests and the superior orders, and a more frequent communion than heretofore of the body of Christ will prove. And since from here there is entrance to the higher orders and to the most sacred mysteries, no one shall be admitted to them whom the promise of knowledge does not show to be worthy of the major orders.[50] These, however, shall not be promoted to sacred orders till a year after the reception of the last of the minor orders, unless necessity or the need of the Church shall in the judgment of the bishop require otherwise.

Chapter XII

THE AGE REQUIRED FOR MAJOR ORDERS; ONLY THOSE WORTHY ARE TO BE ADMITTED

No one shall in the future be promoted to the subdiaconate before the twenty-second, to the diaconate before the

---

48. Cf. *infra,* chap. 13
49. *Ibid.,* chap. 17 and c.3, D.LIX
50. Cc.1, 2, 4, D.LIX

twenty-third, and to the priesthood before the twenty-fifth
year of his age.[51] However, the bishops should know that
not all who have attained that age are to be admitted to
these orders, but those only who are worthy and whose
upright life is as old age. Regulars likewise shall not be
ordained below that age or without a careful examination
by the bishop; all privileges whatsoever in this respect being
completely set aside.

Chapter XIII

WHO MAY BE ORDAINED SUBDEACON AND DEACON; THEIR OBLIGATIONS; ON NO ONE SHALL TWO SACRED ORDERS BE CONFERRED THE SAME DAY

Those shall be ordained subdeacons and deacons who have
a good testimonial,[52] have already been approved in minor
orders, and are instructed in letters and in those things that
pertain to the exercise of the orders. They should hope, with
the help of God, to be able to live continently,[53] should serve
the churches to which they will be assigned, understand
that it is very highly becoming, since they serve at the altar,
to receive holy communion at least on the Lord's days and
on solemn festival days. Those who have been promoted to
the sacred order of subdeacon shall not till they have completed at least one year therein be permitted to ascend to
a higher order,[54] unless the bishop shall judge otherwise.
Two sacred orders shall not be conferred on the same day,
even to regulars,[55] any privileges and indults whatsoever to
whomsoever granted to the contrary notwithstanding.

Chapter XIV

WHO ARE TO BE PROMOTED TO THE PRIESTHOOD; THE OFFICE OF THOSE SO PROMOTED

Those who have conducted themselves piously and faithfully in their performance of earlier functions and are
accepted for the order of priesthood, shall have a good tes-

---

51. C.3, De aet. et qual. et ord. praef. in Clem., I, 6
52. See *1 Tim.* 3:7; c.3, D.LXXVII
53. Cf. c.1, D.XXVIII
54. Cf. *supra,* chap. 11 de ref.
55. Cc.13, 15, X, De temp. ord., I, 11

timonial[56] and be persons who not only have served in the office of deacon for one entire year, unless by reason of the advantage and need of the Church the bishop should judge otherwise, but who also by a previous careful examination have been found competent to teach the people those things which are necessary for all to know unto salvation, and competent also to administer the sacraments, and so conspicuous for piety and purity of morals that a shining example of good works and a guidance for good living may be expected from them. The bishop shall see to it that they celebrate mass at least on the Lord's days and on solemn festivals, but if they have the *cura animarum,* as often as their duty requires. To those who have been promoted *per saltum,*[57] the bishop may for a legitimate reason grant a dispensation, provided they have not exercised the ministry.

Chapter XV

NO ONE SHALL HEAR CONFESSIONS UNLESS APPROVED BY THE ORDINARY

Although priests receive by ordination the power of absolving from sins, nevertheless the holy council decrees that no one, even though a regular, can hear the confessions of seculars, even priests, and that he is not to be regarded as qualified thereto, unless he either holds a parochial benefice or is by the bishops, after an examination, if they should deem it necessary, or in some other manner, judged competent and has obtained their approval,[58] which shall be given gratuitously; any privileges and custom whatsoever, even immemorial, notwithstanding.

Chapter XVI

VAGRANTS AND PERSONS USELESS TO THE CHURCHES SHALL BE EXCLUDED FROM ORDERS

Since no one ought to be ordained who in the judgment of his bishop is not useful or necessary to his churches, the holy council, following the footsteps of the sixth canon of

56. Cf. *1 Tim.* 3:7; c.3, D.LXXVII
57. C.un., D.LII
58. Cf. c.2, VI°, De poenit., V, 10; c.2, De sepult. in Clem., III, 7

the Council of Chalcedon,[59] decrees that no one shall in the future be ordained who is not assigned to that church or pious place for the need or utility of which he is promoted, where he may discharge his duties and not wander about without any fixed abode.[60] But if he shall desert that place without consulting the bishop, he shall be forbidden the exercise of the sacred orders. Furthermore, no cleric who is a stranger shall, without commendatory letters from his ordinary, be admitted by any bishop to celebrate the divine mysteries and to administer the sacraments.[61]

Chapter XVII

IN WHAT MANNER THE EXERCISE OF THE MINOR ORDERS IS TO BE RESTORED

That the functions of holy orders from the deacon to the porter, which have been laudably received in the Church from the times of the Apostles, and which have been for some time discontinued in many localities, may again be restored to use in accordance with the canons,[62] and may not be derided by the heretics as useless, the holy council, burning with the desire to restore the ancient usage, decrees that in the future such functions shall not be exercised except by those constituted in these orders, and it exhorts in the Lord each and all prelates of the churches and commands them that they make it their care to restore these functions, so far as it can be conveniently done, in cathedral, collegiate and parochial churches of their diocese, if the number of people and the revenues of the church are able to bear it. To those exercising these functions they shall assign salaries from a part of the revenues of some simple benefices or of the church treasury if the revenues are adequate, or from the revenues of both, and of these salaries they may, if they prove negligent, be deprived in whole or in part by the judgment of the bishop. In case there should not be at hand unmarried clerics to exercise the functions of the four minor orders, their place may be supplied by married clerics of approved life, provided they have not mar-

---

59. C.1, D.LXX; c. ult., *ibid.*
60. *Ibid., c.*2.
61. Cc.6, 7, 9, D.LXXI *et al.*
62. C.1, D.XXI; Denzinger, nos. 154-58

ried a second time,[63] are competent to discharge the duties, and wear the tonsure and the clerical garb in church.

Chapter XVIII

DIRECTIONS FOR ESTABLISHING SEMINARIES FOR CLERICS, ESPECIALLY THE YOUNGER ONES; IN THEIR ERECTION MANY THINGS ARE TO BE OBSERVED; THE EDUCATION OF THOSE TO BE PROMOTED TO CATHEDRAL AND MAJOR CHURCHES

Since the age of youth, unless rightly trained, is inclined to follow after the pleasure of the world,[64] and unless educated from its tender years in piety and religion before the habits of vice take possession of the whole man, will never perfectly and without the greatest and well-nigh extraordinary help of Almighty God persevere in ecclesiastical discipline, the holy council decrees that all cathedral and metropolitan churches and churches greater than these shall be bound, each according to its means and the extent of its diocese, to provide for, to educate in religion, and to train in ecclesiastical discipline, a certain number of boys of their city and diocese, or, if they are not found there, of their province, in a college located near the said churches or in some other suitable place to be chosen by the bishop.[65] Into this college shall be received such as are at least twelve years of age, are born of lawful wedlock, who know how to read and write competently, and whose character and inclination justify the hope that they will dedicate themselves forever to the ecclesiastical ministry. It wishes, however, that in the selection the sons of the poor be given preference, though it does not exclude those of the wealthy class, provided they be maintained at their own expense and manifest a zeal to serve God and the Church. These youths the bishop shall divide into as many classes as he may deem proper, according to their number, age, and progress in ecclesiastical discipline, and shall, when it appears to him opportune, assign some of them to the ministry of the churches, the others he shall keep in the college to be instructed, and he shall replace by others those who have been withdrawn, so that the college may be a perpetual seminary of minis-

---

63. Cf. tot. tit., X, De big. non ord., I, 21
64. *Gen.* 8:21; cf. c.5, D.XXVIII; c.1, C.XII, q.1
65. Cf. Sess. V, chap. 1 de ref.

ters of God. And that they may be the better trained in the aforesaid ecclesiastical discipline, they shall forthwith and always wear the tonsure and the clerical garb; they shall study grammar, singing, ecclesiastical computation, and other useful arts; shall be instructed in Sacred Scripture, ecclesiastical books, the homilies of the saints, the manner of administering the sacraments, especially those things that seem adapted to the hearing of confessions, and the rites and ceremonies. The bishop shall see to it that they are present every day at the sacrifice of the mass, confess their sins at least once a month, receive the body of Our Lord Jesus Christ in accordance with the directions of their confessor, and on festival days serve in the cathedral and other churches of the locality. All these and other things beneficial and needful for this purpose each bishop shall prescribe with the advice of two of the senior and more reputable canons chosen by himself as the Holy Ghost shall suggest, and they shall make it their duty by frequent visitation to see to it that they are always observed. The disobedient and incorrigible, and the disseminators of depraved morals they shall punish severely, even with expulsion if necessary; and removing all obstacles, they shall foster carefully whatever appears to contribute to the advancement and preservation of so pious and holy an institution. And since for the construction of the college, for paying salaries to instructors and servants, for the maintenance of the youths and for other expenses, certain revenues will be necessary, the bishops shall, apart from those funds which are in some churches and localities set aside for the instruction and maintenance of youths, and which are *eo ipso* to be considered as applied to this seminary under the care of the bishop, with the advice of two of the chapter, of whom one shall be chosen by the bishop, the other by the chapter, and also of two of the clergy of the city, the choice of one of whom shall in like manner be with the bishop, the other with the clergy, deduct a certain part or portion from the entire revenues of the bishop and of the chapter, and of all dignities with and without jurisdiction, offices, prebends, portions, abbeys and priories of whatever order, even though regular, whatever their character and rank; also of hospitals which, according to the constitution of the Council of Vienne, which begins, "Quia contingit,"[66]

---

66. C.2, De relig. dom. in Clem., III, 11

are conferred as title or with a view of administration; also of all benefices, even those of regulars, though they enjoy the right of patronage, even if exempt, or belong to no diocese, or are annexed to other churches, monasteries, hospitals, or to any other pious places even though exempt; also of the treasuries of the churches and of other places, and of all other ecclesiastical revenues or incomes, even those of other colleges (in which, however, the seminaries of students and instructors promoting the common good of the Church are not actually included, for the council wishes these to be exempt, except with reference to such revenues as exceed the expense of the suitable maintenance of these seminaries), or associations or confraternities, which in some localities are called schools; and of all monasteries, except those of the mendicants, also of all tithes belonging in any way to laics, from which ecclesiastical maintenance is customarily paid, and of those also which belong to knights, of whatever military body or order they may be, the brethren of St. John of Jerusalem alone excepted; and the part or portion so deducted, as also some simple benefices, of whatever nature or rank, and prestimonies, or prestimonial portions as they are called, even before they become vacant, without prejudice, however, to the divine service or to those who hold them, they shall apply to and incorporate in this college. This shall have effect whether the benefices be reserved or assigned; and the unions and assignments of these benefices can be neither suspended through resignation nor in any way hindered, but they shall have their effect, any vacancy, even in the Curia, notwithstanding, or any constitution whatsoever. For the payment of this portion the local bishop shall by ecclesiastical censures and other legal means, even with the aid of the secular arm, should he deem it necessary, compel the possessors of benefices, dignities with and without jurisdiction, and each and all of the above-mentioned, whether the revenues are for themselves or for the salaries which they perchance pay to others out of the said revenues, retaining, however, a portion equivalent to that which they have to pay on account of these salaries; any privileges, exemptions, even such as might require a special declaration of annulment, custom, even though immemorial, any appeal and allegation which might hinder the execution of any or all of the above, notwithstanding. But if it should happen that as a result of these unions or otherwise, the seminary should be found to be endowed in whole or in part, then the portion deducted from each benefice, as stated above, and incorporated by the bishop, shall be discontinued in whole or in part as circumstances may require. And if the prelates of cathedrals and other major churches should prove negligent in the erection of the seminary and its maintenance and should decline to pay their portion, it shall be the duty of the archbishop to rebuke the bishop sharply and compel him to comply with all the aforesaid matters, and of the provincial synod to rebuke sharply and compel in like manner the archbishop and superiors, and diligently to see to it that this holy and pious work be, wherever possible, expedited without delay. The bishop shall receive annually the accounts of the revenues of the seminary in the presence of two delegated by the chapter and of as many delegated by the clergy of the city. Furthermore, in order that the establishment of schools of this kind may be procured at less expense, the holy council decrees that bishops, archbishops, primates and other local ordinaries urge and compel, even by the reduction of their revenues, those who hold the position of instructor and others to whose position is attached the function of reading or teaching, to teach those to be educated in those schools personally, if they are competent, otherwise by competent substitutes, to be chosen by themselves and to be approved by the ordinaries.[67] But if these in the judgment of the bishop are not qualified, they shall choose another who is competent, no appeal being permitted; and should they neglect to do this, then the bishop himself shall appoint one. The aforesaid instructors shall teach what the bishop shall judge expedient. In the future, however, those offices or dignities, which are called professorships, shall not be conferred except on doctors or masters or licentiates of Sacred Scripture or canon law and on other competent persons who can personally discharge that office; any appointment made otherwise shall be null and void, all privileges and customs whatsoever, even though immemorial, notwithstanding.

But if in any province the churches labor under such poverty that in some a college cannot be established, then

---

67. Cf. Sess. V, chap. 1 de ref.

the provincial synod or the metropolitan with two of the oldest suffragans shall provide for the establishment of one or more colleges, as he may deem advisable, at the metropolitan or at some other more convenient church of the province, from the revenues of two or more churches in each of which a college cannot be conveniently established, where the youths of those churches might be educated. In churches having extensive dioceses, however, the bishop may have one or more in the diocese, as he may deem expedient; which, however, shall in all things be dependent on the one erected and established in the [metropolitan] city.

Finally, if either with regard to the unions or the appraisement or assignment or incorporation of portions, or for any other reason, any difficulty should happen to arise by reason of which the establishment or the maintenance of the seminary might be hindered or disturbed, the bishop with those designated above or the provincial synod, shall have the authority, according to the custom of the country and the character of the churches and benefices, to decide and regulate all matters which shall appear necessary and expedient for the happy advancement of the seminary, even to modify or augment, if need be, the contents hereof.

ANNOUNCEMENT OF THE NEXT SESSION

Moreover, the same holy Council of Trent announces the next session for the sixteenth day of the month of September, in which it will treat of the sacrament of matrimony and of other matters pertaining to the doctrine of faith, if there be any which can be disposed of; further, it will deal with the collation of bishoprics, dignities and other ecclesiastical benefices and with various articles of reform.

The session was prorogued to the eleventh day of November, 1563.

TWENTY-FOURTH SESSION

which is the eighth under the Supreme Pontiff, Pius IV,
celebrated on the eleventh day of November, 1563

DOCTRINE OF THE SACRAMENT OF MATRIMONY

The perpetual and indissoluble bond of matrimony was
expressed by the first parent of the human race, when, under
the influence of the divine Spirit, he said: *This now is bone
of my bones and flesh of my flesh. Wherefore a man shall
leave father and mother and shall cleave to his wife, and
they shall be two in one flesh.*[1] But that by this bond two
only are united and joined together, Christ the Lord taught
more plainly when referring to those last words as having
been spoken by God, He said: *Therefore now they are not
two, but one flesh,*[2] and immediately ratified the firmness
of the bond so long ago proclaimed by Adam with these
words: *What therefore God has joined together, let no man
put asunder.*[3]

But the grace which was to perfect that natural love, and
confirm that indissoluble union, and sanctify the persons
married, Christ Himself, the instituter and perfecter of the
venerable sacraments, merited for us by His passion, which
Paul the Apostle intimates when he says: *Husbands love
your wives, as Christ also loved the Church, and delivered
himself up for it;*[4] adding immediately: *This is a great sacrament, but I speak in Christ and in the Church.*[5]

Since therefore matrimony in the evangelical law sur-
passes in grace through Christ the ancient marriages, our
holy Fathers, the councils,[6] and the tradition of the universal Church, have with good reason always taught that
it is to be numbered among the sacraments of the New Law;
and since with regard to this teaching ungodly men of this
age, raving madly, have not only formed false ideas concerning this venerable sacrament, but, introducing in con-

---

1. *Gen.* 2:23f. (*Matt.* 19:4ff.; *Mark* 10:6ff.; *Eph.* 5:31f.)
2. *Matt.* 19:6; *Mark* 10:8
3. *Matt., Ibid.; Mark* 10:9
4. *Eph.* 5:25
5. *Ibid.,* 5:32
6. Eugene IV in *decr. ad Armenos* (Denzinger, no. 702).

formity with their habit under the pretext of the Gospel a carnal liberty, have by word and writing asserted, not without great harm to the faithful of Christ, many things that are foreign to the teaching of the Catholic Church and to the usage approved of since the times of the Apostles, this holy and general council, desiring to restrain their boldness, has thought it proper, lest their pernicious contagion should attract more, that the principal heresies and errors of the aforesaid schismatics be destroyed by directing against those heretics and their errors the following anathemas.

CANONS ON THE SACRAMENT OF MATRIMONY

Canon 1. If anyone says that matrimony is not truly and properly one of the seven sacraments of the evangelical law, instituted by Christ the Lord,[7] but has been devised by men in the Church and does not confer grace, let him be anathema.

Canon 2. If anyone says that it is lawful for Christians to have several wives at the same time and that this is not forbidden by any divine law,[8] let him be anathema.

Canon 3. If anyone says that only those degrees of consanguinity and affinity which are expressed in Leviticus can hinder matrimony from being contracted and dissolve it when contracted,[9] and that the Church cannot dispense in some of them or declare that others hinder and dissolve it, let him be anathema.

Canon 4. If anyone says that the Church cannot establish impediments dissolving marriage,[10] or that she has erred in establishing them, let him be anathema.

Canon 5. If anyone says that the bond of matrimony can be dissolved on account of heresy,[11] or irksome cohabitation, or by reason of the voluntary absence of one of the parties, let him be anathema.

Canon 6. If anyone says that matrimony contracted but not consummated is not dissolved by the solemn religious profession of one of the parties,[12] let him be anathema.

Canon 7. If anyone says that the Church errs in that she

---

7. Cf. *supra,* note 1
8. *Matt.* 19:4-6, 9
9. *Lev.* 18:6ff.
10. *Matt.* 16:19; Sess. XXI, chap. 2
11. Cf. c.4, X, De consang., IV, 14; cc.6, 7, X, De divor., IV, 19
12. Cf. c.16, X, De sponsal., IV, 1

taught and teaches that in accordance with evangelical and apostolic doctrine the bond of matrimony cannot be dissolved by reason of adultery on the part of one of the parties, and that both, or even the innocent party who gave no occasion for adultery, cannot contract another marriage during the lifetime of the other, and that he is guilty of adultery who, having put away the adulteress, shall marry another, and she also who, having put away the adulterer, shall marry another,[13] let him be anathema.

Canon 8. If anyone says that the Church errs when she declares that for many reasons a separation may take place between husband and wife with regard to bed and with regard to cohabitation for a determinate or indeterminate period, let him be anathema.

Canon 9. If anyone says that clerics constituted in sacred orders or regulars who have made solemn profession of chastity can contract marriage, and that the one contracted is valid notwithstanding the ecclesiastical law or the vow, and that the contrary is nothing else than a condemnation of marriage, and that all who feel that they have not the gift of chastity, even though they have made such a vow, can contract marriage, let him be anathema, since God does not refuse that gift to those who ask for it rightly, neither does *he suffer us to be tempted above that which we are able.*[14]

Canon 10. If anyone says that the married state excels the state of virginity or celibacy, and that it is better and happier to be united in matrimony than to remain in virginity or celibacy,[15] let him be anathema.

Canon 11. If anyone says that the prohibition of the solemnization of marriages at certain times of the year is a tyrannical superstition derived from the superstition of the heathen,[16] or condemns the blessings and other ceremonies which the Church makes use of therein, let him be anathema.

Canon 12. If anyone says that matrimonial causes do not belong to ecclesiastical judges, let him be anathema.

---

13. *Matt.* 5:32; 19:9; *Mark* 10:11f.; *Luke* 16:18; *1 Cor.* 7:10f.; cc.5-8, 10, C.XXXII, q.7
14. Cf. *1 Cor.* 10:13
15. *Matt.* 19:11f.; *1 Cor.* 7:25f., 38, 40; c.12, C.XXXII, q.1; c.9, C.XXXIII, q.5; c.16, X, De sponsal., IV, 1
16. Cf. *infra,* chap. 10 de ref. matr.

DECREE CONCERNING THE REFORM OF MATRIMONY

Chapter I

THE FORM PRESCRIBED IN THE LATERAN COUNCIL FOR
SOLEMNLY CONTRACTING MARRIAGE IS RENEWED; BISHOPS
MAY DISPENSE WITH THE PUBLICATION OF THE BANNS; WHO-
EVER CONTRACTS MARRIAGE OTHERWISE THAN IN THE PRES-
ENCE OF THE PASTOR AND OF TWO OR THREE WITNESSES,
DOES SO INVALIDLY

Although it is not to be doubted that clandestine marriages
made with the free consent of the contracting parties are
valid and true marriages so long as the Church has not declared
them invalid,[17] and consequently that those persons are justly
to be condemned, as the holy council does condemn them with
anathema, who deny that they are true and valid, and those
also who falsely assert that marriages contracted by children
[minors] without the consent of the parents are invalid, nevertheless the holy Church of God has for very just reasons
at all times detested and forbidden them.[18] But while the
holy council recognizes that by reason of man's disobedience
those prohibitions are no longer of any avail, and considers
the grave sins which arise from clandestine marriages, especially the sins of those who continue in the state of damnation, when having left the first wife with whom they contracted
secretly, they publicly marry another and live with her in
continual adultery, and since the Church which does not judge
what is hidden, cannot correct this evil unless a more effi-
cacious remedy is applied, therefore, following in the footsteps of the holy Lateran Council celebrated under Innocent
III,[19] it commands that in the future, before a marriage is
contracted, the proper pastor of the contracting parties shall
publicly announce three times in the church, during the celebration of the mass on three successive festival days, between
whom marriage is to be contracted; after which publications,
if no legitimate impediment is revealed, the marriage may
be proceeded with in the presence of the people, where the
parish priest, after having questioned the man and the woman

17. C.2, X, De cland. desp., IV, 3
18. C.3, C.XXX, q.5; c.13, C.XXXII, q.2; c.2, C.XXXV, q.6; c.3, X, Qui matr. accus. poss.,
    IV, 18
19. C.3, X, De cland. desp., IV, 3

and heard their mutual consent, shall either say: "I join you together in matrimony, in the name of the Father, and of the Son, and of the Holy Ghost," or he may use other words, according to the accepted rite of each province. But if at some time there should be a probable suspicion that a marriage might be maliciously hindered if so many publications precede it, then either one publication only may be made or the marriage may be celebrated forthwith in the presence of the parish priest and of two or three witnesses. Then before its consummation the publications shall be made in the church, so that if any impediments exist they may be the more easily discovered, unless the ordinary shall deem it advisable to dispense with the publications, which the holy council leaves to his prudence and judgment. Those who shall attempt to contract marriage otherwise than in the presence of the parish priest or of another priest authorized by the parish priest or by the ordinary and in the presence of two or three witnesses, the holy council renders absolutely incapable of thus contracting marriage and declares such contracts invalid and null, as by the present decree it invalidates and annuls them. Moreover, it commands that the parish priest or another priest who shall have been present at a contract of this kind with less than the prescribed number of witnesses, also the witnesses who shall have been present without the parish priest or another priest, and also the contracting parties themselves, shall at the discretion of the ordinary be severely punished. Furthermore, the same holy council exhorts the betrothed parties not to live together in the same house until they have received the sacerdotal blessing in the church;[20] and it decrees that the blessing is to be given by their own parish priest, and permission to impart it cannot be granted to any other priest except by the parish priest himself or by the ordinary, any custom, even though immemorial, which ought rather to be called a corruption, or any privilege notwithstanding. But if any parish priest or any other priest, whether regular or secular, should attempt to unite in marriage or bless the betrothed of another parish without the permission of their parish priest, he shall, even though he may plead that his action was based on a privilege or immemorial custom, remain *ipso jure* suspended until absolved by the ordinary of that

---

20. Cc.2, 3, 5, C.XXX, q.5; c.19, C.XXXV, qq.2, 3

parish priest who ought to have been present at the marriage or from whom the blessing ought to have been received. The parish priest shall have a book in which he shall record the names of the persons united in marriage and of the witnesses, and also the day on which and the place where the marriage was contracted, and this book he shall carefully preserve. Finally, the holy council exhorts the betrothed that before they contract marriage, or at least three days before its consummation, they carefully confess their sins and approach devoutly the most holy sacrament of the Eucharist. If any provinces have in this matter other laudable customs and ceremonies in addition to the aforesaid, the holy council wishes earnestly that they be by all means retained. And that these so salutary regulations may not remain unknown to anyone, it commands all ordinaries that they as soon as possible see to it that this decree be published and explained to the people in all the parish churches of their dioceses, and that this be done very often during the first year and after that as often as they shall deem it advisable. It decrees, moreover, that this decree shall begin to take effect in every parish at the expiration of thirty days, to be reckoned from the day of its first publication in that church.

Chapter II

BETWEEN WHOM SPIRITUAL RELATIONSHIP IS CONTRACTED

Experience teaches that by reason of the large number of prohibitions, marriages are often unknowingly contracted in prohibited cases in which either the parties continue to live, not without great sin, or the marriages are dissolved, not without great scandal. Wherefore, the holy council wishing to provide against this condition, and beginning with the impediment arising from spiritual relationship, decrees that in accordance with the prescriptions of the holy canons,[21] one person only, whether man or woman, or at most one man and one woman, shall act as sponsors in baptism for the one baptized, and spiritual relationship shall be contracted between these only and the one baptized, and his father and mother, and also between the one baptizing and the one baptized and the father and mother of the one baptized. Before

---

21. C.101, D.IV de cons.; c.3, VI°, De cogn. spirit., IV, 3

the parish priest proceeds to confer baptism, he shall carefully inquire of those whom it concerns what person or persons they have chosen to act as sponsors at the font for the
one to be baptized, and he shall permit him or them only to
act as such, shall record their names in the book, and shall
teach them what relationship they have contracted, so that
they may not have any excuse on the score of ignorance. If
any others, besides those designated, should touch the one
being baptized, they shall not in any way contract a spiritual relationship, any constitutions asserting the contrary
notwithstanding.[22] If through the fault or negligence of the
parish priest it should be done otherwise, he shall be punished at the discretion of the ordinary. That relationship also
which is contracted in confirmation is not to be extended
beyond him who confirms, the one confirmed, his father and
mother, and the sponsor;[23] all impediments of this spiritual
relationship between other persons being completely removed.

Chapter III

THE IMPEDIMENT OF PUBLIC HONESTY IS RESTRICTED WITHIN CERTAIN LIMITS

The holy council completely removes the impediment of
justice arising from public honesty where the betrothals are
for any reason not valid.[24] But where they are valid, the
impediment shall not extend beyond the first degree, because
in more remote degrees such a prohibition can no longer be
observed without detriment.

Chapter IV

AFFINITY ARISING FROM FORNICATION IS RESTRICTED TO THE SECOND DEGREE

Moreover, the holy council, moved by the same and other
very grave reasons, restricts the impediment which arises
on account of the affinity contracted from fornication, and
which dissolves the marriage afterward contracted,[25] to those
only who are united in the first and second degree; in more

22. Cc.2, 5, C.XXX, q.3; c.3, X, De cogn. spirit., IV, 11; c.1 h.t. in VI°, IV, 3
23. C.2, C.XXX, q.1; c.1, VI°, De cogn. spirit., IV, 3
24. C. un., VI°, De sponsal., IV, 1
25. Cc.19-24, C.XXXII, q.7; tot. tit. X, De eo, qui cog. consang., IV, 13

remote degrees it ordains that affinity of this kind does not dissolve the marriage afterward contracted.

Chapter V

NO ONE IS TO MARRY WITHIN THE PROHIBITED DEGREES; IN WHAT MANNER DISPENSATION IS TO BE GRANTED THEREIN

If anyone should presume knowingly to contract marriage within the prohibited degrees, he shall be separated and shall have no hope of obtaining a dispensation;[26] and this shall apply much more to him who has dared not only to contract such a marriage but also to consummate it. If he has done this in ignorance and yet has neglected the solemnities required in the contraction of matrimony, he shall be subject to the same penalties; for he who has rashly despised the salutary precepts of the Church, is not worthy to enjoy without difficulty her beneficence. But if after the observance of the solemnities some impediment should afterward be discovered of which he probably had no knowledge, then he may more easily and gratuitously be granted a dispensation. In the contraction of marriages either no dispensation at all shall be granted or rarely, and then for a reason and gratuitously. In the second degree a dispensation shall never be granted except in the case of great princes and for a public cause.

Chapter VI

PUNISHMENTS AGAINST ABDUCTORS ARE PRESCRIBED

The holy council decrees that between the abductor and the one abducted there can be no marriage so long as she remains in the power of the abductor. But if the one abducted is separated from the abductor and is in a free and safe place, and consents to have him for her husband, the abductor may have her for his wife;[27] nevertheless, the abductor and all who have given him advice, aid and approval shall be *ipso jure* excommunicated and forever infamous and disqualified for all dignities of any kind; and if they be clerics, they shall forfeit all rank.[28] The abductor shall, moreover,

---

26. C.3, X, De cland. desp., IV, 3; c. un. in Clem., De consang., IV, un.
27. Cc.7, 11, C. XXXVI, q. 2; c.7, X, De rapt., V, 17
28. Cc.2-6, 10, 11 C.XXXVI, q.2

be bound, whether he marries the one abducted or not, to bestow on her at the discretion of the judge a suitable endowment.[29]

Chapter VII

VAGRANTS ARE TO BE UNITED IN MATRIMONY WITH CAUTION

There are many who are vagrants and have no permanent abode, and, being of unprincipled character, after having abandoned their first wife, marry another, very often several in different localities, during the lifetime of the first. The holy council wishing to put an end to this evil, extends this fatherly admonition to all whom it may concern; namely, not to admit to marriage easily this class of vagrants; it also exhorts the civil magistrates to restrain them vigorously. But it commands parish priests not to be present at the marriage of such persons unless they have first made a diligent inquiry, and after having reported the matter to the ordinary, shall have obtained permission from him to do so.

Chapter VIII

CONCUBINAGE IS SEVERELY PUNISHED

It is a grave sin for unmarried men to have concubines, but it is a most grave sin, and one committed in singular contempt of this great sacrament, when married men live in this state of damnation and have the boldness at times to maintain and keep them in their homes even with their own wives. Wherefore, the holy council, in order to provide suitable remedies against this great evil, decrees that if these concubinaries, whether unmarried or married, whatever may be their state, dignity or profession, have not, after a threefold admonition in reference to this matter by the ordinary, also *ex officio,* put away their concubines and separated themselves from intimacy with them, they shall be punished with excommunication from which they shall not be absolved till they have in fact obeyed the admonition given them.[30] But if, regardless of censures, they shall continue in concubinage for a year, the ordinary shall proceed

---

29. *Exodus* 22:16f., *cit.* in c.1, X, De adult., V, 16
30. C.2, X, De cohab. cler., III, 2; Sess. XXV, chap. 14 de ref.

against them with a severity in keeping with the character of the crime. Women, whether married or unmarried, who live publicly with adulterers or concubinaries, if after a three-fold admonition they do not obey, shall be punished severely in accordance with their guilt by the local ordinaries, even though not called upon by anyone to do so, *ex officio;* and if the ordinaries should deem it expedient, they shall be expelled, even with the aid of the secular arm, if need be, from the city or the diocese; the other penalties imposed on adulterers and concubinaries shall remain in force.

Chapter IX

TEMPORAL LORDS OR MAGISTRATES SHALL NOT ATTEMPT ANYTHING CONTRARY TO THE FREEDOM OF MARRIAGE

Worldly inclinations and desires very often so blind the mental vision of temporal lords and magistrates, that by threats and ill usage they compel men and women who live under their jurisdiction, especially the rich or those who expect a large inheritance, to contract marriage against their will with those whom these lords or magistrates propose to them. Wherefore, since it is something singularly execrable to violate the freedom of matrimony, and equally execrable that injustice should come from those from whom justice is expected,[31] the holy council commands all, of whatever rank, dignity and profession they may be, under penalty of anathema to be incurred *ipso facto,* that they do not in any manner whatever, directly or indirectly, compel their subjects or any others whomsoever in any way that will hinder them from contracting marriage freely.[32]

Chapter X

THE SOLEMNITIES OF MARRIAGES ARE FORBIDDEN AT CERTAIN TIMES

The holy council commands that from the Advent of Our Lord Jesus Christ till the day of the Epiphany, and from Ash Wednesday till the octave of Easter inclusive, the old prohibitions of solemn nuptials be carefully observed by all;[33]

---

31. Cf. cc.14, 17, 29, X, De sponsal., IV, 1
32. Cf. c.6, C.XXXVI, q.2
33. Cc.8-11, C.XXXIII, q.4; c.4, X, De feriis, II, 9

at other times it permits marriages to be celebrated solemnly
and the bishops shall see to it that they are conducted with
becoming modesty and propriety, for matrimony is a holy
thing and is to be treated in a holy manner.

DECREE CONCERNING REFORM

The same holy council, continuing the matter of reform,
decrees that the following be ordained in the present session.

Chapter I

NORMS OF PROCEDURE IN THE ELECTION OF BISHOPS
AND CARDINALS

If in all ecclesiastical grades a prudent and enlightened
attention is necessary in order that in the house of the Lord
there be nothing disorderly and nothing unbecoming, much
more ought we to strive that no error be committed in the
election of him who is constituted above all grades. For the
state and order of the entire household of the Lord will tot-
ter if what is required in the body be not found in the head.
Hence, although the holy council has elsewhere decided to
advantage a number of things concerning those to be promoted to cathedral and major churches,[34] yet it considers
this office to be of such a nature that if viewed in its greatness, there can never be caution enough taken concerning
it. Wherefore it decrees that as soon as a church becomes
vacant, public and private supplications and prayers be made
and be ordered throughout the city and diocese by the chapter, that clergy and people may implore God for a good shepherd. It moreover exhorts and admonishes each and all who
in any manner have a right from the Apostolic See to participate in the promotion of those to be placed in authority,
or who otherwise render assistance (due to the circumstances
of the present time no change being made herein), that they
above all bear in mind that they can do nothing more ser-
viceable to the glory of God and the salvation of the people
than to exert themselves to the end that good and competent shepherds be promoted to the government of the Church,
and that they become partakers in the sins of others and
sin mortally unless they strive diligently that those be pro-

---

34. Cf. Sess. VI, chap. 1 de ref.; VII, chaps, 1, 3 de ref.; XXII, chap. 2 de ref.

moted whom they judge the more worthy and useful to the Church, not moved by entreaties or human affection, or the solicitations of rivals, but because their merits speak for them, whom they know to be persons of lawful wedlock, and whose life, age, learning and all other qualifications meet the requirements of the sacred canons and the decrees of this Council of Trent.[35] But since the taking of the important and competent testimony of upright and learned men regarding the aforesaid qualifications cannot by reason of the diversity of nations, peoples and customs be everywhere uniformly followed, the holy council commands that in the provincial synod to be held by the metropolitan, there be prescribed for each place and province a special or proper form of the examination, investigation or instruction to be made, such as shall appear most useful and suitable for these places and which is to be submitted to the approval of the most holy Roman pontiff; so however, that after the completion of the examination or investigation of the person to be promoted, it shall, after having been put in the form of a public document, be transmitted as soon as possible, with all the attestations and with the profession of faith made by the one to be promoted, to the most holy Roman pontiff, in order that the Roman pontiff himself, with a complete knowledge of the whole matter and of the persons before him, may for the benefit of the Lord's flock provide the churches more profitably if in the examination or investigation they have been found competent. All examinations, investigations, attestations and proofs of whatever kind and by whomever made, even though in the Roman Curia, concerning the qualifications of the one to be promoted and the condition of the church, shall be carefully examined by the cardinal, who shall report thereon to the consistory, and three other cardinals; and this report shall be authenticated by the signature of the cardinal making the report and of the three other cardinals, in which each of the four cardinals shall affirm that, after having given it his careful attention, he has found those to be promoted to possess the qualifications required by law and by this holy council and at the peril of his eternal salvation firmly believes that they are competent to be placed over churches;

---

35. Cf. preceding references.

and the report having been made in one consistory, that the investigation may in the meantime receive more mature consideration, the decision shall be deferred to another consistory, unless the most blessed pontiff shall deem it expedient to act otherwise. Each and all of the particulars relative to the life, age, learning and the other qualifications of those who are to be appointed bishops, which have been determined elsewhere by this council, the same it decrees are to be required in the election of the cardinals of the holy Roman Church, even though they be deacons, whom the most holy Roman pontiff shall, in so far as it can be conveniently done, choose from all the nations of Christendom according as he finds them competent. Finally, the same holy council, moved by so many very grave afflictions of the Church, cannot but call to mind that nothing is more necessary to the Church of God than that the holy Roman pontiff apply that solicitude which by the duty of his office he owes the universal Church in a very special way by associating with himself as cardinals the most select persons only, and appoint to each church most eminently upright and competent shepherds; and this the more so, because Our Lord Jesus Christ will require at his hands the blood of the sheep of Christ that perish through the evil government of shepherds who are negligent and forgetful of their office.

Chapter II

PROVINCIAL SYNODS ARE TO BE CELEBRATED EVERY THREE YEARS, DIOCESAN SYNODS EVERY YEAR; WHO ARE TO CONVOKE THEM AND WHO ARE TO BE PRESENT THEREAT

Provincial synods, wherever they have been omitted, shall be restored for the regulation of morals, the correction of abuses, the settlement of controversies, and for other purposes permitted by the sacred canons.[36] Wherefore the metropolitans in person, or if they are legitimately hindered, the oldest suffragan bishop, shall not neglect to convoke, each in his own province, a synod within a year at least from the termination of the present council and after that at least every third year, after the octave of the resurrection of Our Lord Jesus Christ or at some other more con-

36. Cf. cc.2-7, 9-14, D.XVIII *et al.;* c.25, X, De accus., V, 1

venient time, according to the custom of the province, and which all the bishops and others who by right or custom are under obligation to be present shall be absolutely bound to attend, those being excepted who at imminent danger would have to cross the sea. The bishops of the province shall not in the future be compelled under pretext of any custom whatsoever to go against their will to the metropolitan church. Those bishops likewise who are not subject to any archbishop shall once for all choose some neighboring metropolitan, at whose provincial synod they shall be obliged to be present with the other bishops, and whatever has been decided therein they shall observe and cause to be observed. In all other respects their exemption and privileges shall remain intact and entire. Diocesan synods also are to be celebrated annually; at which also all those exempt, who would otherwise by reason of the cessation of that exemption have to attend, and who are not subject to general chapters, shall be bound to assemble; those also who have charge of parochial or other secular churches, even though annexed, whoever they may be, must be present at the synod. But if the metropolitans and also the bishops and the others mentioned above prove negligent in these matters, they shall incur the penalties prescribed by the sacred canons.

Chapter III

IN WHAT MANNER PRELATES ARE TO MAKE THEIR VISITATION

Patriarchs, primates, metropolitans and bishops shall not neglect to visit their respective dioceses, either personally or, if they are lawfully hindered, through their vicar-general or visitor;[37] if by reason of its extent they are unable to make a visitation of the whole annually, they shall either themselves or through their visitors visit at least the greater part of it, so that the whole may be completed in two years. Metropolitans, even after a complete visitation of their own diocese, shall not visit the cathedral churches or the dioceses of the bishops of their province, except for a cause taken cognizance of and approved by the provincial synod. Archdeacons, deans and other inferiors shall visit those churches in which they have thus far been accustomed legally

---

37. C.11, C.X, q.1.

to make visitations, but from now on with the consent of
the bishop, personally and with the aid of a notary. Also
the visitors delegated by a chapter, where the chapter has
the right of visitation, shall be first approved by the bishop;
thereby, however, the bishop, or if he be hindered, his visitor, shall not be prohibited from visiting those same
churches apart from these, and the archdeacons and other
inferiors shall be bound to render to him an account within
a month of the visitation made by them, and to show him
the depositions of witnesses and the entire proceedings; any
custom, even though immemorial, and any exemptions and
privileges whatsoever notwithstanding. But the chief purpose of all these visitations shall be, after the extirpation
of heresies, to restore sound and orthodox doctrine, to guard
good morals and to correct such as are evil, to animate the
people by exhortations and admonitions with religion, peace
and innocence, and to regulate the rest for the benefit of
the faithful as the prudence of the visitors may suggest,
allowance being made for place, time and occasion.[38] That
these things may be more easily and happily accomplished,
each and all of the aforesaid to whom the right of visitation belongs, are admonished to treat all with a fatherly
love and Christian zeal, and therefore content with a modest train of horses and servants, let them strive to complete the visitation as speedily as possible, yet with due
attention. Meanwhile they shall exercise care that they do
not become troublesome or a burden to anyone by useless
expenses, and neither shall they nor any one of theirs, either
by way of compensation for the visitation or from wills
made for pious purposes, except what is by right due to
them from pious bequests, or under any other name, receive
anything, be it money or gift of whatever kind or in whatever way off offered,[39] any custom, even though immemorial, notwithstanding; with the exception, however, of food,
which shall be furnished them and theirs frugally and in
moderation during the time necessary for the visitation only
and not beyond that.[40] It shall, however, be left to the option
of those who are visited to pay, if they prefer, what in accordance with a fixed assessment they have been accustomed

---

38. C.1 (§ 4), VI°, De cens., III, 20
39. Cc.1, 7, 8, C.X, q.3; c.6, X, De cens., III, 39
40. C.6, VI°, De off. ord., I, 16

to pay in money heretofore, or to furnish the food; inviolate also shall remain the right of old agreements entered into with monasteries or other pious places or with churches not parochial. But in those places or provinces where it is the custom that neither food nor money or anything else be received by the visitors, but that all be done gratuitously, that practice shall continue there. But if anyone, which God forbid, shall presume to receive more in any of the cases mentioned above, in addition to the restitution of double the amount to be made within a month, he shall also incur without hope of pardon the other penalties contained in the constitution of the General Council of Lyons, which begins, "Exigit,"[41] as well as those of the provincial synod at the discretion of that synod. Patrons shall not presume in any way to intrude themselves in those things that pertain to the administration of the sacraments; they shall not interfere with the visitation of the ornaments of the church, or its immovable properties, or the revenues of the buildings, except in so far as they are competent to do this by reason of the institution and foundation; but the bishops themselves shall attend to these things and shall see to it that the revenues of the buildings are devoted to purposes necessary and useful to the church according as they shall deem most expedient.

Chapter IV

BY WHOM AND WHEN THE OFFICE OF PREACHING IS TO BE DISCHARGED. THE PARISH CHURCH IS TO BE ATTENDED TO HEAR THE WORD OF GOD. NO ONE MAY PREACH WITHOUT THE PERMISSION OF THE BISHOP

Desiring that the office of preaching, which belongs chiefly to bishops, be exercised as often as possible for the welfare of the faithful, the holy council, for the purpose of accommodating to the use of the present time the canons published elsewhere on this subject under Paul III,[42] of happy memory, decrees that they themselves shall personally, each in his own church, announce the Sacred Scriptures and the divine law, or, if lawfully hindered, have it done by those whom they shall appoint to the office of preaching; but in

41. C.2, VI°, De cens., III, 20
42. Cf. Sess. V, chap. 2 de ref.

other churches by the parish priests, or, if they are hindered, by others to be appointed by the bishop in the city or in any part of the diocese as they shall judge it expedient, at the expense of those who are bound or accustomed to defray it, and this they shall do at least on all Sundays and solemn festival days, but during the season of fasts, of Lent and of the Advent of the Lord, daily, or at least on three days of the week if they shall deem it necessary; otherwise, as often as they shall judge that it can be done conveniently. The bishop shall diligently admonish the people that each one is bound to be present at his own parish church, where it can be conveniently done, to hear the word of God.[43] But no one whether secular or regular, shall presume to preach, even in churches of his own order, in opposition to the will of the bishop. The bishops shall also see to it that at least on Sundays and other festival days, the children in every parish be carefully taught the rudiments of the faith and obedience toward God and their parents by those whose duty it is, and who shall be compelled thereto, if need be, even by ecclesiastical censures; any privileges and customs notwithstanding. In other respects the things decreed under Paul III concerning the office of preaching shall remain in force.[44]

Chapter V

MAJOR CRIMINAL CAUSES AGAINST BISHOPS SHALL BE TAKEN
COGNIZANCE OF BY THE SUPREME PONTIFF ONLY,
MINOR ONES BY THE PROVINCIAL SYNOD

Graver criminal causes against bishops, also that of heresy, which may God prevent, which merit deposition or deprivation, shall be taken cognizance of and decided by the Roman pontiff only.[45] But if the cause be of such a nature that it must perforce be assigned out of the Roman Curia, it shall not be committed to anyone but metropolitans or bishops to be chosen by the most holy pope. This commission shall be both special and signed by the most holy pontiff's own hand, and he shall never grant more to them than this, that they

---

43. Cc.62, 63, D.I de cons.
44. Cf. Sess. V, chap. 2 de ref.
45. Cf. Sess. XIII, chap. 8 de ref.

take information only of the fact and draw up the process, which they shall transmit immediately to the Roman pontiff, the definitive sentence being reserved to His Holiness. The other things decreed elsewhere under Julius III,[46] of happy memory, concerning these matters, as also the constitution of the general council under Innocent III, which begins, "Qualiter et quando,"[47] and which the holy council renews in the present decree, shall be observed by all. But the minor criminal causes of bishops shall be taken cognizance of and decided in the provincial synod only, or by persons commissioned by the provincial synod.

Chapter VI

AUTHORITY IS GIVEN TO THE BISHOPS TO DISPENSE IN CASES OF IRREGULARITY AND SUSPENSION AND TO ABSOLVE FROM CRIMES

Bishops are authorized to dispense in all cases of irregularity and suspension resulting from a secret crime, except that arising from wilful homicide and those arising from crimes that have found their way before a tribunal, and to absolve gratuitously, after the imposition of a salutary penance, *per se* or through a vicar especially appointed for this purpose *in foro conscientiae* in all occult cases, even those reserved to the Apostolic See, all delinquents subject to them in their diocese. The same is permitted them only, but not their vicars, in the same forum with respect to the crime of heresy.

Chapter VII

THE EFFICACY OF THE SACRAMENTS SHALL BE EXPLAINED BY BISHOPS AND PARISH PRIESTS BEFORE THEY ARE ADMINISTERED TO THE PEOPLE. DURING THE CELEBRATION OF THE MASS THE SACRED SCRIPTURES ARE TO BE EXPLAINED

That the faithful may approach the sacraments with greater reverence and devotion of mind, the holy council commands all bishops that not only when they are themselves about to administer them to the people, they shall

---

46. Cf. Sess. XIII, chaps. 6, 7 de ref.
47. C.24, X, De accus., V, 1

first, in a manner adapted to the mental ability of those who receive them, explain their efficacy and use, but also they shall see to it that the same is done piously and prudently by every parish priest, and in the vernacular tongue, if need be and if it can be done conveniently, in accordance with the form which will be prescribed for each of the sacraments by the holy council in a catechism, which the bishops shall have faithfully translated into the language of the people and explained to the people by all parish priests. In like manner shall they explain on all festivals or solemnities during the solemnization of the mass or the celebration of the divine offices, in the vernacular tongue, the divine commands and the maxims of salvation,[48] and leaving aside useless questions, let them strive to engraft these things on the hearts of all and instruct them in the law of the Lord.

Chapter VIII

PUBLIC SINNERS SHALL DO PUBLIC PENANCE, UNLESS THE
BISHOP SHALL DETERMINE OTHERWISE. A PENITENTIARY IS
TO BE INSTITUTED IN CATHEDRALS

The Apostle admonishes that those who sin publicly are to be reproved publicly.[49] When therefore anyone has publicly and in the sight of many committed a crime by which there is no doubt that others have been offended and scandalized, it is proper that a penance commensurate with his guilt be publicly imposed on him, so that those whom he by his example has led to evil morals, he may bring back to an upright life by the evidence of his correction. The bishop, however, should he judge it advisable, may commute this kind of public penance to one that is secret. In all cathedral churches where it can be conveniently done, let the bishop appoint a penitentiary united with the prebend that shall next become vacant, who shall be a master or doctor or licentiate in theology or canon law and forty years of age, or another who may be found to be more suitable for the character of the place and who, while he is hearing confessions in the church, shall be considered as present in the choir.

---

48. Cf. Sess. XXII, chap. 8
49. See *1 Tim.* 5:20; c.19 (§ 1), C.II, q.1; c.1, X, De poenit., V, 38

Chapter IX

BY WHOM THOSE SECULAR CHURCHES ARE TO BE VISITED THAT BELONG TO NO DIOCESE

What has elsewhere been ordained by this council under Paul III,[50] of happy memory, and lately under our most blessed Lord Pius IV,[51] regarding the attention to be given by ordinaries to the visitation of benefices, even of those exempt, the same is to be observed also with regard to those secular churches which are said to be in no one's diocese, namely, that they be visited by the bishop whose cathedral church is the nearest, if that is agreed upon, otherwise by him, acting as delegate of the Apostolic See, who has once been chosen for this in the provincial synod by the prelate of that place; any privileges and customs whatsoever, even though immemorial, notwithstanding.

Chapter X

THE EXECUTION OF THE VISITATION SHALL NOT BE IMPEDED BY THE SUBJECTS

That the bishops may be better able to keep the people whom they rule in duty and obedience, they shall in all those things that concern visitation and the correction of the morals of their subjects, have the right and authority, also as delegates of the Apostolic See, to decree, regulate, punish and execute, in accordance with the prescriptions of the canons, those things which in their prudence shall appear to them necessary for the emendation of their subjects and for the good of their dioceses. And in these matters, where it is question of visitation and correction of morals, no exemption, inhibition, appeal or complaint, even though submitted to the Apostolic See, shall in any manner whatsoever hinder or suspend the execution of those things which shall have been commanded, decreed or adjudicated by them.[52]

---

50. Cf. Sess. VI, chap. 4 de ref. and VII, chap. 8 de ref.
51. Cf. Sess. XXI, chap. 8 de ref.
52. Cf. Sess. XIII, chap. 1 de ref., XIV, chap. 4 de ref., XXII, chap. 1 de ref.

Chapter XI

HONORARY TITLES OR SPECIAL PRIVILEGES SHALL NOT
DETRACT IN ANY WAY FROM THE RIGHT OF BISHOPS. THE CHAP-
TER "CUM CAPELLA," CONCERNING PRIVILEGES, IS RENEWED

Since privileges and exemptions which are granted to many
persons under various titles, are known to create confusion
nowadays in the jurisdiction of bishops and to give to those
exempt occasion for a more unrestrained life, the holy council decrees that whenever it should be thought proper for
just, weighty and apparently necessary reasons that some
persons be decorated with the honorary titles of Prothono-
tary, Acolyte, Count Palatine, Royal Chaplain, or other such
titles of distinction, whether in or out of the Roman Curia,
as also others granted to any monasteries or in any manner
imparted, whether assumed under the name of servants to
military orders, monasteries, hospitals, colleges, or under any
other title, it is to be understood that by these privileges
nothing is taken away from the ordinaries whereby those persons to whom such privileges have already been granted or
to whom they may be granted in the future cease to be fully
subject in all things to the ordinaries as delegates of the
Apostolic See; and as regards Royal Chaplains, let them be
subject in accordance with the constitution of Innocent III,
which begins, "Cum capella;"[53] those persons, however, being
excepted who are engaged in actual service in the aforesaid
places or in military orders and who reside within their enclosures or houses and live under obedience to them, and those
also who have lawfully and according to the rule of these
military orders made profession, whereof the ordinary must
be certified; notwithstanding any privileges whatsoever, even
those of the order of St. John of Jerusalem and of other military orders. But those privileges which by virtue of the constitution of Eugene[54] they are accustomed to enjoy who reside
in the Roman Curia or who are in the household of cardinals, are by no means to be understood as applying to those
who hold ecclesiastical benefices in regard to those benefices,
but they shall continue to be subject to the jurisdiction of
the ordinaries; any inhibitions whatsoever notwithstanding.

---

53. C.16, X, De privil., V, 33
54. C.3, h.t., Extrav. comm., V, 7; Sess. XXIII, chap. 1 de ref.

Chapter XII

QUALIFICATIONS NECESSARY FOR THOSE WHO ARE TO BE PROMOTED TO THE DIGNITIES AND CANONRIES OF CATHEDRAL CHURCHES AND THE DUTIES OF THOSE SO PROMOTED

Since dignities, especially in cathedral churches, were instituted to maintain and promote ecclesiastical discipline, to the end that those who hold them might be distinguished for piety, be an example to others, and assist the bishops by their labor and service, it is but right that those who are called to them should be such as are able to perform their duty. Wherefore, in the future no one shall be promoted to any dignities whatsoever to which is annexed the *cura animarum,* who has not attained at least the twenty-fifth year of his age, is experienced in the clerical order, and is recommended by the learning necessary for the discharge of his office and the integrity of his morals, conformably to the constitution of Alexander III promulgated in the Council of the Lateran, which begins, "Cum in cunctis." [55] In like manner archdeacons, who are called the eyes of the bishop, [56] shall in all churches where it is possible be masters in theology, or doctors or licentiates in canon law. To other dignities or offices to which no *cura animarum* is annexed, clerics, in other respects qualified, shall not be promoted unless they are twenty-two years of age. Those also who are promoted to any benefices whatever having the *cura animarum,* shall within at least two months from the day of having taken possession be bound to make in the hands of the bishop, or, if he be hindered, in the presence of his vicar-general or official, a public profession of their orthodox faith and to promise solemnly and swear that they will persevere in their obedience to the Roman Church. But those who are promoted to canonries and dignities in cathedral churches, shall be bound to do this not only in the presence of the bishop or his official but also in the chapter; otherwise all those promoted as aforesaid shall not make the fruits their own, neither shall possession be of any avail to them. Furthermore, no one shall in the future be admitted to a dignity, canonry or portion unless he is either already constituted in the

---

55. C.7, X, De elect., I, 6; Sess. VII, chap. 1 de ref., XXII, chap. 2 de ref.
56. C.7, X, De off. archid., I, 23

sacred order which that dignity, prebend or portion requires, or is of such an age as will qualify him for the reception of that order within the time prescribed by law and by this holy council.[57] In all cathedral churches all canonries and portions shall be attached to the order of the priesthood, deaconship or subdeaconship, and the bishop shall with the advice of the chapter designate and distribute, as he shall deem expedient, to which each of the sacred orders is for the future to be attached; so however that at least one half shall be priests and the rest deacons or subdeacons. But where the more laudable custom obtains that the greater part or all shall be priests, this shall by all means be observed. The holy council also exhorts that in provinces where it can be conveniently done, all dignities and at least one half of the canonries in cathedral and prominent collegiate churches be conferred only on masters or doctors, or also on licentiates in theology or canon law. Moreover, those who hold dignities, canonries, prebends or portions in such cathedral or collegiate churches, shall not be permitted by virtue of any statute or custom to be absent from those churches more than three months of each year,[58] saving however the statutes of those churches which require a longer period of service; otherwise every offender shall for the first year be deprived of one half of the fruits which he has made his own even by reason of his prebend and residence. But if he be again guilty of the same negligence, he shall be deprived of all the fruits which he has acquired during that year, and if he should become more contumacious, he shall be proceeded against in accordance with the prescriptions of the sacred canons.[59] Those shall receive distributions who have been present at the appointed hours; the others shall, all collusion and remission being debarred, forfeit them in accordance with the decree of Boniface VIII, which begins, "Consuetudinem,"[60] and which the holy council restores to practice; any statutes or customs whatsoever notwithstanding. All shall be obliged to perform the divine offices in person and not by substitutes;[61] also to assist and serve the

---

57. Cf. Sess. VII, chap. 12 de ref.
58. Cf. Sess. XXIII, chap. 1 de ref.
59. Cf. tot. tit. X, De cler. non resid., III, 4
60. C. un. VI°, De cler. non resid., III, 3; cf. c.32, X, De praeb., III, 5
61. C.3, X, De cler. non resid., III, 4; c.30, De praeb., III, 5; Sess. XXII, chap. 4 de ref.

bishop when celebrating or exercising other pontifical functions, and in the choir instituted for psalmody, to praise the
name of God reverently, distinctly and devoutly in hymns
and canticles. They shall, moreover, wear at all times, both
in and out of church, a becoming dress, shall abstain from
unlawful hunting, fowling, dancing, taverns and games, and
so excel in integrity of morals that they may with justice be
called counsellors of the Church.[62] With regard to matters
that pertain to the proper manner of conducting the divine
offices, the proper way of singing or modulating therein, the
definite rule for assembling and remaining in choir, the things
necessary for those who minister in the church, and such
like, the provincial synod shall prescribe for each province
a fixed form that will be beneficial to and in accordance with
the usage of each province. In the meantime, the bishop,
with the aid of no less than two canons, one chosen by himself, the other by the chapter, may provide in these matters
as he may deem expedient.

Chapter XIII

HOW THE POORER CATHEDRAL AND PARISH CHURCHES ARE TO BE PROVIDED FOR. PARISHES ARE TO BE SEPARATED BY DEFINITE BOUNDARIES

Since the revenues of many cathedral churches are so
limited and scanty that they are in no way in keeping with
the episcopal dignity and insufficient for the needs of the
churches, the provincial synod, having summoned those who
are concerned, shall examine and consider carefully what
churches it may be advisable by reason of their limited
means and poverty to unite to others in the neighborhood
or to provide with additional revenues;[63] and the completed
documents concerning this matter it shall send to the
supreme Roman pontiff, who being informed thereby shall,
as he in his prudence may deem advisable, either unite the
poorly provided churches or by additional revenues improve
them. In the meantime, until the aforesaid provisions are
carried into effect, the supreme pontiff may from certain

---

62. Cf. tot. tit. X, De vit. et hon. cler., III, 1; in VI°, III, 1; in Clem., III, 1; in Extrav.
    comm., III, 1; tit. X, De cler. venat., V, 24
63. Cf. Sess. VII, chaps. 6, 7 de ref., XIV, chap. 9 de ref., XXIV, chap. 15 de ref.

benefices assist those bishops who by reason of the poverty of their diocese are in need of revenues; provided, however, these benefices are not *curae* or dignities or canonries and prebends, or monasteries in which there is regular observance, or which are subject to general chapters or to certain visitors. In parochial churches also in which the revenues are in like manner so small that they are insufficient to meet the necessary obligations, the bishop, if unable to meet the exigency by a union of benefices, not however those of regulars, shall see to it that by the assignment of first fruits or tithes or by the contributions and collections of the parishioners, or in some other way that he shall deem more profitable, as much be collected as may decently suffice for the needs of the rector and the parish. In all unions, however, whether to be made for the aforesaid or other reasons, parochial churches shall not be united to any monasteries whatsoever, or to abbeys or dignities, or prebends of a cathedral or collegiate church, or to other simple benefices, hospitals or military orders, and those so united shall be investigated again by the ordinary in accordance with the decree elsewhere enacted by this council under Paul III,[64] of happy memory, which is to be observed also and in like manner with regard to unions made since that time; notwithstanding whatever forms of words used therein, which shall be considered as sufficiently expressed here. Furthermore, all those cathedral churches whose revenues do not exceed in actual annual value the sum of one thousand ducats, and those parochial churches in which they do not exceed the sum of one hundred ducats, shall not in the future be burdened with taxes or reservations of revenues for this purpose. Also, in those cities and localities where the parochial churches have no definite boundaries, and whose rectors have not their own people whom they may rule but administer the sacraments indiscriminately to all who desire them, the holy council commands the bishops that, for the greater security of the salvation of the souls committed to them, they divide the people into definite and distinct parishes and assign to each its own and permanent parish priest, who can know his people and from whom alone they may licitly receive the sacraments;[65] or that they make other,

---

64. Cf. Ses. VII, chap. 6 de ref.
65. Cf. Sess. XIV, chap. 9 de ref.

more beneficial provisions as the conditions of the locality may require. They shall also see to it that the same is done as soon as possible in those cities and localities where there are no parish churches; any privileges and customs whatsoever, even though immemorial, notwithstanding.

Chapter XIV

NO ONE SHALL BE ADMITTED TO THE POSSESSION OF A
BENEFICE OR OF DISTRIBUTIONS WHEN THE DISTRIBUTION OF
THE FRUITS IS NOT APPLIED TO PIOUS PURPOSES

In many churches, cathedral as well as collegiate and parochial, it is understood to be the practice, derived either from their constitutions or from evil customs, that in the election, presentation, nomination, institution, confirmation, collation or other provision, or upon admission to the possession of a cathedral church or a benefice, of canonries or prebends, or to a portion of the revenues, or to the daily distributions, there are introduced certain conditions or deductions from the fruits, certain payments, promises, or unlawful compensations, or what in some churches is called mutual profits. Since the holy council abhors these practices, it commands the bishops that they prohibit all things of this kind that are not applied to pious purposes and such methods of entering upon offices, which create a suspicion of simoniacal taint or sordid avarice, and that they examine carefully their statutes and customs in regard to the above matter, and retaining only what they approve as laudable, reject and abolish the rest as corrupt and scandalous. It also ordains that those who in any way act in contravention of what is contained in the present decree incur the penalties prescribed against simoniacs by the sacred canons and various constitutions of the supreme pontiffs,[66] all of which it renews; notwithstanding any statutes, constitutions and customs, even though immemorial and confirmed by Apostolic authority, in regard to which any deceit, fraud and defect of intention may be investigated by the bishop as delegate of the Apostolic See.

---

66. Cf. C.I, q.1; tot. tit. X, De sim., III, 5 et Extrav. comm., V, 1

Chapter XV

METHOD OF INCREASING THE SCANTY PREBENDS OF
CATHEDRAL AND PROMINENT COLLEGIATE CHURCHES

In cathedral and prominent collegiate churches where the
prebends are numerous and in relation to the daily distributions so small that they do not suffice for the decent maintenance of the rank of the canons in keeping with the
character of the place and persons,[67] the bishops may with
the consent of the chapter combine them with some simple
benefices, not however with those of regulars, or, if in this
way it cannot be done, they may, with the consent of the
patrons if the right of patronage belongs to laymen, reduce
their number by suppressing some of them and apply the
fruits and proceeds to the daily distributions of the remaining prebends; so however, that such a number remain as
may conveniently serve for the celebration of divine service
and be in keeping with the dignity of the church;[68] any
statutes and privileges, or any reservation whether general
or special, or any expectation notwithstanding. The aforesaid unions or suppressions shall not be frustrated or hindered by any provisions whatsoever, not even by virtue of
resignation or any other derogations or suspensions.

Chapter XVI

WHAT DUTY DEVOLVES UPON THE CHAPTER
DURING THE VACANCY OF A SEE

When a see becomes vacant, the chapter shall, in those
places where the duty of receiving the revenues devolves
upon it, appoint one or more trustworthy and diligent stew-
ards who shall take care of the ecclesiastical properties and
revenues, of which they shall have to give an account to
him whom it will concern. It shall also be strictly bound to
appoint within eight days after the death of the bishop an
official or vicar, or to confirm the incumbent, who shall be
at least a doctor or licentiate in canon law, or otherwise as
competent a person as is available. In case this is not done,
the aforesaid appointment shall devolve upon the metro-

---

67. Cf. chap. 13 de ref. of this sess.
68. C.2, X, De instit., III, 7

politan.[69] But if the church is a metropolitan one or one exempt and the chapter should prove negligent as was said above, then the oldest suffragan bishop in the metropolitan church and the bishop nearest the exempt church shall have the authority to appoint a competent steward and vicar. The bishop who is promoted to the vacant church shall with regard to the matters that pertain to him demand from the steward, vicar and all other officials and administrators who were during the vacancy of the see appointed in his place by the chapter or others, even though they are members of the same chapter, an account of their office, jurisdiction, administration or any other functions, and he shall have the authority to punish those who have been delinquent in their office or administration, even if the aforesaid officials, having turned in their accounts, should have obtained from the chapter or those delegated by it a quittance or discharge. The chapter shall also be bound to render to the bishop an account of documents belonging to the church, if any have come into its possession.

Chapter XVII

THE CONFERRING OF SEVERAL BENEFICES ON AND THEIR RETENTION BY ONE PERSON IS RESTRICTED

Since ecclesiastical order is upset when one cleric holds the offices of several, the sacred canons have piously provided that no one ought to be enrolled in two churches.[70] But since many, led by the passion of ungodly covetousness, deceiving themselves, not God, are not ashamed to evade by various species of deceit what has been beneficially established and to hold several benefices at the same time, the holy council, desiring to restore discipline in the government of the churches, by the present decree, which it commands to be observed by all persons by whatever title distinguished, even though it be the dignity of the cardinalate, ordains that in the future one ecclesiastical benefice only shall be conferred on a person. If that is not sufficient to provide him on whom it is conferred with a decent livelihood, then it is permissible to confer on him another sim-

---

69. Cf. c. ult. in VI°, De suppl. negl. prael., I, 8
70. Cf. Sess. VII, chap. 2 de ref.

ple benefice that will afford a sufficiency, provided both do not require personal residence. These provisions shall apply not only to cathedral churches but also to all other benefices, whether secular or regular, even those held *in commendam,* of whatever title or character they may be. Those who now hold several parochial churches, or one cathedral and one parochial church, shall be strictly bound, all dispensations and unions for life notwithstanding, retaining one parochial church only, or the cathedral church only, to resign the other parochial churches within a period of six months;[71] otherwise the parochial churches and also all the benefices which they hold shall be considered *ipso jure* vacant and as such shall be freely conferred on other competent persons;[72] neither can those who previously held them retain conscientiously the fruits after the time specified. The holy council desires, however, that provision be made in some convenient way, as the supreme pontiff may see fit, for the necessities of those who resign.

Chapter XVIII

ON THE VACANCY OF A PAROCHIAL CHURCH THE BISHOP SHALL
APPOINT THERETO A VICAR UNTIL HE HAS PROVIDED A
PARISH PRIEST. IN WHAT MANNER AND BY WHOM
THOSE APPOINTED TO PAROCHIAL CHURCHES
ARE TO BE EXAMINED

It is highly desirable for the salvation of souls that they be directed by worthy and competent parish priests. That this may be accomplished more diligently and effectively, the holy council decrees that when a parochial church becomes vacant, whether by death or resignation, also in the Curia, or in whatever other manner, it shall be the duty of the bishop immediately upon receipt of information regarding the vacancy of the church to appoint, if need be, a competent vicar to the same, with a suitable assignment, using his own judgment in the matter, of a portion of the fruits thereof, who shall discharge the duties in that church till it has been provided with a rector, even if it be said that the charge of the church belongs to the bishop himself and

---

71. Cf. Sess. VII, chap. 4 de ref.
72. Cf. c.4, Extrav. comm., De praeb., III, 2

is administered by one or more, also in churches called patrimonial or receptive, in which it has been the custom of the bishop to assign the *cura animarum* to one or more, all of whom, it commands, are bound to the examination prescribed below,[73] also if the parochial church be generally or specially reserved or assigned, even by virtue of an indult or privilege in favor of cardinals of the holy Roman Church, or of abbots or chapters. Moreover, the bishop and he who has the right of patronage shall within ten days, or such other term as the bishop shall prescribe, designate in the presence of those to be delegated as examiners some competent clerics who are to rule the church. Furthermore, it shall be permitted to others also who may know any who are fit for the office to make known their names, so that a careful investigation may afterward be made as to the age, morals and sufficiency of each. But if in accordance with the custom of the country it should appear more suitable to the bishop or the provincial synod, those who wish to be examined may be summoned by a public notice. At the expiration of the time specified, all whose names have been entered shall be examined by the bishop,[74] or, if hindered, by his vicar-general, and by other examiners who shall not be fewer than three, to whose votes, in case they are equal or distributed singly, the bishop or his vicar may add his in favor of whomsoever he shall deem most fit. At least six examiners shall be proposed annually by the bishop or his vicar in the diocesan synod, and they must prove satisfactory to it and be approved by it. Upon a vacancy occurring in any church, the bishop shall select three out of that number who shall conduct the examination with him, and on a subsequent vacancy he shall select out of the six aforesaid the same or three others whom he may prefer. These examiners shall be masters or doctors or licentiates in theology or canon law, or other clerics, whether regulars, also of the mendicant orders, or seculars, who appear most competent for the purpose; and all shall take an oath on the holy Gospels of God, that, every human consideration being set aside, they will discharge their duty faithfully. Let them take heed, however, that they do not by reason of this exam-

---

73. Cf. Sess. VII, chap, 13 de ref.
74. Cf. Sess. XXV, chap. 9 de ref.

ination receive anything whatever either before or after, otherwise both they themselves and the givers will be guilty
of the vice of simony, from which they cannot be absolved
till they have resigned the benefices which they in any manner whatever possessed before this act, and they shall, moreover, be rendered disqualified to possess others in the
future.[75] In all these matters they shall be bound to render
an account not only before God but also, if need be, to the
provincial synod, by which, if it has been discovered that
they have done anything in contravention of their duty, they
can at its discretion be severely punished. On the completion of the examination they shall make known how many
they have judged fit in the matter of age, morals, learning,
prudence, and other qualifications suitable for ruling the
vacant church, and from these the bishop shall choose him
whom he shall judge the more competent, and to him and
to none other shall the collation of the church be made by
him to whom such collation pertains.[76] If the church is under
ecclesiastical patronage and the appointment thereto belongs
to the bishop and to no one else, he whom the patron shall
judge the more worthy among those approved by the examiners, shall be bound to present himself to the bishop that
he may be appointed by him.[77] But when the appointment
is to be made by any other than the bishop, then the bishop
only shall choose the worthier among those who are worthy, and the patron shall present him to the one to whom
the appointment belongs. If, however, the church is under
lay patronage, the one presented by the patron must be
examined, as above, by those delegated thereto, and is not
to be admitted unless found competent. In all the above-
mentioned cases, to no other than to one of those examined
and approved by the examiners as aforesaid and in accordance with the above rules shall the church be committed,
and no devolution or appeal, even to the Apostolic See or
the legates, vice-legates or nuncios of that See, or to any
bishops or metropolitans, primates or patriarchs, shall hinder or suspend the execution of the report of the aforesaid
examiners, otherwise the vicar whom the bishop has at his
discretion already appointed for the time being to the vacant

---

75. Cf. c.5, D.XXIV
76. Cf. Sess. XXV, chap. 9 de ref.
77. Cf. Sess. VII, chap. 13 de ref.; Sess. XIV, chap. 13 de ref.

church or whom he may afterward appoint, shall not be removed from the charge and administration of that church until it has been provided for, either by the appointment of the vicar himself or of some other person who has been approved and chosen as stated above. All provisions or appointments made otherwise than in accordance with the above stated form shall be regarded as surreptitious; any exemptions, indults, privileges, anticipations, appropriations, new provisions, indults granted to any universities,[78] also for a certain sum, and any other impediments whatsoever in contravention of this decree, notwithstanding. If, however, the revenues of said parochial churches should be so scanty as not to bear the burden of all this examination, or if no one should care to undergo the examination, or if by reason of open factions or dissensions, which are met with in some localities, more grievous quarrels and disturbances might easily be stirred up, the ordinary may omit this formality and have recourse to a private examination, if in conformity with his conscience and with the advice of the examiners he shall deem this expedient. The other things, however, are to be observed as above prescribed. If the provincial synod should judge that in the above regulations concerning the form of examination something ought to be added or omitted, it shall have the authority to do so.

Chapter XIX

MANDATES CONCERNING PROMOTION, EXPECTANCIES, AND OTHER THINGS OF THIS KIND ARE ABOLISHED

The holy council decrees that mandates concerning promotion and favors which are called expectancies, shall no longer be granted to anyone, even to colleges, universities, senators, or to any individuals whatsoever, even under the name of an indult, or for a certain sum, or under any other pretext; neither shall it be permitted to anyone to make use of those thus far granted.[79] Neither shall mental reservations nor other favors whatsoever with regard to future vacancies, or indults respecting churches belonging to oth-

---

78. Cf. Sess. XXV, chap. 9 de ref.
79. Cf. Sess. XXV, chap. 9 de ref., and tot. tit. X, De conc. praeb. non vac., III, 8; in VI°, III, 7; in Clem., III, 3

ers, or monasteries, be granted to anyone, not even to cardinals of the holy Roman Church, and those hitherto granted shall be considered abolished.

Chapter XX

THE MANNER OF CONDUCTING CAUSES PERTAINING TO THE ECCLESIASTICAL FORUM IS PRESCRIBED

All causes belonging in any way whatever to the ecclesiastical forum, even if they relate to benefices, shall be taken cognizance of in the first instance before the local ordinaries only, and shall be completely terminated within at least two years from the day that the suit was instituted; otherwise, at the expiration of that term the parties, or either of them, shall be free to have recourse to superior, but otherwise competent, judges, who shall take up the cause as it then stands and shall see to it that it is terminated as soon as possible. Before that term they shall neither be committed to others nor withdrawn; any appeals introduced by the parties shall not be received by any superior judges, neither shall any assignment or restriction be issued by them except upon a definitive sentence or one having the force of such a sentence, and the grievance arising therefrom cannot be repaired by an appeal from the definitive sentence. From the above are to be excepted those causes which according to the prescriptions of the canons are to be dealt with before the Apostolic See,[80] or which the supreme Roman pontiff shall for an urgent and reasonable cause judge advisable to assign or withdraw by a special rescript provided with the signature of His Holiness signed with his own hand. Furthermore, matrimonial and criminal causes shall not be left to the judgment of a dean, archdeacon or other inferiors, even in the course of their visitation, but shall be reserved to the examination and jurisdiction of the bishop only (even though there should at the time be a dispute, in whatever instance it may be, between the bishop and the dean or archdeacon or other inferiors regarding the examination of those causes), and if in the same matrimonial cause one of the parties should in the presence of the bishop really prove his poverty, he

---

80. Cf. c.7, C.VI, q.4; Sess. XXV, chap. 10 de ref.

shall not be compelled to litigate his case either in the second or third instance outside the province, unless the other party is prepared to provide for his maintenance and bear the expenses of the trial. In like manner, legates, also those *de latere,* nuncios, ecclesiastical governors or others, shall not only not presume by virtue of any authority whatsoever to hinder bishops in the aforesaid causes, or in any manner take away the exercise of or disturb their jurisdiction, but they shall not even proceed against clerics or other ecclesiastical persons until the bishop has first been approached and has proved himself negligent in the matter; otherwise their proceedings and decisions avail nothing and they shall be bound to make satisfaction to the parties for the damage sustained. Moreover, if anyone should appeal in cases permitted by the law,[81] or make a complaint regarding some grievance, or otherwise by reason of the lapse of two years, as was said above, have recourse to another judge, he shall be bound to transfer at his own expense to the judge of appeal all the acts of the proceedings conducted in the presence of the bishop, having previously, however, notified the bishop, so that if anything appears suitable to him for the direction of the cause, he may communicate it to the judge of appeal. But if the appellee appears, he shall also be bound to bear his proportion of the expenses of transferring the acts if he wishes to use them, unless it is a local custom to act otherwise, namely, that the entire costs are borne by the appellant. Furthermore, the notary shall be bound on receipt of a suitable fee to furnish the appellant as soon as possible and within at least one month with a copy of the proceedings, and should he through delay in supplying such copy be guilty of fraud, he shall at the discretion of the ordinary be suspended from the administration of his office and shall be compelled to pay double the costs of the suit, which is to be divided between the appellant and the poor of the locality. But if the judge himself should be aware of this delay, or should participate therein, or should in any other way hinder the delivery of the entire proceedings to the appellant within the time specified above, he shall be bound to the same penalty of paying double the costs, as was stated above; any

---

81. Cf. tot. tit. X, De appell., II, 28; in VI°, II, 15; in Clem., II, 12

privileges, indults, agreements which bind only their authors, and any other customs whatsoever to the contrary in respect to all matters dealt with above, notwithstanding.

Chapter XXI

IT IS DECLARED THAT BY CERTAIN WORDS USED ABOVE, THE USUAL MANNER OF TREATING MATTERS IN GENERAL COUNCILS IS NOT CHANGED

The holy council, desiring that no occasion for doubt arise at any future time from decrees which it has published, in explaining those words contained in a decree published in the first session under our most blessed Lord, Pius IV, namely, "which at the suggestion and under the presidency of the legates shall appear suitable and proper to the holy council for alleviating the calamities of these times, adjusting religious controversies, restraining deceitful tongues, correcting the abuses of depraved morals, and to bring about true Christian peace in the world,"[82] declares that it was not its intention that by the foregoing words the usual manner of treating matters in general councils should in any part be changed, or that anything new besides that which has so far been established by the sacred canons or the prescriptions of general councils, should be added to or taken away from anyone.

ANNOUNCEMENT OF THE NEXT SESSION

Moreover, the same holy council ordains and decrees that the next session be held on the Thursday after the conception of the Blessed Virgin Mary, which will be the ninth day of the coming December, with the authority, however, of abbreviating that time. In this session will be considered the sixth chapter now deferred to it and the remaining chapters on reform which have already been set forth and other matters related thereto. If it appears opportune and time will permit, some dogmas may also be considered, as in their turn they will be proposed in the congregations.

The time appointed for the session was abridged.

---

82. Cf. Sess. XVII at the beginning.

TWENTY-FIFTH SESSION

which is the ninth and last under the Supreme Pontiff,
Pius IV, begun on the third and closed on the fourth day
of December, 1563

DECREE CONCERNING PURGATORY

Since the Catholic Church, instructed by the Holy Ghost,
has, following the sacred writings and the ancient tradition of the Fathers, taught in sacred councils and very
recently in this ecumenical council that there is a purgatory,[1] and that the souls there detained are aided by the
suffrages of the faithful and chiefly by the acceptable sacrifice of the altar, the holy council commands the bishops
that they strive diligently to the end that the sound doctrine of purgatory, transmitted by the Fathers and sacred
councils,[2] be believed and maintained by the faithful of
Christ, and be everywhere taught and preached. The more
difficult and subtle questions, however, and those that do
not make for edification and from which there is for the
most part no increase in piety, are to be excluded from popular instructions to uneducated people.[3] Likewise, things
that are uncertain or that have the appearance of falsehood they shall not permit to be made known publicly and
discussed. But those things that tend to a certain kind of
curiosity or superstition, or that savor of filthy lucre, they
shall prohibit as scandals and stumblingblocks to the faithful. The bishops shall see to it that the suffrages of the living, that is, the sacrifice of the mass,[4] prayers, alms and
other works of piety which they have been accustomed to
perform for the faithful departed, be piously and devoutly
discharged in accordance with the laws of the Church, and
that whatever is due on their behalf from testamentary
bequests or other ways, be discharged by the priests and
ministers of the Church and others who are bound to ren-

---

1. Cf. Sess. VI, can. 30 and Sess. XXII, chap. 2 and can. 3
2. Cf. cc.4, 5, D.XXV; Eugene IV in the Council of Florence (Denzinger, *Enchiridion*,
no. 693)
3. See *1 Tim.* 1:4; *2 Tim.* 2:23; *Titus* 3:9
4. Cf. *infra*, chap. 4 de ref.

der this service not in a perfunctory manner, but diligently
and accurately.

ON THE INVOCATION, VENERATION, AND RELICS OF SAINTS, AND ON SACRED IMAGES

The holy council commands all bishops and others who
hold the office of teaching and have charge of the *cura animarum,* that in accordance with the usage of the Catholic
and Apostolic Church, received from the primitive times of
the Christian religion, and with the unanimous teaching of
the holy Fathers and the decrees of sacred councils, they
above all instruct the faithful diligently in matters relating
to intercession and invocation of the saints, the veneration
of relics, and the legitimate use of images, teaching them
that the saints who reign together with Christ offer up their
prayers to God for men, that it is good and beneficial sup-
pliantly to invoke them and to have recourse to their prayers,
assistance and support in order to obtain favors from God
through His Son, Jesus Christ Our Lord, who alone is our
redeemer and saviour;[5] and that they think impiously who
deny that the saints who enjoy eternal happiness in heaven
are to be invoked, or who assert that they do not pray for
men, or that our invocation of them to pray for each of us
individually is idolatry, or that it is opposed to the word of
God and inconsistent with the honor of the *one mediator of
God and men, Jesus Christ,*[6] or that it is foolish to pray
vocally or mentally to those who reign in heaven. Also, that
the holy bodies of the holy martyrs and of others living with
Christ, which were the living members of Christ and the
temple of the Holy Ghost,[7] to be awakened by Him to eternal life and to be glorified, are to be venerated by the faithful,[8] through which many benefits are bestowed by God on
men, so that those who maintain that veneration and honor
are not due to the relics of the saints, or that these and
other memorials are honored by the faithful without profit,
and that the places dedicated to the memory of the saints
for the purpose of obtaining their aid are visited in vain,
are to be utterly condemned, as the Church has already long

---

5. Cf. Sess. XXII, chap. 3
6. See *1 Tim.* 2:5
7. See *1 Cor.* 3:16; 6:19; *2 Cor.* 6:16
8. Cf. II Council of Nicaea (787), can. 7

since condemned and now again condemns them. Moreover, that the images of Christ, of the Virgin Mother of God, and of the other saints are to be placed and retained especially in the churches, and that due honor and veneration is to be given them; not, however, that any divinity or virtue is believed to be in them by reason of which they are to be venerated, or that something is to be asked of them, or that trust is to be placed in images, as was done of old by the Gentiles who placed their hope in idols;[9] but because the honor which is shown them is referred to the prototypes which they represent, so that by means of the images which we kiss and before which we uncover the head and prostrate ourselves, we adore Christ and venerate the saints whose likeness they bear. That is what was defined by the decrees of the councils, especially of the Second Council of Nicaea,[10] against the opponents of images.

Moreover, let the bishops diligently teach that by means of the stories of the mysteries of our redemption portrayed in paintings and other representations the people are instructed and confirmed in the articles of faith, which ought to be borne in mind and constantly reflected upon; also that great profit is derived from all holy images, not only because the people are thereby reminded of the benefits and gifts bestowed on them by Christ, but also because through the saints the miracles of God and salutary examples are set before the eyes of the faithful, so that they may give God thanks for those things, may fashion their own life and conduct in imitation of the saints and be moved to adore and love God and cultivate piety. But if anyone should teach or maintain anything contrary to these decrees, let him be anathema. If any abuses shall have found their way into these holy and salutary observances, the holy council desires earnestly that they be completely removed, so that no representation of false doctrines and such as might be the occasion of grave error to the uneducated be exhibited. And if at times it happens, when this is beneficial to the illiterate, that the stories and narratives of the Holy Scriptures are portrayed and exhibited, the people should be instructed that not for that reason is the divinity represented in pic-

---

9. *Psalms* 134:15ff.
10. Sess. III, IV, VI

ture as if it can be seen with bodily eyes or expressed in colors or figures. Furthermore, in the invocation of the saints, the veneration of relics, and the sacred use of images, all superstition shall be removed,[11] all filthy quest for gain eliminated, and all lasciviousness avoided, so that images shall not be painted and adorned with a seductive charm, or the celebration of saints and the visitation of relics be perverted by the people into boisterous festivities and drunkenness, as if the festivals in honor of the saints are to be celebrated with revelry and with no sense of decency.[12] Finally, such zeal and care should be exhibited by the bishops with regard to these things that nothing may appear that is disorderly or unbecoming and confusedly arranged, nothing that is profane, nothing disrespectful, since holiness becometh the house of God.[13] That these things may be the more faithfully observed, the holy council decrees that no one is permitted to erect or cause to be erected in any place or church, howsoever exempt, any unusual image unless it has been approved by the bishop; also that no new miracles be accepted[14] and no relics recognized[15] unless they have been investigated and approved by the same bishop, who, as soon as he has obtained any knowledge of such matters, shall, after consulting theologians and other pious men, act thereon as he shall judge consonant with truth and piety. But if any doubtful or grave abuse is to be eradicated, or if indeed any graver question concerning these matters should arise, the bishop, before he settles the controversy, shall await the decision of the metropolitan and of the bishops of the province in a provincial synod; so, however, that nothing new or anything that has not hitherto been in use in the Church, shall be decided upon without having first consulted the most holy Roman pontiff.

CONCERNING REGULARS AND NUNS

The same holy council, continuing the work of reform, has thought fit that the following matters be decided.

---

11. Cf. c.ult., X, De reliq. et ven. sanct., III, 45
12. C.2, D.III de cons.
13. *Psalms* 92:5
14. Cf. c.1, X, De reliq. et ven. sanct., III, 45
15. Cf. c.ult., X, h.t., De reliq.

Chapter I

ALL REGULARS SHALL ADJUST THEIR LIFE IN ACCORDANCE WITH THE REQUIREMENTS OF THE RULE WHICH THEY HAVE PROFESSED; SUPERIORS SHALL SEDULOUSLY SEE TO IT THAT THIS IS DONE

Since the holy council is not ignorant of how great a splendor and usefulness accrues to the Church of God from monasteries piously regulated and properly administered, it has, to the end that the old and regular discipline may be the more easily and promptly restored where it has collapsed, and may be the more firmly maintained where it has been preserved, thought it necessary to command, as by this decree it does command, that all regulars, men as well as women, adjust and regulate their life in accordance with the requirements of the rule which they have professed, and especially that they observe faithfully whatever pertains to the perfection of their profession, as the vows of obedience, poverty, and chastity,[16] and any other vows and precepts peculiar to any rule and order and belonging to the essence thereof, as well as the preservation of the common life, food and clothing. Superiors shall use all care and diligence, in general and provincial chapters as well as in their visitations, which they shall not neglect to make at the proper times, that these things are not departed from, for it is evident that they cannot make any relaxations in those things that pertain to the substance of the regular life. For if those things that constitute the basis and foundation of all regular discipline are not strictly observed, the whole edifice must necessarily fall.

Chapter II

PRIVATE OWNERSHIP IS ABSOLUTELY FORBIDDEN TO REGULARS

To no regular, therefore, whether man or woman, shall it be lawful to possess or to hold as his own or even in the name of the convent any movable or immovable property, of whatever nature it may be or in whatever manner acquired;[17] but the same shall be handed over immediately

---

16. Cf. c.1 (§ *Quum igitur in primis*), in Clem., De verb. sig., V, 11
17. Cf. cc.11, 13, C.XII, q.1; cc.2, 6, X, De statu monach., III, 35

to the superior and be incorporated in the convent. Neither
shall it in the future be lawful for superiors to grant immovable property to any regular, not even the usufruct or use,
or the administration thereof or as *commendam*. But the
administration of the property of monasteries or convents
shall belong to the officials thereof only, who are removable
at the will of their superiors. Superiors shall so permit the
use of movable goods that the furniture is consistent with
the state of poverty which they have professed; there shall
be nothing superfluous, neither shall anything that is necessary be denied them. But should anyone be discovered or
convicted of possessing something in any other manner, he
shall be deprived for two years of his active and passive
voice and shall also be punished in accordance with the prescriptions of his rule and order.

Chapter III

ALL MONASTERIES, SAVE THOSE HEREIN EXCEPTED, MAY
POSSESS IMMOVABLE PROPERTY, THE NUMBER OF PERSONS IN
THEM IS TO BE DETERMINED BY THE AMOUNT OF REVENUES
OR ALMS. NO MONASTERIES MAY BE ERECTED WITHOUT
THE PERMISSION OF THE BISHOP

The holy council grants that all monasteries and houses,
of men as well as of women, and of mendicants, even those
that were forbidden by their constitutions or that had not
received permission to this effect by Apostolic privilege, with
the exception of the houses of the brethren of St. Francis,[18]
the Capuchins, and those called Minor Observants, may in
the future possess immovable property. But if any of the
aforesaid places, to which it has been granted by Apostolic
authority to possess such property, have been deprived
thereof, it decrees that the same shall be wholly restored
to them. But in the aforesaid monasteries and houses, of
men as well as of women, whether they do or do not possess immovable properties, only such a number of persons
shall be determined upon and retained in the future as can
be suitably maintained either from the revenues of the
monasteries or from the customary alms;[19] neither shall

18. Cf. c.3 (§ Porro), VI°, De verb. sig., V, 12; c.1, h.t. in Clem., V, 11
19. Cf. c.9, X, De vit. et hon. cler., III, 1; c.1, X, De instit., III, 7; c. un. (§ 1), VI°, De
    stat. regul., III, 16.

such places be erected in the future unless the permission of the bishop in whose diocese they are to be established has first been obtained.

Chapter IV

NO REGULAR SHALL WITHOUT THE PERMISSION OF HIS SUPERIOR ENTER THE SERVICE EITHER OF ANOTHER PLACE OR PERSON, OR WITHDRAW FROM HIS MONASTERY, WHEN ABSENT BY REASON OF STUDY HE SHALL RESIDE IN A MONASTERY

The holy council forbids that any regular under the pretext of preaching or lecturing or of any pious work, place himself at the service of any prelate, prince, university, community, or of any other person or place whatsoever without the permission of his superior,[20] any privilege or authority obtained from others regarding these matters shall avail him nothing. Should he act in contravention of this he shall at the discretion of his superior be punished as disobedient. Neither shall it be lawful for regulars to leave their convents, even under pretext of going to their superiors, unless they have been sent or summoned by them. Anyone discovered without having obtained the aforesaid command in writing, shall be punished by the local ordinaries as a deserter of his institute. Those who for reasons of study are sent to universities, shall reside in convents only, otherwise the ordinaries shall take action against them.

Chapter V

PROVISION IS MADE FOR THE ENCLOSURE OF NUNS, ESPECIALLY THOSE WHO RESIDE OUTSIDE THE CITIES

The holy council, renewing the constitution of Boniface VIII, which begins, "Periculoso,"[21] commands all bishops that by the judgment of God to which it appeals and under threat of eternal malediction, they make it their special care that in all monasteries subject to them by their own authority and in others by the authority of the Apostolic See, the enclosure of nuns be restored wherever it has been violated

---

20. Cf. c.35, C.XVI, q.1; c.7, X, De off. jud. ord., I, 31; cc.3, 4, X, Ne cler. vel monach., III, 50; c.1 (§ 5), in Clem., De stat. monach., III, 10
21. C. un., VI°, De stat. regul., III, 16

and that it be preserved where it has not been violated; restraining with ecclesiastical censures and other penalties, every appeal being set aside, the disobedient and gainsayers, even summoning for this purpose, if need be, the aid of the secular arm. The holy council exhorts all Christian princes to furnish this aid, and binds thereto under penalty of excommunication to be incurred *ipso facto* all civil magistrates. No nun shall after her profession be permitted to go out of the monastery, even for a brief period under any pretext whatever, except for a lawful reason to be approved by the bishop;[22] any indults and privileges whatsoever notwithstanding. Neither shall anyone, of whatever birth or condition, sex or age, be permitted, under penalty of excommunication to be incurred *ipso facto,* to enter the enclosure of a monastery without the written permission of the bishop or the superior.[23] But the bishop or superior ought to grant permission in necessary cases only, and no other person shall in any way be able to grant it, even by virtue of any authority or indult already granted or that may be granted in the future. And since monasteries of nuns situated outside the walls of a city or town are often without any protection exposed to the rapacity and other crimes of evil men, the bishops and other superiors shall make it their duty to remove, if they deem it expedient, the nuns from those places to new or old monasteries within cities or more populous towns, summoning, if need be, the aid of the secular arm. Those who hinder or disobey them, they shall compel to submission by ecclesiastical censures.

Chapter VI

THE MANNER OF CHOOSING SUPERIORS

That all things may be done properly and without fraud in the election of superiors, temporary abbots and other officials and generals, as also abbesses and other superioresses, the holy council above all things strictly commands that all the aforesaid must be chosen by secret ballot, so that the names of individual voters may never become known. Neither shall it be lawful in the future to appoint provincials,

---

22. Cf. c. un., VI°, De stat. regular., III, 16
23. C.8, X, De vit. et hon. cler., III, 1

abbots, priors, or any other titled persons whatsoever with a view of determining the election to be made, nor to add the votes and approvals of those absent. But if anyone should be elected contrary to the prescription of this decree, such an election shall be invalid, and he who has permitted himself to be chosen provincial, abbot, or prior in the aforesaid manner, shall from that time on be disqualified to hold any offices whatsoever in the order; any faculties that have been granted in these matters shall be considered as *eo ipso* nullified, and should any others be granted in the future, they shall be regarded as surreptitious.

Chapter VII

WHO MAY BE ELECTED ABBESSES AND SUPERIORESSES BY WHATEVER NAME KNOWN AND HOW THEY ARE TO BE ELECTED. NO ONE SHALL BE APPOINTED OVER TWO MONASTERIES

No one shall be elected abbess or prioress, or by whatever other name the one appointed or the superioress may be known, who is less than forty years of age and who has not lived commendably during the eight years after having made her profession. If no one is found in a monastery possessing these qualifications, then one may be chosen from another of the same order. But if the superior who presides over the election should judge even this inconvenient, with the consent of the bishop or other superior one of those in the same monastery who is beyond her thirtieth year and has lived commendably at least five years since her profession may be chosen.[24] No one, however, shall be appointed over two monasteries. If anyone is in any way in possession of two or more, she shall, retaining one, be compelled to resign the remainder within six months, and in case she has not resigned within that period, all shall be *ipso jure* vacant. He who presides at the election, whether it be the bishop or other superior, shall not enter the enclosure of the monastery, but shall hear or receive the vote of each at the little window of the grating. In other matters the constitutions of each order or monastery shall be observed.

---

24. Cf. c.43, VI°, De elect., I, 6

Chapter VIII

HOW THE GOVERNMENT OF MONASTERIES WHICH HAVE NO REGULARS AS ORDINARY VISITORS IS TO BE CONDUCTED

All monasteries which are not subject to general chapters or to bishops, and which have not regular visitors who belong to the order, but have been accustomed to be governed under the immediate protection and direction of the Apostolic See, shall be bound within a year from the dissolution of the present council and thereafter every three years, to assemble in congregations in accordance with the form of the constitution of Innocent III published in the general council, which begins, "In singulis";[25] and they shall there authorize certain regulars who shall deliberate and decide on the manner and order of establishing the aforesaid congregations and also the rules to be therein observed. But if they should prove negligent in these matters, then the metropolitan in whose province the aforesaid monasteries are located, as the delegate of the Apostolic See, shall convoke them for the above named purpose. If, however, there is not a sufficient number of such monasteries within the confines of one province to establish a congregation, the monasteries of two or three provinces may form one congregation. When these congregations have been established, their general chapters and the superiors and visitors elected by them shall have the same authority over the monasteries of their congregation and over the regulars residing therein as other superiors and visitors have in other orders, and they shall be bound to visit the monasteries of their congregation frequently, to apply themselves to their reform, and to observe whatever has been decreed in the sacred canons[26] and in this holy council. But if at the request of the metropolitan they fail to take steps to carry the aforesaid matters into effect, then they shall be subject to the bishops, as the delegates of the Apostolic See, in whose dioceses the aforesaid places are situated.

---

25. Cf. c.7, X, De stat. monach., III, 35
26. Cf. tot. tit. X, De stat. monach., III, 35, De stat. regul. in VI°, III, 16, De stat, monach. in Clem., III, 10

Chapter IX

MONASTERES OF NUNS IMMEDIATELY SUBJECT TO THE
APOSTOLIC SEE SHALL BE SUPERVISED BY THE BISHOP;
OTHERS, BY THOSE DELEGATED IN GENERAL CHAPTERS
OR BY OTHER REGULARS

Monasteries of nuns which are immediately subject to the
Apostolic See, also those known by the name of Chapters of
St. Peter or of St. John or by any other name, shall be supervised by the bishops as delegates of that See, anything to
the contrary notwithstanding. Those, however, that are supervised by persons delegated in general chapters or by other
regulars, shall be left under their charge and protection.

Chapter X

NUNS SHALL CONFESS AND COMMUNICATE ONCE A MONTH. AN
EXTRAORDINARY CONFESSOR SHALL BE PROVIDED FOR THEM
BY THE BISHOP. AMONG THEM THE EUCHARIST SHALL NOT
BE RESERVED OUTSIDE THE PUBLIC CHURCH

Bishops and other superiors of monasteries of nuns shall
take special care that the nuns, as they are admonished in
their constitutions, confess their sins and receive the most
holy Eucharist at least once a month,[27] so that they may
fortify themselves by that salutary safeguard valiantly to
overcome all the assaults of the devil. In addition to the
ordinary confessor, the bishop and other superiors shall provide twice or three times a year an extraordinary one, whose
duty it shall be to hear the confessions of all. The holy council forbids, however, that the holy body of Christ be reserved
within the choir or the enclosure of the monastery and not
in the public church; any indult or privilege notwithstanding.

Chapter XI

THE BISHOP SHALL VISIT MONASTERIES TO WHICH IS ANNEXED
THE *CURA* OF SECULARS BESIDES THOSE WHO BELONG TO THEIR
HOUSEHOLD, AND HE SHALL, WITH CERTAIN EXCEPTIONS,
EXAMINE THOSE WHO ARE TO EXERCISE THAT *CURA*

In monasteries or houses of men or women to which is

---

27. C.1 (§ 2) in Clem., De stat. monach., III, 10

annexed the *cura animarum* of secular persons other than
those who belong to the household of those monasteries or
places, those persons, whether regulars or seculars, who exercise that *cura* shall in all things that pertain to that *cura*
and to the administration of the sacraments be subject immediately to the jurisdiction, visitation, and correction of the
bishop in whose diocese they are located. Neither may anyone, not even such as are removable at any moment, be
appointed thereto except with his consent and after having
been previously examined by him or by his vicar;[28] the
monastery of Cluny with its territories being excepted, and
excepted also are those monasteries or places in which the
abbots, generals, or heads of orders ordinarily have their
principal residence, and other monasteries or houses in which
abbots or other superiors of regulars exercise episcopal and
temporal jurisdiction over the parish priests and parishioners;
saving the right, however, of those bishops who exercise a
greater jurisdiction over the places or persons named above.

Chapter XII

IN THE OBSERVANCE OF EPISCOPAL CENSURES AND DIOCESAN
FEASTS, REGULARS SHALL ACT IN ACCORD WITH
THE SECULAR CLERGY

Not only the censures and interdicts that have emanated
from the Apostolic See but also those promulgated by the
ordinaries, shall on the bishop's command be published and
observed by the regulars in their churches.[29] The feast days
also which the bishop shall command to be observed in his
diocese, shall be observed by all those exempt, also by the
regulars.[30]

Chapter XIII

DISPUTES CONCERNING PRECEDENCE THE BISHOP SHALL
SETTLE IMMEDIATELY. EXEMPT PERSONS WHO DO NOT LIVE IN
VERY STRICT ENCLOSURES, ARE OBLIGED TO ATTEND THE
PUBLIC PRAYERS

All disputes concerning precedence which very often and

28. Cf. c.11, C.XVIII, q.2
29. C.1, in Clem., De sent. excomm., V, 10
30. C.13, D.XII

not without grave scandal arise among ecclesiastics, both secular and regular, at public processions as well as the burial of the dead, as also in the matter of carrying the canopy and other things of this kind, the bishop shall settle to the exclusion of every appeal; anything to the contrary notwithstanding. All exempt persons, secular as well as regular clerics, also monks, summoned to public processions, shall be obliged to attend; those only being excepted who live permanently in strict enclosure.

Chapter XIV

BY WHOM PUNISHMENT IS TO BE IMPOSED ON A REGULAR GUILTY OF A PUBLIC OFFENSE

A regular not subject to the bishop and living within the enclosure of a monastery, who has outside of that enclosure committed so notorious an offense as to be a scandal to the people, shall at the instance of the bishop be severely punished by his superior within the time specified by the bishop, and the superior shall report to the bishop concerning this punishment. Otherwise he shall be deprived of his office by his superior and the delinquent may be punished by the bishop.[31]

Chapter XV

PROFESSION SHALL NOT BE MADE EXCEPT AFTER ONE YEAR'S PROBATION AND ON THE COMPLETION OF THE SIXTEENTH YEAR

In no religious order whatever, whether of men or of women, shall profession be made before the completion of the sixteenth year, and no one shall be admitted to profession who has been under probation less than a year after the reception of the habit.[32] Any profession made sooner is null and imposes no obligation to the observance of any rule either of a religious body or an order, neither does it entail any other effects whatsoever.[33]

---

31. Cf. c. ult., X, De stat. monach., III, 35
32. Cf. c.1, C.XVII, q.2; c.16, X, De regular., III, 31; c.2, h.t. in VI°, III, 14
33. Cf. c.8, X, h.t., III, 31; c.1, h.t., in VI°, III, 14

Chapter XVI

A RENUNCIATION MADE OR AN OBLIGATION ASSUMED TWO
MONTHS BEFORE PROFESSION IS NULL. THE PROBATION COM-
PLETED, THE NOVICES SHALL BE EITHER PROFESSED OR DIS-
MISSED. IN THE PIOUS INSTITUTE OF CLERICS OF THE SOCIETY
OF JESUS NOTHING NEW IS INTRODUCED, NO PART OF THE
PROPERTY OF A NOVICE SHALL BE GIVEN TO THE MONASTERY
BEFORE PROFESSION

Moreover, no renunciation or obligation previously made,
even upon oath or in favor of any pious cause whatsoever,
shall be valid, unless it be made with the permission of the
bishop or his vicar within two months immediately preceding profession, and it shall not be understood otherwise to
have effect unless the profession followed; but if made in
any other manner, even with the express renunciation of
this favor, also upon oath, it shall be invalid and of no effect.
When novices have completed their novitiate, the superiors
shall admit to profession those novices found qualified; the
others they shall dismiss from the monastery. Hereby, however, the holy council does not intend to innovate or prohibit something that will hinder the order of clerics of the
Society of Jesus from serving the Lord and His Church in
accordance with their pious institute approved by the holy
Apostolic See. Before the profession of a novice, whether
male or female, nothing shall under any pretext whatever
be given to the monastery from the property of the same,
either by parents, relatives or guardians, except for food and
clothing during the time of probation, lest the novice should
be unable to leave for the reason that the monastery possesses the whole or greater part of his substance, and he
would be unable easily to recover it in case he should leave.
The holy council, therefore, commands under penalty of
anathema both givers and receivers that this be in no wise
done, and that to those who leave before profession everything that was theirs be restored. All of which, that it may
be done properly, the bishop shall, if need be, enforce with
ecclesiastical censures.

Chapter XVII

IF A GIRL WHO IS MORE THAN TWELVE YEARS OF AGE WISHES TO TAKE THE HABIT OF REGULARS, SHE SHALL BE EXAMINED BY THE ORDINARY, AND AGAIN BEFORE PROFESSION

The holy council, having in view the freedom of the profession of virgins who are to be dedicated to God, ordains and decrees that if a girl more than twelve years of age wishes to take the habit of regulars, she shall not take that habit, neither shall she nor any other at a later period make profession,[34] until the bishop, or, if he be absent or hindered, his vicar, or someone delegated by them at their expense, has carefully examined the wish of the virgin, whether she has been forced or enticed, or knows what she is doing;[35] and if her will is found to be pious and free and she has the qualifications required by the rule of that monastery and order, and also if the monastery is a suitable one for her, she shall be permitted freely to make profession. And that the bishop may not be ignorant of the time of the profession, the superioress of the monastery shall be bound to give him notice thereof a month beforehand; but if she fails to make the matter known to him, she shall be suspended from office for as long a period as the bishop shall deem proper.

Chapter XVIII

NO ONE SHALL, EXCEPT IN THE CASES PERMITTED BY LAW, COMPEL A WOMAN TO ENTER A MONASTERY OR PREVENT HER IF SHE WISHES TO ENTER. THE CONSTITUTIONS OF THE PENITENTS OR CONVERTS ARE TO BE OBSERVED

The holy council anathematizes each and all persons, of whatever character or rank they may be, whether clerics or laics, seculars or regulars, and with whatever dignity invested, who shall, except in the cases permitted by law,[36] in any way force any virgin or widow, or any other woman whatsoever, to enter a monastery against her will, or to take the habit of any religious order or to make profession; those

---

34. C.12, X, De regular., III, 31
35. C.10, C.XX, q.1; c.1, X, De regular., III, 31
36. Cf. cc.18, 19, X, De conv. conjug., III, 32

also who give advice, aid or encouragement, as well as those who, knowing that she does not enter the monastery or receive the habit, or make profession voluntarily, shall in any way take part in that act by their presence, consent or authority. Similarly does it anathematize those who shall in any way and without a just cause impede the holy wish of virgins or other women to take the veil or pronounce the vows.[37] Each and all of those things which must be done before profession or at the profession itself shall be observed not only in monasteries subject to the bishop but also in all others. From the above, however, are excepted the women who are called penitents or converts, whose own constitutions shall be observed.

Chapter XIX

HOW TO PROCEED IN THE CASE OF THOSE WHO DESERT AN ORDER

Any regular who shall pretend that he entered a religious order through compulsion and fear, or shall allege that he was professed before the proper age or something similar,[38] and wishes for some reason to lay aside the habit, or departs with the habit without the permission of his superior, shall not be listened to unless it be within five years only from the day of his profession, and not even then unless he has submitted to his superior and to the ordinary the reasons for his pretensions. But if before doing this he has of his own accord laid aside the habit, he shall under no circumstances be admitted to assign any reason whatever, but shall be compelled to return to his monastery and be punished as an apostate, and in the meantime he shall not have the benefit of any privilege of his order. Moreover, no regular shall in virtue of any authority whatsoever be transferred to an order less rigorous,[39] neither shall permission be granted to any regular to wear the habit of his order secretly.

---

37. C.2, C.XX, q.2; c.16, C.XXXII, q.2
38. C.8, C.XX, q.1; c.12, X, De regular., III, 31
39. Cf. Sess. XIV, chap. 11 de ref.

Chapter XX

SUPERIORS OF ORDERS NOT SUBJECT TO BISHOPS SHALL VISIT
AND CORRECT INFERIOR MONASTERIES, EVEN THOSE
PROVISIONALLY COLLATED

Abbots who are heads of orders and other superiors of the aforesaid orders who are not subject to bishops but have a lawful jurisdiction over other inferior monasteries or priories, shall, each in his own locality and order, visit *ex officio* those monasteries and priories that are subject to them, also if held *in commendam*. Since these are subject to the heads of their orders, the holy council declares that they are not to be included in what has been decided elsewhere concerning the visitation of monasteries held *in commendam*,[40] and all superiors of the monasteries of the aforesaid orders shall be bound to receive the above named visitors and to execute their commands. Those monasteries also which are the heads of orders shall be visited in accordance with the constitutions of the holy Apostolic See and of each order. And so long as such provisional collations continue, there shall be appointed by the general chapters or by the visitors of the orders cloistral priors, or subpriors in the priories that have a convent, who shall correct and exercise spiritual authority. In all other things the privileges and faculties of the above named orders, which concern their persons, places and rights, shall remain firm and undisturbed.

Chapter XXI

MONASTERIES SHALL BE CONFERRED ON REGULARS, HEAD OR
PRINCIPAL MONASTERIES SHALL NOT IN THE FUTURE BE
CONFERRED ON ANYONE *IN COMMENDAM*

Since most monasteries, also abbeys, priories, and provostries, have suffered no little loss both in spiritual and temporal things through the maladministration of those to whom they have been entrusted, the holy council desires to restore them entirely to a discipline becoming the monastic life. But the present state of the times is so adverse and so full of difficulties that a remedy cannot be applied to all at once, or a common one everywhere, as it desired. Nev-

---

40. Cf. Sess. XXI, chap. 8 de ref.

ertheless, that it may not omit anything that may in time provide advantageously for the aforesaid, it trusts in the first place that the most holy Roman pontiff will according to his piety and prudence make it his care, so far as he sees the times will permit, that regulars expressly professed in the same order and capable of guiding and governing the flock be placed over those monasteries which are now held *in commendam* and which have their own convents. Those which in the future become vacant shall be conferred only on regulars of approved virtue and holiness.[41] With regard to those monasteries which are the head and chief ones of the orders, whether their filiations be called abbeys or priories, they who now hold them *in commendam* shall be bound, if a regular has not been appointed as successor thereto, to make within six months a solemn profession of the vows peculiar to those orders or to resign; otherwise the aforesaid places held *in commendam* shall be considered *ipso jure* vacant. But that in each and all of the aforesaid matters no fraud may be perpetrated, the holy council decrees that in the appointments to the monasteries mentioned the character of each person be expressly stated, and any appointment made otherwise shall be considered surreptitious and shall not be protected by any subsequent possession, even though this covers a period of three years.

Chapter XXII

WHAT HAS BEEN SAID CONCERNING THE REFORM OF REGULARS SHALL BE CARRIED INTO EXECUTION WITHOUT DELAY

The holy council commands that each and all of the matters contained in the foregoing decrees be observed in all convents and monasteries, colleges and houses of all monks and regulars whatsoever, as also of all religious virgins and widows, even though they live under the guidance of military orders, also that (of St. John) of Jerusalem, and by whatever name they may be designated, under whatever rule or constitutions and under whatever protection or administration they may be, or in whatever subjection to, union with, or dependence on any order whatsoever, whether of mendi-

---

41. Cf. Sess. XIV, chap. 10 de ref.

cants or non-mendicants, or of other regular monks or canons whatsoever; any privileges of each and all of those above mentioned in whatever form of words expressed, even those known as *mare magnum* and those obtained at their foundation, also constitutions and rules, even though subscribed to under oath, and also customs and prescriptions, even though immemorial, notwithstanding. But if there are regulars, men as well as women, who live under a stricter rule or statutes, except with regard to the permission to possess immovable property in common, the holy council does not intend to hinder them in their rule and observance. And since the holy council desires that each and all of the aforesaid matters be put into effect as soon as possible, it commands all bishops that in the monasteries subject to them and in all others specifically committed to them in the foregoing decrees, and all abbots, generals and other superiors of the aforesaid orders, that they put into execution the foregoing matters immediately. And if there be anything that is not put into execution, the provincial synods shall supplement and correct the negligence of the bishops. The negligence of the regulars, their provincial and general chapters, and in default of the general chapters, the provincial synods shall attend to by delegating certain persons of the same order. The holy council also exhorts and in virtue of holy obedience commands all kings, princes, governments and magistrates to deign to lend, as often as requested, their help and influence in support of the aforesaid bishops, abbots, generals, and other superiors in the execution of the reform indicated above, so that they may without hindrance properly put into effect the foregoing matters to the praise of Almighty God.

DECREE CONCERNING REFORM

Chapter I

CARDINALS AND ALL PRELATES OF THE CHURCHES SHALL HAVE PLAIN FURNITURE AND TABLE. THEY SHALL NOT ENRICH THEIR RELATIONS AND DOMESTICS FROM THE PROPERTY OF THE CHURCH

It is to be desired that those who assume the episcopal office know what are their duties, and understand that they have been called not for their own convenience, not for riches

or luxury, but to labors and cares for the glory of God. For
it is not to be doubted that the rest of the faithful will be
more easily roused to religion and innocence, if they see
those who are placed over them concentrate their thoughts
not on the things of this world but on the salvation of souls
and on their heavenly country. Since the holy council considers these things to be of the greatest importance in the
restoration of ecclesiastical discipline, it admonishes all bishops that they reflect often on these things and also by the
actions and behavior of their life, which is a sort of perpetual sermon, give evidence that their deportment is consistent with their office; but above all that they so regulate
their whole conduct that others may derive therefrom examples of moderation, modesty, continency, and of that holy
humility which recommends us so to God.[42] Wherefore, after
the example of our Fathers in the Council of Carthage,[43] it
commands not only that bishops be content with modest
furniture and a frugal table, but also that they take heed
that in the rest of their manner of living and in their whole
house, nothing appears that is at variance with this holy
ordinance, or that does not manifest simplicity, zeal for God
and a contempt for vanities. But above all does it forbid
them to attempt to enrich their relations or domestics from
the revenues of the Church,[44] since the canons of the Apostles also forbid that ecclesiastical goods, which belong to
God, be given to relations;[45] but if they are poor, let them
distribute to them as poor, but they shall not alienate or
waste these goods for their sake. Indeed, the holy council
admonishes them to the utmost of its ability that they lay
aside completely all this human affection of the flesh toward
brothers, nephews, and relations, which is the nursery of
many evils in the Church. And what has been said of bishops is to be observed not only by all who hold ecclesiastical benefices, whether secular or regular, according to the
nature of the rank of each, but it decrees that it applies
also to the cardinals of the holy Roman Church, for since
the administration of the universal Church is supported by
their advice to the most holy Roman pontiff, it can appear

42. Cf. *Psalms* 101:18; *Ecclus.* 3:20; 35:21; *Matt.* 18:3f.
43. C.7, D.XLI
44. C.23, C.XII, q.1; c.19, C.XII, q.2
45. Cf. Apost. can. 39

wicked if they do not shine in the splendor of the virtues and in discipline of life, which should justly draw upon them the eyes of all.

Chapter II

BY WHOM PARTICULARLY THE DECREES OF THE COUNCIL ARE TO BE SOLEMNLY RECEIVED AND TAUGHT

The distress of the times and the malice of increasing heresies make it necessary that nothing be left undone which may appear to be for the edification of the faithful and for the defense of the Catholic faith. Wherefore, the holy council commands patriarchs, primates, archbishops, bishops, and all others who by right or custom ought to be present at the provincial synod,[46] that in the very first provincial synod to be held after the close of the present council, they receive publicly each and all of the matters which have been defined and decreed by this holy council; also that they promise and profess true obedience to the supreme Roman pontiff and at the same time publicly express their hatred of and anathematize all the heresies that have been condemned by the sacred canons and general councils and especially by this council. The same shall in the future be observed by all who are promoted to patriarchal, primatial, archiepiscopal and episcopal sees, in the first provincial synod at which they are present. But if anyone of all the aforesaid should refuse, which God forbid, the comprovincial bishops shall be bound under penalty of divine indignation to give notice thereof immediately to the supreme Roman pontiff, and shall in the meantime abstain from communion with that person. All others who now hold or hereafter will hold ecclesiastical benefices, whose duty it is to assemble in diocesan synod, shall do and observe in the first synod to be held the same as was prescribed above, otherwise they shall be punished in accordance with the prescriptions of the sacred canons. Furthermore, all those to whom pertains the care, visitation, and reform of universities and of [houses of] general studies, shall diligently see to it that the canons and decrees of this holy council are integrally received by the universi-

---

46. Cf. Sess. XXIV, chap. 2 de ref.

ties and that the masters, doctors, and others in those universities teach and interpret the things that are of Catholic faith in conformity therewith, and at the beginning of each year bind themselves by solemn oath to the observance of this ordinance;[47] and if there be any other matters in the aforesaid universities that need correction and reform, they shall for the advancement of religion and ecclesiastical discipline be reformed and put in order by those to whom it pertains. Those universities, however, that are immediately subject to the protection and visitation of the supreme Roman pontiff, His Holiness will provide for in the matters of visitation and reform through his delegates in the manner aforesaid and as shall seem to him most beneficial.

Chapter III

THE SWORD OF EXCOMMUNICATION IS NOT TO BE USED RASHLY. WHERE IN THINGS AND PERSONS THE END CAN BE OBTAINED, CENSURES ARE TO BE ABSTAINED FROM AND THE CIVIL AUTHORITY HAS NO RIGHT TO INTRUDE

Although the sword of excommunication is the nerve of ecclesiastical discipline and very salutary for holding the people in their duty, it is, however, to be used with moderation and great discretion, since experience teaches that if wielded rashly or for trifling reasons, it is more despised than feared and is productive of destruction rather than of salvation. Wherefore, those excommunications which after previous admonitions are customarily imposed for the purpose of eliciting a so-called disclosure, or by reason of properties squandered or alienated, shall be issued by absolutely no one but the bishop, and even then not except by reason of an unusual circumstance and after a diligent and very complete examination by the bishop of the cause which moves his mind thereto.[48] Neither shall he allow himself to be moved to their imposition by the authority of any secular person, even though a magistrate, but the entire matter shall be left to his own judgment and conscience, whether, after considering the circumstances, place, person or time, he shall himself deem it advisable to impose them. With re-

---

47. Cf. Sess. V, chap. 1 de ref.
48. Cf. cc.8, 41, 42, C.XI, q.3; c.48, X, De sent. excomm., V, 39

gard to judicial causes, all ecclesiastical judges, of whatever dignity they may be, are commanded that both during the proceedings and in rendering decisions, they abstain from ecclesiastical censures or interdict whenever the action can in each stage of the process be completed by themselves through their own authority; but in civil causes belonging in any way to the ecclesiastical forum, they may, if they deem it advisable, proceed against all persons, also laics, and terminate suits by pecuniary fines, which shall as soon as they have been collected be without further ado assigned to the pious places of the locality, or by distress of property, or by restraint of the persons, to be effected by their own or other agents, or even by the deprivation of benefices and other legal means. But if the action against the guilty party cannot be completed in this way and there be contumacy toward the judge, he may then in addition to other penalties chastise them also with the sword of anathema, if he should deem it expedient. In criminal causes also where a suit can be completed as was stated above, censures are to be abstained from. But if that effect cannot be easily obtained, it shall be lawful for the judge to make use of this spiritual sword against delinquents, provided the nature of the offense, preceded by at least two admonitions, even by an edict, requires it. But it shall not be lawful for any civil magistrate to prohibit an ecclesiastical judge from excommunicating anyone, or to command him to revoke an excommunication that has been imposed, under the pretext that the contents of the present decree have not been observed, since the investigation of this matter does not pertain to seculars but to ecclesiastics. But every excommunicated person who after the legitimate admonitions does not repent, shall not only be excluded from the sacraments and from intercourse and from friendship with the faithful, but if, bound with censure, he shall with obdurate heart remain therein for a year, he may also be proceeded against as suspected of heresy.[49]

---

49. Cf. cc.18, 19, 25, 26, C.XI, q.3; cc.8, 9, 15, 18, 29-31, 38, 39, X, De sent. excomm., V, 39

Chapter IV

WHERE THE NUMBER OF MASSES TO BE CELEBRATED IS TOO
GREAT, BISHOPS, ABBOTS AND GENERALS OF ORDERS SHALL
MAKE SUCH DISPOSITION AS THEY SHALL DEEM EXPEDIENT

It often happens in some churches that by reason of various bequests from deceased persons either so great a number of masses to be celebrated is left with them that it is not possible to take care of them on the particular days specified by the testators, or that the alms given for their celebration is so small that it is not easy to find one who is willing to accept this obligation; the result being that the pious intentions of the testators are defeated and occasion is given of burdening the consciences of those to whom the aforesaid obligations pertain. The holy council, desirous that these bequests for pious purposes be satisfied in the fullest and most useful manner possible, empowers bishops in the diocesan synod and likewise abbots and generals of orders in their general chapters, to decide with regard to the aforesaid churches, which they shall find to stand in need of regulation in this matter, whatever in their consciences they shall after a diligent examination of the circumstances judge to be most beneficial for the honor and service of God and the good of the churches;[50] so, however, that a commemoration be always made of the departed who for the welfare of their souls have left those bequests for pious purposes.

Chapter V

FROM WELL ESTABLISHED FOUNDATIONS WITH AN OBLIGATION
ANNEXED NOTHING SHALL BE REMOVED

Reason requires that from those things which have been well established nothing be withdrawn by contrary ordinances. When, therefore, in virtue of the erection or foundation of any benefices whatsoever or other constitutions, certain qualifications are required or certain obligations are attached to them, then in the collation of the benefices or in any other arrangement whatsoever nothing shall be taken from them. The same is to be observed in the matter of prebends for theologians, masters, doctors, priests, deacons,

50. Cf. Sess. XXII, chap. 6 de ref.

and subdeacons whenever they have been so established, so that in any provision nothing shall be altered with regard to their qualifications and orders, and any provision made otherwise shall be considered surreptitious.

Chapter VI

HOW THE BISHOP OUGHT TO ACT WITH REGARD TO THE VISITATION OF EXEMPT CHAPTERS

The holy council ordains that in all cathedral and collegiate churches the decree published under Paul III, of happy memory, which begins, "Capitula cathedralium,"[51] be observed, not only when the bishop makes his visitation but also as often as he proceeds *ex officio* or at the request of one against anyone of those included in said decree; so, however, that when he institutes proceedings outside of visitation all the following particulars shall be observed, namely, that the chapter at the beginning of each year choose two of its members, with whose counsel and consent the bishop or his vicar shall be bound to proceed both in shaping the process and in all other transactions connected therewith to the end of the action inclusively, in the presence, however, of the bishop's notary and in his residence or in the customary court of justice. These two, however, shall have only one vote, and one of them may cast his with the bishop. But if in any transaction or interlocutory or definitive sentence both should disagree with the bishop, then they shall within six days choose in union with the bishop a third party; and should they disagree also in the choice of that third party, the selection shall devolve on the nearest bishop and the point on which they disagreed shall be decided in favor of the opinion with which the third party agrees. Otherwise the proceedings and what followed therefrom shall be null and without effect in law. In criminal cases, however, arising from incontinency, of which mention has been made in the decree dealing with *concubinarii,*[52] and in the more outrageous crimes that demand deposition and degradation, where it is feared that judgment may be evaded by flight and the detention of the person is there-

---

51. Cf. Sess. VI, chap. 4 de ref.; Sess. XIV, chap. 4 de ref.
52. Cf. Sess. XXIV, chap. 8 de ref. Matr. and chap. 14 *infra.*

fore necessary, the bishop may in the beginning proceed alone to a summary investigation and the necessary detention, observing, however, the above order in the rest. But in all cases consideration is to be given to this, that the delinquents be confined in a suitable place in keeping with the nature of the crime and the character of the persons. Moreover, everywhere there shall be given to the bishops the honor which is in keeping with their dignity; to them belongs the first seat in the choir, in the chapter, in processions, and in other public functions,[53] and the place which they themselves may select, and theirs shall be the chief authority in everything that is to be done. If they propose something to the canons for deliberation and the matter is not one that is of benefit to them or theirs, the bishops themselves shall convoke the chapter, examine the votes, and decide according to them.[54] But in the absence of the bishop this shall be done entirely by those of the chapter to whom it by law or custom pertains, and the vicar of the bishop is not to be admitted to this. In all other things the jurisdiction and power of the chapter, if it perchance has any, and the administration of properties shall be left absolutely unimpaired and intact. All those, however, who do not possess dignities and do not belong to the chapter, shall in ecclesiastical causes be subject to the bishop, notwithstanding, with regard to what has been said above, privileges, even those accruing from a foundation, or customs, even though immemorial, or judgments, oaths, pacts, which bind only the authors thereof; the privileges, however, which have been granted to universities of general studies or to the persons attached thereto, shall in all things remain intact. But each and all of these things shall not have effect in those churches in which the bishops or their vicars, in virtue of constitutions, privileges, customs, pacts, or any other right, possess a power, authority, and jurisdiction greater than that included in the present decree; these the holy council does not intend to impair.

---

53. C.10, D.XCV
54. Cf. cc.4, 5, X, De his, quae fiunt a prael., III, 10

Chapter VII

ACCESS AND REGRESS TO BENEFICES ARE ABOLISHED. HOW, TO WHOM AND FOR WHAT REASON A COADJUTOR IS TO BE GRANTED

Since whatever in the matter of ecclesiastical benefices has the appearance of hereditary succession is odious to the sacred constitutions and contrary to the decrees of the Fathers,[55] no access or regress to any ecclesiastical benefice of whatever kind shall in future, even with consent, be granted to anyone, and those thus far granted shall not be suspended, extended, or transferred. And this decree shall apply to all ecclesiastical benefices whatsoever and to all persons, even though distinguished with the dignity of the cardinalate. In the case of coadjutors with future succession also the same shall hereafter be observed, so that they shall not be permitted to anyone in any ecclesiastical benefices whatsoever. But if at any time urgent necessity or the manifest interest of a cathedral church or of a monastery should demand that a coadjutor be given to a prelate, he shall not be given with the right of future succession until the reason therefore has first been diligently investigated by the most holy Roman pontiff,[56] and until it is certain that he possesses all the qualifications which by law and by the decrees of this holy council are required in bishops and prelates;[57] otherwise the concessions made in these matters shall be considered surreptitious.

Chapter VIII

DUTY OF THE ADMINISTRATORS OF HOSPITALS, BY WHOM AND HOW THEIR NEGLIGENCE IS TO BE PUNISHED

The holy council admonishes all who hold ecclesiastical benefices, whether secular or regular, to accustom themselves, so far as their revenues will permit, to exercise with promptness and kindness the office of hospitality so often commended by the holy Fathers;[58] being mindful that those

---

55. Cf. cc.5, 7, C.VIII, q.1; cc.7, 10, 11, 13, X, De fil. presb., I, 17; cc.6, 15, X, De jur. patr., III, 38
56. Cf. Sess. XXI, chap. 6 de ref.; cc.1, 14, C.VII, q.1
57. Cf. Sess. VII, chaps. 1, 3 de ref. and XXII, chap. 2 de ref.
58. Cf. c.2, D.XLII; c. un. D.LXXXV; c.2, D.LXXXIX; c.30, C. XII, q. 2

who love hospitality receive Christ in their guests.[59] Those who hold *in commendam,* by way of administration or under any other title whatsoever, or also have united to their own churches institutions commonly called hospitals, or other pious places established especially for the benefit of pilgrims, of the infirm, the aged or the poor, or if parish churches perchance united to hospitals or converted into hospitals have been handed over to their patrons to be administered by them, it strictly commands that they discharge the office and duty imposed on them and actually exercise the hospitality that they owe from the revenues set aside for that purpose, in accordance with the constitution of the Council of Vienne, renewed elsewhere by this same council under Paul III, of happy memory, which begins, "Quia contingit."[60] But if these hospitals were established to receive a certain class of pilgrims, infirm persons or others, and in the place in which they are located there are no such persons or very few to be found, it commands further that their revenues be diverted to some other pious purpose that is more closely related to their foundation and the more useful in respect of place and time, as shall appear most expedient to the ordinary, aided by two of the chapter experienced in the administration of property and to be chosen by himself; unless it has perchance been specified otherwise, even with regard to this event, in their foundation or institution, in which case the bishop shall see to it that what has been prescribed be observed, or if that is not possible he shall, as above, regulate the matter in a beneficial manner. If, therefore, any or all of the aforesaid, of whatever rank, order and dignity, even if they be laics, who have the administration of hospitals, not however subject to regulars where regular observance is in force, shall, after having been admonished by the ordinary, actually neglect to discharge the duty of hospitality in the fulness to which they are bound, they may be compelled thereto not only by ecclesiastical censures and other legal means, but may also be deprived forever of the administration and care of the hospital and others shall be put in their place by those to whom this pertains. The aforesaid persons, moreover, shall be bound in conscience to

---

59. *Matt.* 25:35
60. Cf. Sess. VII, chap. 15 de ref.; c.2 in Clem., De relig. dom., III, 11

the restitution of the revenues which they have received in violation of the institution of these hospitals, which shall not be pardoned by any remission or agreement; neither shall the administration or government of such places be in the future entrusted to one and the same person for a longer period than three years, unless it be otherwise provided for in their foundation; notwithstanding, with regard to all of the aforesaid, any union, exemption and custom, even though immemorial, to the contrary, or any privileges or indults whatsoever.

Chapter IX

HOW THE RIGHT OF PATRONAGE IS TO BE PROVED. ON WHOM THE OFFICE OF PATRONS MAY BE CONFERRED. ACCESSIONS PROHIBITED. BY WHOM THAT RIGHT MAY NOT BE ACQUIRED

Just as it is not equitable to take away the legitimate rights of patronage and to infringe upon the pious intentions of the faithful in their institution, so also is it not to be permitted that under this pretext ecclesiastical benefices be reduced to a state of servitude, as is impudently done by many. That, therefore, in all things a proper procedure may be observed, the holy council decrees that the title of the right of patronage is based on a foundation or on an endowment and is to be proved from an authentic document and by other proofs required by law;[61] or also by repeated presentations during a period of time so remote that it goes beyond the memory of man, or by other methods, as the law may direct. But in the case of those persons, communities or universities in which that right is for the most part usually presumed to have been acquired by usurpation, a more complete and more precise proof shall be required to establish the true title; and even the proof derived from immemorial time shall avail them nothing unless, in addition to the other things necessary for it, it shall be proved from authentic documents that presentations have been made without interruption during a period of no less than fifty years, all of which have been carried into effect. All other rights of patronage relating to benefices, secular as well as regular, or parochial, or in regard to dignities, or any other benefices

---

61. Cf. Sess. XIV, chap. 12 de ref.; c.25, X, De jur. patr., III, 38

whatsoever in a cathedral or collegiate church, as also faculties and the privileges granted in virtue of patronage or with any other right whatsoever to nominate, elect, and present to the same when vacant, shall be understood as completely abrogated and nullified *in totum,* together with the quasi-possession that followed therefrom, and benefices of this kind shall be conferred as being free by their collators and such appointments shall have full effect; excepted are the rights of patronage that belong to cathedral churches and those that belong to the emperor, or to kings, or to those possessing supreme jurisdiction, and to other high and preeminent princes who have the rights of sovereignty within their own dominions, and those which have been granted in favor of general studies.[62] Moreover, it shall be lawful for the bishop to reject those presented by the patrons if they are incompetent. But if the appointment belongs to inferiors, they [the presentees] shall nevertheless be examined by the bishop, in accordance with what has elsewhere been decreed by this holy council;[63] otherwise the appointment made by inferiors shall be null and void. The patrons of benefices, however, of whatever order and dignity, also if they are communities, universities, colleges of clerics or laics, shall by no means or for any reason or under any pretext interfere with the receiving of the fruits, revenues and dues of any benefices whatsoever,[64] even if they are by virtue of foundation or endowment truly under their right of patronage, but they shall leave them to be distributed freely by the rector or the incumbent, any custom whatsoever notwithstanding. Neither shall they contrary to the prescriptions of the canons presume to transfer to others the said right of patronage under the title of sale or under any other title.[65] If they act otherwise, they shall be subject to the penalties of excommunication and interdict and shall be *ipso jure* deprived of that right of patronage. Furthermore, the accessions made by way of union of free benefices with churches that are subject to the right of patronage, even of laics, whether they are parochial churches or benefices of any other kind whatsoever, even simple benefices, or dignities,

---

62. Cf. Sess. XXIV, chap. 19 de ref.
63. Cf. Sess. XIV, chap. 13 de ref. and XXIV, chap. 18 de ref.
64. Cf. c. un., X, Ut eccles. benef. sine demin. confer., III, 12
65. Cc.6, 16, X, De jur. patr., III, 38

or hospitals, in such wise that the aforesaid free benefices are made to be of the same nature as those to which they are united and placed under the right of patronage, if they have not yet been carried into full effect, or shall in the future be made at the instance of any person, by whatever authority they shall have been granted, even the Apostolic, they shall, together with the unions themselves, be considered as having been obtained surreptitiously, notwithstanding any form of words therein or any derogation which might be considered as equivalent to being expressed; neither shall they be any more carried into execution, but the benefices so united shall, when vacant, be freely conferred as heretofore. Those, however, which have been made within the last forty years and have obtained their full effect and complete incorporation, shall nevertheless be inquired into and examined by the ordinaries as delegates of the Apostolic See, and those which are found to have been obtained surreptitiously or deceitfully shall together with the unions be declared null and the benefices shall be separated and conferred on others.[66] In like manner also all rights of patronage over churches and all other benefices, also over dignities formerly free, which were acquired within the last forty years, or that may in the future be acquired, whether through an increase in the endowment or in consequence of new construction or through some similar reason, even though with the authority of the Apostolic See, shall be carefully examined by the ordinaries as delegates aforesaid, who shall not in these matters be hindered by the authority or privileges of anyone; and those which they shall find to have been not legitimately established for a very manifest necessity of the church, benefice or dignity, they shall revoke *in totum,* and, without detriment to the incumbents thereof and after restoration to the patrons of whatever they may have given therefor, they shall restore benefices of this kind to their former state of liberty; any privileges, constitutions, and customs, even though immemorial, notwithstanding.

---

66. Cf. Sess. VII, chap. 6 de ref.

Chapter X

JUDGES TO BE DELEGATED BY THE APOSTOLIC SEE ARE TO BE
DESIGNATED BY THE SYNOD; BY THEM AND BY THE OR-
DINARIES CAUSES ARE TO BE TERMINATED SPEEDILY

Since by reason of the malicious suggestions of petitioners and sometimes by reason of the distance of places an
adequate knowledge of the persons to whom causes are committed cannot be obtained, and hence local causes are at
times referred to judges who are not altogether competent,
the holy council decrees that in all provincial and diocesan
synods some persons who possess the qualifications required
by the constitution of Boniface VIII, which begins, "Statu-
tum,"[67] and who are otherwise suited thereto be designated,
so that to them also, besides the local ordinaries, may hereafter be committed ecclesiastical and spiritual causes and
such as belong to the ecclesiastical forum which have to be
referred to their districts. And if one of those designated
should happen to die in the meantime, then the local ordinary shall with the advice of the chapter appoint another
in his place till the next provincial or diocesan synod, so
that each diocese may have at least four or even more
approved and qualified persons, as specified above, to whom
causes of this kind may be committed by any legate or nun-
cio and also by the Apostolic See. Moreover, after the des-
ignation has been made, which the bishops shall transmit
at once to the supreme Roman pontiff, all assignments of
other judges made to others than these shall be regarded
as surreptitious. The holy council furthermore admonishes
the ordinaries and all other judges to strive to terminate
causes in as brief a time as possible,[68] and to meet in every
way, either by prescribing a definite time or by some other
available method, the artifices of the litigants, whether it
be in delaying the admission of the suit or in any other part
of the trial.

---

67. C.11 VI°, De rescript., I, 3
68. Cf. cc.5, 10, X, De dolo et cont., II, 14; c.2, X, De sent. et re jud., II, 27; Sess.
XXIV, chap. 20 de ref.

Chapter XI

VARIOUS LEASES OF ECCLESIASTICAL PROPERTY ARE FORBIDDEN; SOME ALREADY MADE ARE INVALIDATED

It usually brings great ruin on churches when their property is, to the disadvantage of those who succeed, leased to others on the present payment of a sum of money. Wherefore, all such leases, if made for payments in advance, shall be in no way considered valid to the disadvantage of those who succeed,[69] any indult or privilege whatsoever notwithstanding; neither shall such leases be confirmed in the Roman Curia or elsewhere. It shall furthermore not be lawful to lease ecclesiastical jurisdiction or the authority to nominate or delegate vicars in matters spiritual,[70] or for the lessees to exercise them *per se aut alios,* and any concessions made otherwise, even by the Apostolic See, shall be considered surreptitious. The holy council declares invalid, even if confirmed by Apostolic authority, leases of ecclesiastical goods made within thirty years, for a long time, or as they are designated in some localities, for twenty-nine or for twice twenty-nine years, which the provincial synod or its delegates shall judge to have been contracted to the detriment of the church and contrary to the prescriptions of the canons.[71]

Chapter XII

TITHES ARE TO BE PAID IN FULL; THOSE WHO WITHHOLD THEM ARE TO BE EXCOMMUNICATED. THE RECTORS OF POOR CHURCHES ARE TO BE PIOUSLY SUPPORTED

Those are not to be tolerated who strive by various devices to withhold the tithes due to the churches, or who rashly take possession of and apply to their own use tithes to be paid by others, since the payment of tithes is due to God, and those who refuse to pay them or hinder those who pay them usurp the property of others.[72] Therefore, the holy council commands all, of whatever rank or condition, on whom rests the obligation to pay tithes, that they in the

---

69. C.6, C.X, q.2
70. Cc. 1, 2, X, ne prael. vices suas, V, 4
71. Cf. c. un., De reb. eccl. non al. in Extrav. comm., III, 4
72. *Exodus* 22:29; *Lev.* 27:30f.; *Num.* 18:21ff.; *Tobias* 1:6; *Mal.* 3: 10; c.66, C.XVI, q.1; cc.6, 7, C.XVI, q.7; cc.14, 23, 26, X, De decimis, III, 30

future pay in full, to the cathedral or to whatever other churches or persons to whom they are legitimately due, the tithes to which they are bound by law. Those who withhold them or hinder their payment shall be excommunicated, and they shall not be absolved from this crime until full restitution has been made.[73] It further exhorts each and all in Christian charity and the duty they owe their pastors, that they do not regard it a burden to assist liberally, out of the things given them by God, the bishops and priests who preside over the poorer churches, for the honor of God and the maintenance of the dignity of their pastors who watch over them.

Chapter XIII

THE CATHEDRAL OR PARISH CHURCHES SHALL RECEIVE A FOURTH PART OF FUNERAL DUES

The holy council decrees that in whatever places it has for forty years been the custom to pay to the cathedral or parochial church a fourth of the funeral dues,[74] as they are called, but has subsequently by virtue of any privilege whatever been granted to other monasteries, hospitals, or any pious places whatsoever, the same shall in the future, with unimpaired right and in the same proportion as was formerly the custom, be paid to the cathedral or parochial church; all concessions, favors, privileges, even those called *mare magnum,* or any others notwithstanding.

Chapter XIV

THE MANNER OF PROCEEDING AGAINST CLERICS WHO KEEP CONCUBINES IS PRESCRIBED

How shameful and how unworthy it is of the name of clerics who have dedicated themselves to the service of God to live in the filth of impurity and unclean cohabitation, the thing itself sufficiently testifies by the common scandal of all the faithful and the supreme disgrace on the clerical order. Wherefore, that the ministers of the Church may be brought back to that continency and purity of life which is

---

73. Cf. c.5, C.XVI, q.7; cc.5, 22, 25, 32, X, De decimis, III, 30; C,1, in Clem., h.t., III, 8
74. Cf. c.8, X, De sepult., III, 28; c.2, h.t. in VI°, III, 12; c.2, h.t. in Clem., III, 7

proper to them, and that for this reason the people may learn to reverence them the more, the more honorable they see them in their conduct, the holy council forbids all clerics whatsoever to presume to keep concubines or other women concerning whom suspicion can be had in their house or elsewhere, or to presume to have any association with them; otherwise they shall be punished with the penalties imposed by the sacred canons or the statutes of the churches.[75] But if after being admonished by their superiors they do not keep away from them, they shall be *ipso facto* deprived of the third part of the fruits, revenues and dues of all their benefices and of their salaries, which shall be applied to the treasury of the church or to another pious place according to the judgment of the bishop.[76] If, however, they should persist in the same crime with the same or another woman and not obey even the second admonition, then they shall not only forfeit *eo ipso* all the fruits and revenues of their benefices and their salaries, which shall be applied to the aforesaid places, but they shall also be suspended from the administration of the benefices for as long a period as the ordinary, also as the delegate of the Apostolic See, shall deem advisable; and if those so suspended shall still not put them away or shall still associate with them, then they shall be forever deprived of their ecclesiastical benefices, portions, offices and salaries of whatever kind, and shall be declared disqualified and unworthy to hold any honors, dignities, benefices and offices whatsoever in the future, until after a manifest amendment of life it appears good to their superiors on justifiable grounds to grant them a dispensation. But if, after having once put them away, they should presume to renew the interrupted intercourse or to take to themselves other scandalous women of this kind, they shall, in addition to the aforesaid penalties, be chastised with the sword of excommunication.[77] Nor shall any appeal or exemption hinder or suspend the aforesaid execution, and the investigation of all the aforesaid shall pertain not to the archdeacons, or to the deans or other inferiors, but to the bishops themselves, who may proceed summarily and solely in accordance with the truth of the fact ascertained. Clerics who have no ecclesiastical benefices or

---

75. Cf. tot. tit: X, De cohab. cler. et mul., III, 2
76. Cf. cc.4, 6, h.t.
77. Cf. cc.2, 3, h.t.

salaries shall be punished in accordance with the character of their crime and contumacy and their persistence therein by the bishop himself with imprisonment, suspension from order, disqualification to hold benefices, or in other ways conformable to the sacred canons. Bishops also, if, which God forbid, they do not abstain from crime of this nature and, after being admonished by the provincial synod, do not amend, are *ipso facto* suspended;[78] and if they persist therein, they shall be reported by that synod to the most holy Roman pontiff, who shall punish them according to the nature of the crime, even with deprivation if necessary.

Chapter XV

FROM WHAT BENEFICES THE ILLEGITIMATE SONS OF CLERICS ARE EXCLUDED

That the memory of the incontinency of the fathers may be banished as far as possible from places consecrated to God, where purity and holiness are most especially becoming, it shall not be lawful for sons of clerics, not born in lawful wedlock, to hold in those churches in which their fathers have or had some ecclesiastical benefice, any benefice whatsoever, even though a different one, or to minister in any way in those churches, or to have salaries from the revenues of the benefices which their fathers hold or formerly have held.[79] But if a father and son shall be found at the present time to hold benefices in the same church, the son shall be compelled to resign his benefice, or within three months to exchange it for another in another church, otherwise he shall be *ipso jure* deprived of it and any dispensation in this matter shall be considered surreptitious. Furthermore, any reciprocal resignations made in the future by fathers who are clerics in favor of their sons that one may obtain the benefices of the other, shall in every respect be considered as an evasion of this decree and of the prescriptions of the canons; nor shall the collations that followed by virtue of resignations of this kind, or of any others whatsoever made fraudulently, be of any avail to sons of clerics.

---

78. C.1, D.XXXIV; cc. 13, 16, D.LXXXI
79. Cf. tot. tit. X, De fil. presb., I, 17

Chapter XVI

BENEFICES WITH THE *CURA* ANNEXED SHALL NOT BE
CONVERTED INTO SIMPLE BENEFICES. A SUITABLE PORTION
SHALL BE AS-SIGNED TO HIM TO WHOM THE *CURA ANIMARUM*
HAS BEEN COMMITTED. VICARIATES SHALL COME TO AN
END WHEN THE *CURA* IS REUNITED TO THE BENEFICE

The holy council decrees that secular ecclesiastical
benefices, by whatever name they may be designated, which
by virtue of their original institution or in any other manner whatever have the *cura animarum,* shall not in the
future be converted into a simple benefice, even though a
suitable portion be assigned to a perpetual vicar; notwithstanding any favors whatsoever which have not obtained
their plenary effect. With regard to those, however, in which
contrary to their institution or foundation the *cura animarum*
has been transferred to a perpetual vicar, even though they
are found to have been in this state from time immemorial,
if a suitable portion of the fruits has not been assigned to
the vicar of the church, by whatever name he may be designated, it shall be assigned as soon as possible and within
a year at least from the end of the present council, as the
ordinary shall see fit, in accordance with the form of the
decree made under Paul III, of happy memory.[80] But if this
cannot be conveniently done, or if within that term it has
not been done, then as soon as the benefice or vicariate shall
have become vacant either by the retirement or death of the
vicar or rector, or in any other way, the benefice shall again
receive the *cura animarum* and be restored to its former
state, and the name of vicariate shall be discontinued.

Chapter XVII

BISHOPS SHALL MAINTAIN THEIR DIGNITY WITH SERIOUSNESS
OF MANNERS, AND SHALL NOT CONDUCT THEMSELVES WITH
UNWORTHY SERVILITY TOWARD MINISTERS OF KINGS,
PRINCES OR BARONS

The holy council cannot but be deeply distressed when it
hears that some bishops, forgetful of their state, dishonor
the episcopal dignity by conducting themselves, both in and

---

80. Cf. Sess. VII, chap. 7 de ref.

out of the church, with an unbecoming servility toward the ministers of kings, princes and barons, and as inferior ministers of the altar not only most unworthily give them precedence but even serve them in person. Wherefore, the holy council, detesting these and similar things, renews all the sacred canons, general councils and other Apostolic ordinances that relate to the decorum and esteem of the episcopal dignity, and commands that in the future bishops abstain from such things, and that both in and out of the church, having before their eyes their rank and order, they bear in mind everywhere that they are fathers and pastors; the rest, princes as well as all others, it commands that they pay them paternal honor and due reverence.

Chapter XVIII

THE CANONS SHALL BE STRICTLY OBSERVED. IF AT ANY TIME A
DISPENSATION IS TO BE GRANTED WITH REGARD TO THEM, IT
SHALL BE DONE VALIDLY, WITH MATURE
CONSIDERATION AND *GRATIS*

Just as the public good requires that the fetters of the law be at times relaxed in order that cases and necessities which arise may be met more fully for the common good, so to dispense too frequently from the law and to yield to petitioners by reason of precedent rather than through a certain discrimination of persons and things is nothing else than to open the way for each one to transgress the laws. Wherefore, be it known to all that the most sacred canons are to be accurately observed by all and, so far as this is possible, without distinction. But if an urgent and just reason and at times a greater good should require that one or another be dispensed, this is to be granted after the matter has been investigated and after the most mature deliberation and *gratis* by those to whom that dispensation pertains, and any dispensation granted otherwise shall be regarded as surreptitious.

Chapter XIX

DUELING IS PUNISHED WITH THE SEVEREST PENALTIES

The abominable practice of dueling, introduced by the contrivance of the devil, that by the cruel death of the body he may bring about also the destruction of the soul, should be utterly eradicated from the Christian world. Emperor, kings, dukes, princes, marquises, counts, and temporal rulers by whatever other name known, who shall within their territories grant a place for dueling between Christians, shall be *eo ipso* excommunicated and shall be understood to be deprived of the jurisdiction and dominion obtained from the Church over any city, castle or locality in which or at which they have permitted the duel to take place, and if they are fiefs they shall forthwith revert to their direct rulers. Those who entered the combat as well as those who are called their seconds shall incur the penalty of excommunication, the confiscation of all their property, and perpetual infamy, and are in conformity with the sacred canons to be punished as homicides, and if they are killed in the combat they shall be forever deprived of Christian burial.[81] Those also who give advice in the matter of a duel, whether in questions of right or of fact, or in any other way whatever persuade anyone thereto, as also those who are present, shall be bound by the fetters of excommunication and everlasting malediction; any privilege whatsoever or evil custom, even though immemorial, notwithstanding.

Chapter XX

THE RIGHTS OF THE CHURCH ARE RECOMMENDED TO THE PRINCES FOR OBSERVANCE AND PROTECTION

The holy council, desirous that ecclesiastical discipline be not only restored among the Christian people, but also forever preserved unimpaired against all obstacles, besides those things which it has ordained concerning ecclesiastical persons, has deemed it proper that secular princes also be admonished of their duty; being confident that as Catholics whom God has willed to be protectors of the holy faith and the Church,[82] they will not only allow that the Church be restored her right but also will lead back all their subjects to due reverence toward the clergy, parish priests and the higher orders, and will not permit their officials or inferior

---

81. Cf. c.22, C.II, q.5; tot. tit. X, De torneam., V, 13, De cler. pugn. in duello, V, 14, et De homicid., V, 12
82. Cf. c.20, C.XXIII, q.5

magistrates through any spirit of covetousness or impru-
dence to violate the immunity of the Church and of ecclesiastical persons, which has been established by the authority
of God and the ordinances of the canons, but that they,
together with the princes themselves, render due obedience
to the sacred constitutions of the supreme pontiffs and councils. It ordains therefore and commands that the sacred
canons and all the general councils, as also other Apostolic
ordinances published in the interest of ecclesiastical persons, the liberty of the Church, and against the violators
thereof, all of which it renews by the present decree, be
accurately observed by all. And hence it admonishes the
emperor, kings, states, princes, and each and all, of whatever state or dignity they may be, that the more bountifully
they are adorned with temporal goods and with power over
others, the more religiously should they respect those things
that are of ecclesiastical right as ordinances of God and as
covered by His protection; and that they suffer them not to
be infringed by any barons, members of their families, governors, or other temporal lords or magistrates, and above
all by the ministers of the princes, but that they punish
severely those who obstruct her liberty, immunity and jurisdiction. To these they themselves should be an example in
the matter of piety, religion and protection of the churches,
in imitation of their predecessors, those most excellent and
religious princes, who not only defended the Church against
injuries by others but by their authority and munificence
promoted her interests in a special manner. Wherefore, let
each one discharge his duty sedulously in this matter so
that divine worship may be celebrated devoutly and the
prelates and other clerics may remain quietly and without
hindrances in their residences and in the discharge of their
duties for the benefit and edification of the people.

Chapter XXI

IN ALL THINGS THE AUTHORITY OF THE APOSTOLIC SEE SHALL REMAIN INTACT

Lastly, the holy council declares that each and all of the
things which under whatever clauses and words have been
established in this holy council in the matter of reform of

morals and ecclesiastical discipline, under the supreme po॥
tiffs Paul III and Julius III, of happy memory, as well as
under the most blessed Pius IV, have been so decreed that
in these matters the authority of the Apostolic See is and
is understood to be intact.[83]

DECREE CONCERNING THE CONTINUATION OF THE SESSION ON THE FOLLOWING DAY

Since all the things that were to be considered in the present session cannot by reason of the lateness of the hour
be conveniently dispatched, the things that remain are
deferred till tomorrow by continuing this same session, as
was resolved by the Fathers in a general congregation.

CONTINUATION OF THE SESSION ON THE FOURTH DAY OF DECEMBER DECREE CONCERNING INDULGENCES

Since the power of granting indulgences was conferred by
Christ on the Church,[84] and she has even in the earliest
times made use of that power divinely given to her, the holy
council teaches and commands that the use of indulgences,
most salutary to the Christian people and approved by the
authority of the holy councils, is to be retained in the Church,
and it condemns with anathema those who assert that they
are useless or deny that there is in the Church the power
of granting them. In granting them, however, it desires that
in accordance with the ancient and approved custom in the
Church moderation be observed, lest by too great facility
ecclesiastical discipline be weakened. But desiring that the
abuses which have become connected with them, and by reason of which this excellent name of indulgences is blas-
phemed by the heretics, be amended and corrected, it ordains
in a general way by the present decree that all evil traffic
in them, which has been a most prolific source of abuses
among the Christian people, be absolutely abolished.[85] Other
abuses, however, of this kind which have sprung from superstition, ignorance, irreverence, or from whatever other source,
since by reason of the manifold corruptions in places and
provinces where they are committed, they cannot conveniently be prohibited individually, it commands all bishops

---

83. Cf. Sess. VII de ref. at the beginning
84. *Matt.* 16: 19; *John* 20:23
85. C.2, in Clem., De poenit. et remiss., V, 9

diligently to make note of, each in his own church, and report them in the next provincial synod,[86] so that after having been examined by the other bishops also they may forthwith be referred to the supreme Roman pontiff, by whose authority and prudence that may be ordained which is expedient for the universal Church; that thus the gift of holy indulgences may be dispensed to all the faithful piously, holly, and without corruption.

CONCERNING THE CHOICE OF FOODS; FASTS AND FESTIVAL DAYS

The holy council exhorts furthermore, and by the most holy Advent of Our Lord and Saviour conjures all pastors, that like good soldiers they sedulously commend to all the faithful all those things which the holy Roman Church, the mother and mistress of all churches, has decreed; also those things which have been established in this council and in the other ecumenical councils, and to make every effort that they comply with all these things, particularly those which tend to mortify the flesh, as the choice of foods and fasts, also those that serve to increase piety, as the devout and religious celebration of festival days; often admonishing the people to obey those placed over them, since those who hear them will hear God as a rewarder, while those who despise them will feel God as an avenger.[87]

CONCERNING THE INDEX OF BOOKS AND THE CATECHISM, BREVIARY AND MISSAL

The holy council in the second session,[88] celebrated under our most holy Lord, Pius IV, commissioned some Fathers to consider what ought to be done concerning various censures and books either suspected or pernicious and to report to this holy council. Hearing now that they have put the finishing hand to this work, which, however, by reason of the variety and multitude of books the holy council cannot distinctly and easily estimate, it commands that whatever has been done by them be given over to the most holy Roman pontiff, that it may by his judgment and authority be completed and made public. The same it commands shall be

---

86. Cf. Sess. XXI, chap. 9 de ref.
87. *Luke* 10:16; *Heb.*13:17; c.9, D.XCIII
88. Cf. Sess. XVIII at the beginning

done with regard to the catechism by the Fathers to whom it was assigned,[89] and likewise with regard to the missal and breviary.

CONCERNING THE PLACE OF AMBASSADORS

The holy council declares that by the place assigned to ambassadors, ecclesiastics as well as seculars, whether in the sessions, processions, or in any other acts whatsoever, no prejudice has been created with regard to any of them,[90] but that all their rights and prerogatives, as well as those of the emperor, their kings, states, and princes are unimpaired and intact and continue in the same state in which they were before the present council.

CONCERNING THE ACCEPTANCE AND OBSERVANCE OF THE DECREES OF THE COUNCIL

So great have been the misfortunes of these times and such the inveterate malice of the heretics, that in the statement of our faith there has been nothing so clearly and so certainly defined, which they at the instigation of the enemy of the human race have not defiled with some kind of error. For which reason the holy council has taken very special care to condemn and anathematize the chief errors of the heretics of our time and to transmit and teach the true and Catholic doctrine, as it has condemned, anathematized, and decreed. And since so many bishops, summoned from the various provinces of the Christian world, cannot for so long a time without great loss to the flock committed to them and without universal danger be absent from their churches, and since there is no hope that the heretics who have been so often invited, even provided with a safe-conduct which they desired,[91] and have been so long expected, will come here later, and it is therefore necessary finally to bring this holy council to an end, it remains now that it admonish in the Lord all princes, which it hereby does, so to direct their activity as not to permit the things that it has established to be corrupted or mutilated by the heretics, but that they be devoutly received and faithfully observed by them and by all others. But if with regard to their acceptance any difficulty

---

89. Cf. Sess. XXIV, chap. 7 de ref.
90. Cf. Sess, II at the end
91. Cf. Sess. XIII, XV, XVIII

should arise, or something should turn up which requires explanation or definition, which does not appear probable, the holy council trusts that besides the other remedies established in this council, the most blessed Roman pontiff will see to it that for the glory of God and the tranquillity of the Church, the necessities of the provinces be provided for either by summoning, especially from those provinces where the difficulty has arisen, the persons whom he shall judge competent to discuss the matter, or by the celebration of a general council if he should deem it necessary, or in any other way as shall seem to him more suitable.

THE READING OF THE DECREES OF THE COUNCIL UNDER PAUL III AND JULIUS III IN THE SESSION

Since at different times under Paul III as well as under Julius III, of happy memory, many things relative to dogma and the reform of morals have been decreed and defined in this council,[92] the holy council wishes that they be now recited and read.

They were read.

THE END OF THE COUNCIL AND THE REQUEST FOR CONFIRMATION FROM OUR MOST HOLY LORD

Most illustrious Lords and most reverend Fathers, does it please you that to the praise of Almighty God an end be put to this holy ecumenical council and that the confirmation of each and all of the things which have been decreed and defined therein under the Roman pontiffs, Paul III and Julius III, of happy memory, as well as under our most holy Lord, Pius IV, be sought in the name of this holy council by the presidents and the legates of the Apostolic See from the most blessed Roman pontiff?

They replied: It pleases us.

Hereupon the most illustrious and most reverend Cardinal Morone, the first legate and president, blessing the holy council, said: After having given thanks to God, most reverend Fathers, go in peace.

They replied: Amen.

---

92. Cf. Sess. V—VII, XIII, XIV

ACCLAMATIONS OF THE FATHERS AT THE CLOSE OF
THE COUNCIL

The Cardinal of Lorraine: To the most blessed Pius, Pope and Our Lord, pontiff of the holy universal Church, many years and eternal memory.

Reply of the Fathers: O Lord God, do Thou preserve very long, for many years, the most holy Father to thy Church.

The Cardinal: To the souls of the most blessed sovereign pontiffs, Paul III and Julius III, by whose authority this holy, general council was begun, peace from the Lord, and eternal glory, and happiness in the light of the saints.

Reply: Be their memory in benediction.

The Cardinal: May the memory of the Emperor Charles V and of the most serene kings, who have promoted and protected this universal council, be in benediction.

Reply: Amen, Amen.

The Cardinal: To the most serene Emperor Ferdinand, ever august, orthodox, and peaceful, and to all our kings, states, and princes, many years.

Reply: Preserve, O Lord, the pious and Christian Emperor; O, heavenly Emperor, protect earthly kings, the preservers of the right faith.

The Cardinal: To the legates of the Apostolic See, and the presidents of this council, many years and many thanks.

Reply: Many thanks; the Lord reward them.

The Cardinal: To the most reverend cardinals and most illustrious ambassadors.

Reply: Many thanks; many years.

The Cardinal: To the most holy bishops, life and a happy return to their churches.

Reply: To the heralds of truth perpetual memory; to the orthodox senate many years.

The Cardinal: The holy, ecumenical Council of Trent; let us confess its faith; let us always observe its decrees.

Reply: Let us always confess, always observe.

The Cardinal: We all believe thus, we all think the same, agreeing therein and embracing them, we all subscribe. This is the faith of blessed Peter and of the Apostles; this is the faith of the Fathers; this is the faith of the orthodox.

Reply: Thus we believe; thus we think; thus we subscribe.

The Cardinal: Adhering to these decrees, may we be made worthy of the mercies and grace of the first and great supreme priest, Jesus Christ God; our inviolate Lady, the holy Mother of God, and all the saints interceding.

Reply: So be it, so be it, Amen, Amen.

The Cardinal: Anathema to all heretics.

Reply: Anathema, anathema.

After this the legates presiding commanded all the Fathers under penalty of excommunication, that they before leaving the city of Trent subscribe with their own hand the decrees of the council, or approve them by some public instrument; all then subscribed, and they were in number two hundred and fifty-five, namely, four legates, two cardinals, three patriarchs, twenty-five archbishops, one hundred and sixty-eight bishops, seven abbots, thirty-nine procurators of absentees with lawful commission, seven generals of orders.

PRAISE BE TO GOD

It agrees with the original; in faith whereof we have subscribed:

I, Angelus Massarellus, Bishop of Telese, secretary of the holy Council of Trent.

I, Marcus Antonius Peregrinus, of Como, notary of the same council.

I, Cynthius Pamphilius, cleric of the diocese of Camerino, notary of the same council.

ORATION
delivered in the ninth and last Session of the
COUNCIL OF TRENT
celebrated on the third and fourth day of December, 1563
under the Supreme Pontiff, Pius IV.
by the most Reverend Jerome Ragazonus, of Venice,
Bishop of Nazianzus and Coadjutor of Famagusta

WHEREIN ALL THAT WAS DEFINED IN THE COUNCIL OF TRENT
PERTAINING TO FAITH AND MORALS IS SUMMARIZED

"Hear these things, all ye nations; give ear all ye inhabitants of the world."[1]

The Council of Trent which was begun long ago, was for a time suspended, often postponed and dispersed, now at

---

1. *Psalms* 48:2.

last through a singular favor of Almighty God and with a complete and wonderful accord of all ranks and nations has come to a close. This most happy day has dawned for the Christian people; the day in which the temple of the Lord, often shattered and destroyed, is restored and completed, and this one ship, laden with every blessing and buffeted by the worst and most relentless storms and waves, is brought safely into port. Oh, that those for whose sake this voyage was chiefly undertaken had decided to board it with us; that those who caused us to take this work in hand had participated in the erection of this edifice! Then indeed we would now have reason for greater rejoicing. But it is certainly not through our fault that it so happened.

For that reason we chose this city, situated at the entrance to Germany, situated almost at the threshold of their homes; we have, in order to give them no ground for suspicion that the place is not entirely free, employed no guard for ourselves; we granted them that public security which they requested and which they themselves had drawn up; for a long time we awaited them and never did we cease to exhort them and plead with them to come here and learn the truth. Indeed, even in their absence we were, I think, sufficiently concerned about them. For since in a twofold respect medicine had to be applied to their weak and infirm spirits, one, the explanation and confirmation of the teaching of the Catholic and truly evangelical faith in those matters upon which they had cast doubt and which at this time appeared opportune for the dispersion and destruction of all the darkness of errors; the other, the restoration of ecclesiastical discipline, the collapse of which they claim was the chief cause of their severance from us, we have amply accomplished both so far as was in our power and so far as the conditions of the times would permit.

At the beginning, after having in accordance with a laudable custom of our forefathers made a profession of faith, in order to lay a foundation, as it were, for subsequent transactions and to point out by what witnesses and evidence the definition of articles of faith must be supported, this holy council scrupulously and prudently enumerated, after the example of the most approved ancient councils, the books of the Old and New Testaments which must be accepted without a doubt; and that no difficulty might arise as regards the wording of various translations, it approved a trust-worthy and certain translation from the Greek and Hebrew. Thereupon, attacking the pillar and bulwark of all heresies concerning the original corruption of human nature, it stated what the truth itself would express if it could speak. Then, with reference to justification, an important matter and assailed in a striking manner by heretics of ancient as well as modern times, it defined, with such wonderful order and admirable wisdom that the spirit of God is easily discerned therein, those things by which the most pernicious opinions of this kind might be refuted and the correct manner of thinking pointed out. Through this most extraordinary decree in the memory of man well-nigh all heresies are strangled and, as darkness before the sun, dispersed and dissipated, and the truth appears with such clearness and splendor that no one can any longer pretend not to see so great a light. Hereupon followed the consideration of the seven sacra-ments of the Church; first in general, then each one in par-ticular. Who does not see here how exactly, how clearly, copiously, resplendently, and, what is most important, how truly the nature of these heavenly mysteries is summed up? Who can in this body of doctrine, so great and rich in con-tent, in any way still wish for something which is to be observed or avoided? Who will in all this find room or occa-sion to go astray? Who finally can henceforth entertain any doubt as to the power and efficacy of these sacraments, since it is clear that that grace which daily like trickling water flows through them into the souls of the faithful was then so abundantly present in us? Thereupon followed the deci-sions concerning the most holy sacrifice of the mass, com-munion under both species and for little children, than which we have nothing holier, nothing more beneficial, so that they appear to have fallen from heaven rather than to have been composed by men. To these is added today the true teach-ing concerning purgatory, the veneration and invocation of saints, images and relics, whereby not only the deceptions and calumnies of heretics are opposed but also the con-sciences of pious Catholics fully satisfied.

These things, dealing with matters that pertain to our salvation and known as dogmas, have been successfully and happily accomplished, and in this respect nothing more will be expected of us at this time.

But since in the administration of some of the foregoing matters there were some things which were not rightly and properly observed, you have, most esteemed Fathers, very carefully provided that they be carried out in a correct and untarnished manner and in accordance with the usages and institutions of the Fathers. You have thereby removed from the celebration of the mass all superstition, all greed for lucre and all irreverence; forbidden vagrant, unknown and depraved priests to offer this holy sacrifice; removed its celebration from private homes and profane places to holy and consecrated sanctuaries; you have banished from the temple of the Lord the more effeminate singing and musical compositions, promenades, conversations and business transactions; you have thus prescribed for each ecclesiastical rank such laws as leave no room for the abuse of the orders divinely conferred. You have likewise removed some matrimonial impediments which seemed to give occasion for violating the precepts of the Church, and to those who do not enter the conjugal union legitimately you have closed the easy way of obtaining forgiveness. And what shall I say about furtive and clandestine marriages? For myself I feel that if there had been no other reason for convoking the council, and there were many and grave reasons, this one alone would have provided sufficient ground for its convocation. For since this is a matter that concerns all, and since there is no corner of the earth which this plague has not invaded, provision had to be made by which this common evil might be remedied by common deliberation. By your clear-sighted and well-nigh divine direction, most holy Fathers, the occasion for innumerable and grave excesses and crimes has been completely removed, and the government of the Christian commonweal most wisely provided for. To this is added the exceedingly salutary and necessary prohibition of many abuses connected with purgatory, the veneration and invocation of the saints, images and relics, and also indulgences, abuses which appeared to defile and deform in no small measure the beautiful aspect of these objects.

The other part, in which was considered the restoration of the tottering and well-nigh collapsed ecclesiastical discipline, was most carefully performed and completed. In the future only those who are known for their virtues, not for their ambition, who will serve the interests of the people, not their own, and who desire to be useful rather than invested with authority, will be chosen for the discharge of ecclesiastical offices. The word of God, which is more penetrating than any two-edged sword,[2] will be more frequently and more zealously preached and explained.

The bishops and others to whom the *cura animarum* has been committed, will remain with and watch over their flocks and not wander about outside the districts entrusted to them. Privileges will no longer avail anyone for an impure and wicked life or for evil and pernicious teaching; no crime will go unpunished, no virtue will be without its reward. The multitude of poor and mendicant priests have been very well provided for; everyone will be assigned to a definite church and to a prescribed field of labor whence he may obtain sustenance.

Avarice, than which there is no vice more hideous,[3] especially in the house of God, will be absolutely banished therefrom, and the sacraments, as is proper, will be dispensed gratuitously. From one Church many will be established and from many one, according as the welfare of the people and circumstances demand. Questors of alms, as they are called, who, seeking their own and not the things of Jesus Christ, have brought great injury, great dishonor upon our religion, will be completely removed from the memory of men, which must be regarded as a very great blessing. For from this our present calamity took its beginning; from it an endless evil did not cease to creep in by degrees and daily take a wider course, nor have precautionary and disciplinary measures of many councils thus far been able to suppress it. Wherefore, who will not agree that for this reason it was a very prudent undertaking to cut off this member, on whose restoration to health much labor had been vainly spent, lest it corrupt the remainder of the body?

Moreover, divine worship will be discharged more purely and promptly, and those who carry the vessels of the Lord will be so chastened that they will move others to follow their example. In connection with this point plans were skillfully devised whereby those who are to be promoted to

---

2. *Heb.* 4:12
3. *Ecclus.* 10:9

sacred orders might in every church be from their youth up instructed in the habits of Christian life and knowledge, so that in this way a sort of seminary of all virtues might be established. In addition, provincial synods were restored; visitations reintroduced for the welfare of the people, not for the disturbance and oppression of them; greater faculties granted to the pastors for guiding and feeding their flocks; public penance again put into practice; hospitality recommended to ecclesiastical persons as well as to pious foundations; in the bestowal upon priests of the *cura animarum* a memorable and well-nigh heavenly method was adopted; plurality of benefices abolished; the hereditary possession of the sanctuary of God prohibited; excommunication restricted and the manner of its imposition determined; first judgments assigned to the places where the disputes arise; duels forbidden; a sort of bridle put on the luxury, greed and licentiousness of all people, particularly the clergy, which cannot be easily shaken off; kings and princes diligently reminded of their duties, and other things of a similar nature were enacted with the greatest discernment. Who does not see that you, most illustrious Fathers, have also in these matters done your duty in the fullest measure? Oftentimes in earlier councils our faith was explained and morals corrected, but I do not know whether ever more carefully and more clearly. We had here, especially during these two years, from all peoples and nations by whom the truth of the Catholic religion is recognized, not only Fathers but also ambassadors. And what men! If we consider science, the most learned; practice, the most experienced; mental gifts, the most penetrating; piety, the most religious; and deportment, the most irreproachable. The number also was such that if the present distresses of the Christian world are considered, this assembly appears the largest in attendance of all that preceded it. Here the individual wounds of all were uncovered, morals exposed, nothing was concealed. The propositions and arguments of our adversaries were so treated that it appeared as if their case not ours was the point under consideration. Some things were discussed three and even four times; debates were carried on with the greatest vehemence, for the purpose, namely, that as gold is tried in the fire, so might the power and vigor of the truth be proved through such contests. For how

could there be discords among those who have the same
view and the same aim?

That being the case, though it was very much desired, as
I said in the beginning, to discuss these things conjointly
with those for whose sake they were chiefly discussed, nevertheless such provision was made for the welfare and salvation of the absentees that it appears it could not have
been otherwise even if they had been present. Let them read
with humility, as becomes a Christian, what we have defined
concerning our faith, and if some light should come upon
them, let them not turn away the face; if they should hear
the voice of the Lord, let them not harden their hearts, and
if they should wish to return to the common embrace of
mother Church from which they severed themselves, they
may rest assured that every indulgence and sympathy will
be extended to them. But the best way, most esteemed
Fathers, to win the minds of those who differ with us and
to hold in the faith and duty those who are in union with
us is this, that we in our churches translate into action the
enactments which we have here expressed in language. Laws
may be the best, they are, however, but mute entities. Of
what avail to the Hebrew people were the laws that came
from the mouth of God Himself? What advantage did the
laws of Lycurgus bring to the Lacedaemonians, those of
Solon to the Athenians, for the preservation of liberty, the
sole purpose for which they were written? But why do I
make mention of such alien and ancient instances? What
further instructions and precepts for good and holy living
can we or should we desire in the life and teaching of Our
Lord Christ? Likewise, what was omitted by our forefathers
that belongs either to the true faith or to a commendable
conduct? For a long time we have had the salutary medicine, properly mixed and prepared; but if it is to drive out
disease it must be taken and through the veins find its way
throughout the entire body. From this cup of salvation, dear-
est brethren, let us first satiate ourselves, and let us be living and vocal laws, a model and rule by which the actions
and aspirations of others may be guided, and so each one
may convince himself that nothing will be gained from the
advantage and honor of the Christian commonweal unless
he zealously contributes in so far as is in him.

If this was our solicitude in the past, it must be more

scrupulously so in the future. For if after the example of our
Master and Saviour we must first do and then teach,[4] what
can be our excuse if after we have taught we fail to practice
our teaching? Who could endure and tolerate us if after we
have pointed out that theft is forbidden we ourselves steal?
that adultery is forbidden and we ourselves commit adultery?
It is certainly not proper that saints turn away from the holy
council, the innocent and virtuous from the precepts of virtue
and innocence, the strong and steadfast in the faith from the
firmly established teaching of our faith. And such are we
expected to be by our people, who, for a long time anxiously
awaiting our return, have consoled themselves with the consideration that we on our return will with greater zeal repair
this absence. This you will do, I hope, most holy Fathers, with
zealous endeavor; and as you have done here so will you also
at home render due service to God and to the people.

Now let us first of all, so far as time will permit, express
and render our most fervent and undying thanks to the great
and eternal God, who has recompensed us not according to
the sins that we have committed nor according to our transgressions,[5] but in His great goodness has granted us not
only to see this most joyful day, which many desired to see,
but also to celebrate it with the full and unqualified consent and approval of the entire Christian people. Then we
must give special and everlasting thanks to our great and
illustrious pontiff, Pius IV, who, as soon as he had ascended
the chair of St. Peter, was so kindled with the desire to
reconvene this council that he directed to it all his energy
and attention. He immediately dispatched as delegates the
most experienced men to announce the council to those
provinces and nations for whose benefit it was chiefly convoked. These traversed nearly all the countries of the North,
entreated, implored and adjured; they promised every security and friendship, and even passed over into England.
Later, since he could not himself be present at the council,
as he so ardently wished, he sent legates distinguished for
piety and learning, two of whom, whose memory is in benediction, he wished to be here on the day appointed, though
scarcely any bishops had yet arrived. These, together with

---

4. *Acts* 1:1
5. *Psalms* 102:10

a third added shortly after, spent nine inactive months in this place waiting for the arrival of an adequate number of bishops to open the council. In the meantime the Pope himself did nothing and contemplated nothing other than that very many and very distinguished Fathers should come here as soon as possible and all kings and princes of Christendom should send their ambassadors, so that by the common desire and deliberation of all this common matter, the gravest and most important of all, might be fully considered. And what did he later omit in the way of attention, anxiety and expenses that seemed in any manner to contribute to the greatness, liberty and success of this council? Oh, the extraordinary piety and prudence of our pastor and father! Oh, the fullest happiness to him by whose authority and under whose protection this long tossed about and distracted council found stability and rest! You who have passed away, Paul III and Julius, you I ask, how long and with what yearning have you desired to see what we see! at what costs and labor have you brought this about! Wherefore, most holy and most blessed Pius, we truly and heartily congratulate you that the Lord has reserved to you such great joy, to your name such high honor, which is the greatest proof of God's benevolence toward you; and with united prayers and supplications we beseech Him that He will for the honor and ornament of His holy Church very speedily restore you to us in good health and preserve you for many years. To the most illustrious Emperor also we must by every right extend our thanks and congratulations. Having won as a basic point the good will of the most powerful rulers who were kindled with such wonderful zeal for the propagation of the Christian religion, he has kept this city free from all danger and by his vigilance has seen to it that we might enjoy a safe and undisturbed peace; by the constant presence of his three representatives, men of the highest character, which was almost a pledge to us, he brought great security to our minds. In conformity with his eminent piety he was singularly solicitous about our affairs. He spared no labor to bring out of the densest darkness in which they dwell those who differed from him and from us in matters of faith and to lead them to see the bright light of this holy council. We must, moreover, hold in grateful remembrance the exceedingly pious disposition of the Christian kings and princes in honoring this council with the presence of their highly esteemed ambassadors and in committing their power to your authority. Finally, who is it, most illustrious legates and cardinals, who does not acknowledge his great obligation to you? You have been the most trustful leaders and directors of our deliberations. With incredible patience and perseverance you have taken care that our freedom either in the discussions or the decisions might not appear to be infringed upon. You have spared no bodily labor, no mental effort, that the business which many others like you have attempted in vain might be brought to the desired termination as soon as possible. In this, you, most illustrious and distinguished Morone, must feel a special and peculiar joy, you who twenty years ago laid the first stone for this magnificent edifice, and now, after many other master-builders have been employed at this work, you have fortunately by your extraordinary and almost divine wisdom put the final hand to it. This remarkable and singular deed of yours will be forever celebrated in words and no age will ever maintain its silence regarding your renown. What shall I say about you, most holy Fathers? How well you have merited by these your most marvelous deliberations in the interests of the Christian state! What commendation, what glory will be given to the name of each one of you by the entire Christian people! All will acknowledge and proclaim you true fathers, true pastors; everyone will cheerfully reward you for the preservation of his life and the attainment of salvation. Oh, how happy and joyful will that day be for our people, when on our return home from erecting this temple of the Lord they can again for the first time see and embrace us!

But thou Lord, our God, grant that we may by noble needs justify so generous an opinion of ourselves, and that the seed which we have sown in Thy field may yield abundant fruit and Thy word issue forth as dew, and that what Thou hast promised may take place during our time, that there be one fold and one shepherd of all, and he preferably Pius IV, to the eternal glory of Thy name. Amen.

PETITION FOR THE CONFIRMATION OF THE COUNCIL

We, Alexander of Farnese, cardinal-deacon of St. Lawrence in Damasus, vice-chancellor of the holy Roman Church, do certify and attest that on this day, Wednesday, the twenty-sixth of January, 1564, in the fifth year of the pontificate of our most holy Lord Pius IV, by the providence of God, Pope, my most reverend Lords, the Cardinals Morone and Simoneta, lately returned from the holy Council of Trent, at which they had presided as legates of the Apostolic See, did in a secret consistory held at St. Peter's petition our most holy Lord as follows:

"Most blessed Father, in a decree regarding the close of the ecumenical Council of Trent, published on the fourth of December last, it was declared that through the legates and presidents of Your Holiness and of the holy Apostolic See, confirmation of each and all of the things which were therein established and defined under Paul III and Julius III, of happy memory, as well as under Your Holiness, should be requested in the name of the Council from Your Holiness. Wherefore, we, Cardinal John Morone and Cardinal Louis Simoneta, who were then legates and presidents, wishing to execute what is ordained in that decree, do humbly petition in the name of the said ecumenical Council of Trent that Your Holiness deign to confirm each and all of the things which have been decreed and defined therein under Paul III and Julius III, of happy memory, as well as under Your Holiness."

Upon hearing which His Holiness, after having seen and read the contents of the said decree, and after having obtained the advice of my most reverend Lords, the cardinals, replied in these words:

"We, yielding to the petition made to us by the aforesaid legates in the name of the ecumenical Council of Trent regarding the confirmation thereof, with Apostolic authority and with the advice and assent of our venerable brethren, the cardinals, having previously had mature deliberation with them, confirm each and all of the things which have been decreed and defined in said Council under our predecessors, Paul III and Julius III, of happy memory, as well as during the time of our pontificate, and we command that they be received and inviolately observed by all the faithful of Christ, in the name of the Father and of the Son and of the Holy Ghost. Amen."

Thus it is.

A. Farnese, Cardinal, Vice-Chancellor.

BULL

Pius, Bishop, servant of the servants of God, for a
perpetual remembrance hereof

"Blessed be the God and Father of Our Lord Jesus Christ,
the Father of mercies and the God of all comfort,"[1] who,
having deigned to look upon His holy Church, agitated and
tossed by so many storms and tempests and day by day
more sorely distressed, has at length come to her aid with
a suitable and longed-for remedy. To extirpate so many and
most destructive heresies, to reform morals and restore
ecclesiastical discipline, to bring about peace and harmony
among the Christian people, an ecumenical and general council had already a long time ago been summoned by our predecessor, Paul III, of happy memory, to meet in the city of
Trent and had been begun by holding several sessions.
Recalled by his successor Julius to the same city, it was,
after the celebration of several sessions, by reason of various hindrances and difficulties that prevented its continuance, for a long time interrupted, not without the greatest
grief on the part of all pious persons, since the Church day
by day increased her prayers for the success of that remedy. But after having assumed the government of the Apostolic See, we, trusting in the divine mercy, undertook to
accomplish, as our pastoral solicitude directed us, so necessary and salutary a work, and supported by the pious zeal
of our most beloved son in Christ, Ferdinand, Emperor-elect
of the Romans, and of other Christian kings, states and
princes, we at length attained that for which we did not
cease to labor in watchfulness day and night and for which
we have assiduously besought the Father of lights. For since
a very large assembly of bishops and other distinguished
prelates, one worthy of an ecumenical council, had, by our
letters of convocation and impelled also by their piety, gath-
ered from all Christian nations in that city, together with
very many other pious persons pre-eminent for their knowl-

---

1. Cf. *2 Cor.* 1:3

edge of sacred letters and divine and human law, under the
presidency in that council of the legates of the Apostolic
See, and since we so favored the freedom of the council that
we by letters to our legates voluntarily left the council free
to deal with matters properly reserved to the Apostolic See,
those things which remained to be considered, defined and
decreed regarding the sacraments and other matters which
seemed necessary for the refutation of heresies, removal of
abuses, and reform of morals, were dealt with and accurately and very deliberately defined, explained and decreed
by the holy council with the fullest freedom and thoroughness.
On the completion of these matters the council was brought
to a close with so great unanimity on the part of all who
participated therein, that it was manifest that such agreement was *the Lord's doing, and it was very wonderful in
our eyes*[2] and in those of all. For this so singular favor of
God we at once ordered public prayers in this fair city in
which the clergy and people participated with great devotion, and we made it our care that praises and thanksgivings so justly due be paid to the divine majesty, since the
close of the council has brought with it a great and well-
nigh assured hope that greater fruits will day by day accrue
to the Church from its decrees and constitutions. But since
the holy council itself, in its reverence toward the Apostolic
See and following in this also the footsteps of the ancient
councils, has, in a decree made in public session, petitioned
us for the confirmation of all its decrees made in our time
and in that of our predecessors, we, having been made
acquainted with the request of the council, first by the letters of our legates, then, on their return, by what they diligently reported in the name of the council, after mature
deliberation thereon with our venerable brethren, the cardinals of the holy Roman Church, and, above all, having
invoked the aid of the Holy Ghost, after we had ascertained
that all those decrees were Catholic, useful and salutary to
the Christian people, to the praise of Almighty God, with
the advice and assent of our brethren aforesaid, have this
day in our secret consistory confirmed by Apostolic authority each and all, and have decreed that they be received
and observed by all the faithful of Christ, as we also, for

---

2. *Psalms* 117:23

the clearer knowledge of all men, do by the contents of this letter confirm them and decree that they be received and observed by all. Moreover, in virtue of holy obedience and under the penalties prescribed by the holy canons, and others more severe, even of deprivation, to be imposed at our discretion, we command each and all of our venerable brethren, patriarchs, archbishops, bishops, and all other prelates of churches, whatever may be their state, rank, order and dignity, even though distinguished with the honor of the cardinalate, to observe diligently the said decrees and ordinances in their churches, cities and dioceses both in and out of the court of justice, and to cause them to be observed inviolately, each by his own subjects whom it may in any way concern; restraining all opponents and obstinate persons by means of judicial sentences, censures and ecclesiastical penalties contained in those decrees, every appeal being set aside, calling in also, if need be, the aid of the secular arm. We admonish and by the bowels of the mercy of Our Lord Jesus Christ conjure our most beloved son the Emperor-elect and the other Christian kings, states and princes, that they, with the same piety and zeal which they manifested through their ambassadors at the council, for the honor of God and the salvation of their people, in reverence also toward the Apostolic See and the holy council, support, if need be, with their aid and encouragement, the prelates in enforcing and observing the decrees of the council, and not to permit opinions contrary to the sound and salutary doctrine of the council to be received by the people under their jurisdiction, but to forbid them absolutely. Furthermore, to avoid the perversion and confusion which might arise if everyone were allowed to publish, as he saw fit, his commentaries on and interpretations of the decrees of the council, we by Apostolic authority forbid all persons, ecclesiastics, of whatever order, condition or rank they may be, as well as laics, with whatever honor and power invested, prelates, indeed, under penalty of being prohibited entrance into the church, and others, whoever they may be, under penalty of excommunication *latae sententiae,* to presume without out our authority to publish in any form any commentaries, glosses, annotations, scholia on, or any kind of interpretation whatsoever of the decrees of this council, or to decide something under whatever name, even under pretext of greater corroboration or better execution of the decrees, or under any other color or pretext. But if anything therein should appear to anyone to have been expressed and defined in an obscure manner and for that reason stands in need of some interpretation or decision, *let him go up to the place which the Lord has chosen,*[3] namely, to the Apostolic See, the mistress of all the faithful, whose authority the holy council also has so reverently acknowledged. For if difficulties and controversies relative to those decrees shall arise, their explanation and decision we reserve to ourselves, as the holy council itself has also decreed; being prepared, as that council has justly confided to us, to provide for the necessities of all the provinces as it shall appear to us most suitable; at the same time we declare null and void whatever should be attempted to the contrary in these matters, whether knowingly or unknowingly, by any authority whatsoever. But that these things may come to the knowledge of all and that no one may plead ignorance as an excuse, we wish and command that this letter be read publicly and in a loud voice by some officials of our court in the Vatican Basilica of the Prince of the Apostles and in the Lateran Church at a time when the people are accustomed to assemble there for the celebration of the masses; and after having been read, let it be affixed to the doors of those churches and also to those of the Apostolic Chancery and at the usual place in the Campo di Fiore, and let it be left there for some time that it may be read and come to the knowledge of all; but when removed thence, copies being according to custom left there, let it be committed to the press in the fair city that it may be more conveniently made known throughout the provinces and kingdoms of Christendom. We command and decree also that an unwavering faith be given to the transcripts thereof, written or subscribed by the hand of a notary public and authenticated by the seal and signature of some person constituted in ecclesiastical dignity. Let no one, therefore, infringe this our letter of confirmation, admonition, inhibition, will, commands and decrees, or with foolhardy boldness oppose it. But if anyone shall presume to attempt this, let him know that he will incur the indignation of Almighty God and of His blessed Apostles Peter and

---

3. *Deut.* 17:8

Paul. Given at Rome at Saint Peter's in the year 1564 of the Lord's incarnation on the twenty-sixth of January, in the fifth year of our pontificate.

I, Pius, Bishop of the Catholic Church.

I, F. Card, Pisanus, Bishop of Ostia, Dean.
I, Fed. Card, Caesius, Bishop of Porto.
I, Jo, Card. Moronus, Bishop of Tusculum.
I, A. Card. Farnesius, Vice-Chancellor, Bishop of Sabina.

I, R, Card. S. Angeli, Major Penitentiary.

I, Jo, Card. S. Vitalis.
I, Jo, Michael Card. Sarasenus.

I, Jo, B, Cicada, Card. S. Clementis.
I, Scipio Card. Pisarum.
I, Jo, Card. Romanus.
I, F. M. G. Card, Alexandrinus.
I, F, Clemens Card, Arae Coeli.
I, Jo. Card. Sabellus.

I, B. Card. Salviatus.
I, Philip. Card. Aburd.
I, Lud. Card. Simoneta.

I, F, Card, Pacieccus y de Tol.
I, M, A, Card. Amulius.
I, Jo. Franc. Card. de Gambara.
I, Carolus Card. Borromaeus.
I, M. S. Card. Constant.
I, Alph. Card. Gesualdus.
I, Hipp. Card. Ferrar.
I, Franciscus Card. Gonzaga.

I, Gui. Asc. Diac. Card. Cam.
I, Vitellotius Card, Vitellius.

Ant. Florebellus Lavellinus.
H. Cumyn.

TEN RULES CONCERNING PROHIBITED BOOKS DRAWN UP BY
THE FATHERS CHOSEN BY THE COUNCIL OF TRENT AND
APPROVED BY POPE PIUS[1]

I

All books which have been condemned either by the
supreme pontiffs or by ecumenical councils before the year
1515 and are not contained in this list, shall be considered
condemned in the same manner as they were formerly condemned.

II

The books of those heresiarchs, who after the aforesaid
year originated or revived heresies, as well as of those who
are or have been the heads or leaders of heretics, as Luther,
Zwingli, Calvin, Balthasar Friedberg, Schwenkfeld, and others like these, whatever may be their name, title or nature
of their heresy, are absolutely forbidden. The books of other
heretics, however, which deal professedly with religion are
absolutely condemned. Those on the other hand, which do
not deal with religion and have by order of the bishops and
inquisitors been examined by Catholic theologians and
approved by them, are permitted. Likewise, Catholic books
written by those who afterward fell into heresy, as well as
by those who after their fall returned to the bosom of the
Church, may be permitted if they have been approved by
the theological faculty of a Catholic university or by the
general inquisition.

III

The translations of writers, also ecclesiastical, which have
till now been edited by condemned authors, are permitted
provided they contain nothing contrary to sound doctrine.
Translations of the books of the Old Testament may in the
judgment of the bishop be permitted to learned and pious
men only, provided such translations are used only as elu-
cidations of the Vulgate Edition for the understanding of
the Holy Scriptures and not as the sound text. Translations
of the New Testament made by authors of the first class of
this list shall be permitted to no one, since great danger

---

1. Cf. Sess. XXV, decree concerning the index of books

and little usefulness usually results to readers from their perusal. But if with such translations as are permitted or with the Vulgate Edition some annotations are circulated, these may also, after the suspected passages have been expunged by the theological faculty of some Catholic university or by the general inquisition, be permitted to those to whom the translations are permitted. Under these circumstances the entire volume of the Sacred Books, which is commonly called the *biblia Vatabli,* or parts of it, may be permitted to pious and learned men. From the Bibles of Isidore Clarius of Brescia, however, the preface and introduction are to be removed, and no one shall regard its text as the text of the Vulgate Edition.

IV

Since it is clear from experience that if the Sacred Books are permitted everywhere and without discrimination in the vernacular, there will by reason of the boldness of men arise therefrom more harm than good, the matter is in this respect left to the judgment of the bishop or inquisitor, who may with the advice of the pastor or confessor permit the reading of the Sacred Books translated into the vernacular by Catholic authors to those who they know will derive from such reading no harm but rather an increase of faith and piety, which permission they must have in writing. Those, however, who presume to read or possess them without such permission may not receive absolution from their sins till they have handed them over to the ordinary. Book dealers who sell or in any other way supply Bibles written in the vernacular to anyone who has not this permission, shall lose the price of the books, which is to be applied by the bishop to pious purposes, and in keeping with the nature of the crime they shall be subject to other penalties which are left to the judgment of the same bishop. Regulars who have not the permission of their superiors may not read or purchase them.

V

Those books which sometimes produce the works of heretical authors, in which these add little or nothing of their own but rather collect therein the sayings of others, as lexicons, concordances, apothegms, parables, tables of contents and such like, are permitted if whatever needs to be elim-

inated in the additions is removed and corrected in accordance
with the suggestions of the bishop, the inquisitor and
Catholic theologians.

VI

Books which deal in the vernacular with the controversies
between Catholics and heretics of our time may not be permitted indiscriminately, but the same is to be observed with
regard to them what has been decreed concerning Bibles
written in the vernacular. There is no reason, however, why
those should be prohibited which have been written in the
vernacular for the purpose of pointing out the right way to
live, to contemplate, to confess, and similar purposes, if they
contain sound doctrine, just as popular sermons in the vernacular are not prohibited. But if hitherto in some kingdom
or province certain books have been prohibited because they
contained matter the reading of which would be of no benefit to all indiscriminately, these may, if their authors are
Catholic, be permitted by the bishop and inquisitor after
they have been corrected.

VII

Books which professedly deal with, narrate or teach things
lascivious or obscene are absolutely prohibited, since not
only the matter of faith but also that of morals, which are
usually easily corrupted through the reading of such books,
must be taken into consideration, and those who possess
them are to be severely punished by the bishops. Ancient
books written by heathens may by reason of their elegance
and quality of style be permitted, but may by no means be
read to children.

VIII

Books whose chief contents are good but in which some
things have incidentally been inserted which have reference
to heresy, ungodliness, divination or superstition, may be
permitted if by the authority of the general inquisition they
have been purged by Catholic theologians. The same decision holds good with regard to prefaces, summaries or annotations which are added by condemned authors to books not
condemned. Hereafter, however, these shall not be printed
till they have been corrected.

IX

All books and writings dealing with geomancy, hydromancy, aeromancy, pyromancy, oneiromancy, chiromancy, necromancy, or with sortilege, mixing of poisons, augury, auspices, sorcery, magic arts, are absolutely repudiated. The bishops shall diligently see to it that books, treatises, catalogues determining destiny by astrology, which in the matter of future events, consequences, or fortuitous occurrences, or of actions that depend on the human will, attempt to affirm something as certain to take place, are not read or possessed.[2] Permitted, on the other hand, are the opinions and natural observations which have been written in the interest of navigation, agriculture or the medical art.

X

In the printing of books or other writings is to be observed what was decreed in the tenth session of the Lateran Council under Leo X.[3] Wherefore, if in the fair city of Rome any book is to be printed, it shall first be examined by the vicar of the supreme pontiff and by the Master of the Sacred Palace or by the persons appointed by our most holy Lord. In other localities this approbation and examination shall pertain to the bishop or to one having a knowledge of the book or writing to be printed appointed by the bishop and to the inquisitor of the city or diocese in which the printing is done, and it shall be approved by the signature of their own hand, free of charge and without delay under the penalties and censures contained in the same decree, with the observance of this rule and condition that an authentic copy of the book to be printed, undersigned by the author's hand, remain with the examiner. Those who circulate books in manuscript form before they have been examined and approved, shall in the judgment of the Fathers delegated by the council be subject to the same penalties as the printers, and those who possess and read them shall, unless they make known the authors, be themselves regarded as the authors. The approbation of such books shall be given in writing and must appear authentically in the front of the

2. For the mode of procedure suggested to the bishops and local inquisitors, cf. the bull *Coeli et terrae,* of Sixtus V, 5 Jan., 1586
3. Fifth Lateran, Hardouin, IX, pp. 1775-77; Schroeder, *Disciplinary Decrees of the General Councils,* pp. 504, 644f.

written or printed book and the examination, approbation and other things must be done free of charge. Moreover, in all cities and dioceses the houses or places where the art of printing is carried on and the libraries offering books for sale, shall be visited often by persons appointed for this purpose by the bishop or his vicar and also by the inquisitor, so that nothing that is prohibited be printed, sold or possessed. All book dealers and venders of books shall have in their libraries a list of the books which they have for sale subscribed by the said persons, and without the permission of the same appointed persons they may not under penalties of confiscation of the books and other penalties to be imposed in the judgment of the bishops and inquisitors, possess or sell or in any other manner whatsoever supply other books. Venders, readers and printers shall be punished according to the judgment of the same. If anyone brings into any city any books whatsoever he shall be bound to give notice thereof to the same delegated persons, or in case a public place is provided for wares of that kind, then the public officials of that place shall notify the aforesaid persons that books have been brought in. But let no one dare give to anyone a book to read which he himself or another has brought into the city or in any way dispose of or loan it, unless he has first exhibited the book and obtained the permission of the persons appointed, or unless it is well known that the reading of the book is permitted to all. The same shall be observed by heirs and executors of last wills, so, namely, that they exhibit the books left by those deceased, or a list of them, to the persons delegated and obtain from them permission before they use them or in any way transfer them to other persons. In each and all of such cases let a penalty be prescribed, covering either the confiscation of books or in the judgment of the bishops or inquisitors another that is in keeping with the degree of the contumacy or the character of the offense.

With reference to those books which the delegated Fathers have examined and expurgated or have caused to be expurgated, or under certain conditions have permitted to be printed again, the book dealers as well as others shall observe whatever is known to have been prescribed by them. The bishops and general inquisitors, however, in view of the authority which they have, are free to prohibit even those books which appear to be permitted by these rules, if they should deem this advisable in their kingdoms, provinces or dioceses. Moreover, the secretary of those delegated has by order of our most holy Lord [the pope] to hand over in writing to the notary of the holy universal Roman inquisition the names of the books which have been expurgated by the delegated Fathers as well as the names of those to whom they committed this task.

Finally, all the faithful are commanded not to presume to read or possess any books contrary to the prescriptions of these rules or the prohibition of this list. And if anyone should read or possess books by heretics or writings by any author condemned and prohibited by reason of heresy or suspicion of false teaching, he incurs immediately the sentence of excommunication. He, on the other hand, who reads or possesses books prohibited under another name shall, besides incurring the guilt of mortal sin, be severely punished according to the judgment of the bishops.

INDEX

Abbess: duty in matter of profession, 231; Election of, 225; may not preside over two monasteries, 225

Abbeys commendatory: obligation toward seminary, 178; on whom to be conferred, 233; Visitation of, 142, 233

Abbots
Decrees concerning regulars, 233
Duty of preaching, 27
Election of, 224
In motherhouses of orders, 233
Lectureship in Scripture, 25
Letters dimissory, 172
Minor orders, 172
Presence at degradation, 83
Privileges abrogated, 172, 209
Right of visitation, 233
Satisfaction of masses, 240

Absence from churches
Brief, 167
Contumacy, 48, 168
Dispensations, 49
Grievous sin of, 168
Necessity of, 166
Penalty for, 48, 168
Report to Roman pontiff, 48
When and how long permitted to: bishops, 48, 166; canons and others, 204; curates, 48, 168

Absence in matter of matrimony, 183
Absolution from sin, 95
By faith alone, 35, 44, 96, 104
Judicial act, 95, 104
Minister of, 95, 104
Mortis articulo, 96
Public crimes, 84
Reserved cases, 96, 104, 198
Usurpers of church property, 160
When null, 93, 96

Abuses: in honor paid to saints, 218; indulgences, 144, 257; preaching, 26; quest of alms, 28, 144; sacrifice of mass, 150

Access to benefices, 243
Accession by way of union, 246
Acclamations of the Fathers, 261
Acolyte, Order of, 163
Acts of the first instance: expense of transfer, 215; to be given gratis, 83; within what time, 83, 215

Adam, Sin of: free will, 29, 43; how transfused, 22; how taken away, 23; injured entire human race, 21, 30

Administration of monastic property, 222

Administrators: of episcopal revenues. 207; hospitals, 61, 159, 243; pious places, 159

Admonitions, 190, 235, 248.
Adoration of Christ in Eucharist, 76, 80
Adultery, 184: Punishment of, 190
Affinity: restricted, 188; Spiritual, 187
Age: dignities and canonries, 203; entrance to seminary, 177; major orders, 173; to obtain benefice, 170

Alexander III, Constitutions of: *Ad audientiam, 566; Cum in cunctis,* 558, 573; *Quia nonnulli,* 558

Alienation: of church property, 235; of patrimony, 138

Alms: Administration of, 159; for the dead, 213; Importunate demands for, 156; questors of, 28, 144

Altar called table by St. Paul, 147
Ambassadors, 259
Ambulations during mass, 153
Anathema of heresies regarding
Baptism, 53
Communion, 136
Confirmation, 55
Eucharist, 79
Extreme unction, 105
Justification, 42
Matrimony, 183
Order, 164
Original sin, 21
Penance, 102
Sacraments in general, 51
Sacrifice of the mass, 151

Annoyance of bishops, 84
Antiquity of little children's communion, 136

Apostasy, Occasion of, 116
Apostates, Punishment of, 232
Apostles: instituted priests, 147, 149; power of consecrating the Eucharist, 162; power of remitting sins. 89

Apostolic traditions, 17, 29, 34, 51, 78, 89, 100, 148, 151, 163, 176, 183, 217

Appeals
Acts of first instance, 83, 214